Ways to Truth

A view of Hindu Tradition

Ways to Truth

A view of Hindu Tradition

Ananda Wood

D.K.Printworld (P) Ltd.
New Delhi

Cataloging in Publication Data — DK
[Courtesy: D.K. Agencies (P) Ltd. <docinfo@dkagencies.com>]

Wood, Ananda E. (Ananda Evelyn), 1947-
Ways to truth : a view of Hindu tradition / by Ananda Wood.
x, 269 p. 23 cm.
Includes bibliographical references (p.)
Includes indexes.
ISBN 8124604355

1. Advaita. 2. Vedanta. 3. Philosophy, Hindu. 4. Civilization, Hindu. I. Title.

DDC 181.4 22

ISBN 81-246-0435-5 (Hardbound)
ISBN 81-246-0439-8 (Paperback)
First published in India in 2008

Published and printed by:
D.K. Printworld (P) Ltd.
Regd. Office: 'Sri Kunj', F-52, Bali Nagar
Ramesh Nagar Metro Station
New Delhi-110 015
Phones: (011) 2545-3975; 2546-6019; *Fax*: (011) 2546-5926
E-mail: dkprintworld@vsnl.net
Website: www.dkprintworld.com

Contents

Preface

This book is one of many attempts to make some sense of Hinduism as a living tradition, which is now joining into a globalizing world. This particular attempt is centred on the philosophy of Advaita Vedānta, so it provides only one of many points of view. Each view has its insights to contribute for a general audience, including those who might see things quite differently.

A general reader will notice that diacritical marks are often used, to transliterate words that come from Sanskrit. These marks show how to pronounce the Sanskrit letters, as indicated roughly in the footnote below.[1] The reader need not worry too much about this, because English equivalents are provided repeatedly, to help avoid the need for Sanskrit terms.

In the end, it doesn't really matter whether Sanskrit terms are used or avoided. What matters is a willingness to investigate beliefs and assumptions that are taken blindly for granted, by force of unexamined habit, in one's own language and ideas and attitudes.

---

[1] First, when there is a bar above a vowel, it shows that the vowel is long. Thus, 'i' is pronounced as in the English 'hit', but 'ī' is like 'ee' in 'sweet'; 'a' is like 'u' in 'hut', but 'ā' is like 'a' in 'father'; 'u' is like 'u' in 'put', 'ū' like 'oo' in 'root'. The vowels 'e' and 'o' are always long, like 'ay' in 'day' and 'o' in 'go'.

Second, when there is a dot underneath a consonant, it shows a retroflex version of the consonant, with the tongue doubled back and touching the top of the palate. So 't' is like the soft Italian 't' in 'pasta', but 'ṭ' is more like the hard English 't' in 'table'. Similarly, 'd' is pronounced as in the Italian 'dolce', 'ḍ' more like in the English 'desk'.

Third, the letter 'h' is always used to indicate a breathy 'h' sound. Thus 'th' is not pronounced like 'th' in 'this'. Instead it is like the 'th-h' in 'bath-house'. And 'ṭh' is like the 't-h' in 'goat-herd'.

Fourth, 'ś' and 'ṣ' are each pronounced like the 'sh' in 'shine'; 'c' like 'ch' in 'chat'; 'ṛ' and 'ḷ' like 'ri' and 'li' in 'Krishna' and 'clip'; and 'ñ' followed by a vowel like 'ny' in 'banyan'.

All arguments and inference
depend upon intelligence.
They're nothing but the power of words.

Where formal logic blindly follows
words expressed in outward speech,
it's just a verbal mimicking
that ties no concrete meaning down.
It cannot record anything.
Such logic is not found in texts
of genuine authority.

From Bhartṛhari's *Vākyapadīya*, 1.137
(see page 184)

Part 1 — Learning from the Past

History and Learning among Hindus

Living History

Hindus have a strong sense of history. Their past goes back a long way; and they often think of it, in the present. However, there is a complication. The Hindu tradition tells us many stories about its own past; but these stories are not plain history. They are not plain records of past events. As the stories were told, a large element of myth and legend was intimately woven in.

This was of course an imaginative device, which was used to convey many subtle kinds of knowledge. Today, we live in a kind of society that depends on printing and other modern media, to organize information and to spread it widely among different classes of people. In this modern kind of society, an intellectual education is far more widely available than it could be in traditional times, before the introduction of printing. Then, of necessity, the ability to think in abstract terms was confined to an elite few. So there was far more use of myths and legends. They were used as creative metaphors — to represent an underlying subtlety of knowledge, in a more concrete way than the abstractions of intellectual thought.

In the Hindu tradition, this mythical element was particularly strong. It helped to pass on knowledge; but it complicated the recording of ordinary facts in the external world of physical space and time. As compared with the West or the Middle East or China, the Hindu tradition provides us with little by way of chronicles that are plainly and straightforwardly historical.

Before the nineteenth century, Hindus did not take much to the habit of writing plain history, with the primary purpose of chronicling their lives and times. They passed down many myths and legends, many inspiring works of art, some profound ways of thought, many practical techniques for the cultivation of mind and body, and many idealized prescriptions of how things ought to be done. But, in this rich heritage, there is a curious lack of plain description, to tell us ordinary facts about historical persons and the events that took place in their lives.

For chronicles of Hindu history, we often have to rely on the accounts of travellers to India. For the early classical period of the Mauryas and their successors, we have ancient Greek and Persian accounts, from Alexander's invasion and the contacts that it opened up. For the later classical period of the Guptas and their successors, we have the accounts of Chinese pilgrims, who came to visit the birthplace of the Buddha. For the medieval period, we have accounts by Islamic historians and scholars, who were associated with invasions from the Middle East. And for the colonial period, there are Christian and European accounts, which have set out a modern framework for writing Indian history.

But these are all accounts from the outside. They describe the Hindu tradition through foreign eyes. That leaves us with a delicate question. How does the tradition tell its own story? Where can we ask how it sees itself, from the inside?

One answer is simple and obvious. We can look in the living tradition, as it is practised today. Through rituals and exercises, through questions and discussions, through stories and values, the tradition has a long history of handing over knowledge, from person to person. That knowledge is very much alive in those individuals who take to it and make it their own today.

It is here that Hinduism comes to life and tells its own story: as a tradition of knowledge that keeps renewing itself, from generation to generation. That is its living history, telling us of a long past where knowledge has similarly been kept alive.

'Heard' and 'Remembered' Texts

According to an old convention, the Hindu tradition is founded upon a collection of texts called Śruti. The word 'śruti' means 'direct hearing' or 'immediate listening'. It implies that these texts had a special religious status. They were not meant to be *read,* as the written-down records of various personal authors. Instead, they were meant to be *heard,* as direct expressions of a divine principle that speaks through them spontaneously. They were meant for direct listening — to a timeless principle that is always fresh and alive, beyond all time-worn records of passing events and persons.

Of the Śruti texts, the earliest are the four Vedas. Their main use was for chanting, in the performance of Vedic rituals. This ritual performance and its results are described in a second set of Śruti texts, which are called the Brāhmaṇas. In a third set, called the Āraṇyakas, the rituals are interpreted as symbolic, of a deeper and broader meaning that involves the entire universe. And finally, there is a fourth set of Śruti texts, called the Upaniṣads, where the rituals are left behind. They are seen as outward acts — directed towards temporary and superficial results — in a questionable world. So there is a reflection back, to ask for clear knowledge of underlying truth.

The Śruti texts are very old. In classical times, they were already old; and they were seen as representing the authentic source of true knowledge. From this basic source, further systems and branches of learning were developed: as ways of explaining and supplementing the fundamental principles that the Śrutis had already revealed. These further systems and branches of learning were described in a second category of texts, which were called Smṛti.

The word 'smṛti' means 'memory' or 'calling to mind'. It implies the indirectness of recalling something from the past, and having to interpret it in the present. The Smṛti texts were recognized as personal and cultural compositions, created by various authors. And it was recognized that these texts were indirect, that they depended upon interpretation. The interpretations were made in a wide range of disciplines that developed along with the texts.

We can think of the texts as having three main uses. First, they codified customs and prescribed systems of practice: as for example in the codes of conduct called Dharma-śāstras, or in Patañjali's *Yoga-sūtras*. Second, they analysed ideas and built intellectual systems: as in the schools of philosophy called Darśanas. And third, they recorded the telling of imaginative and instructive stories: as in the *Rāmāyaṇa* and the *Mahābhārata* epics, or in the religious myths of the Purāṇas.

For a modern reader, the distinction of Śruti and Smṛti can be rather puzzling. Why were the Śruti texts so special that they were supposed to be heard directly from a divine principle? Why refuse to accept that they must be interpreted as the compositions of various personal authors, just like the Smṛtis or like any other text? Clearly, this is a traditional convention which a modern reader does not have to take literally. But then, what does it show?

In the first place, it shows a distinction between two kinds of knowledge: direct and indirect. Direct knowledge was represented by the Śruti texts. As founding texts for the whole, diverse tradition, they stood for a central source and a common basis that underlies all experience. And, in calling them 'śruti' or 'immediate listening', this common basis was identified as direct knowledge — where no uncertain faculties of body or mind, nor any cultural constructions can get in the way of clear truth.

The Smṛti texts were recognized as cultural compositions, built by our partial faculties of feeling, thought and action. By calling them 'smṛti' or 'memory', they were identified as indirect and partial expressions, which need interpretation through a variety of disciplines. So they stood for differing ways of approach, towards an ultimate truth that was also their common foundation. In a direct sense, they did not represent knowledge itself, but only ways of expressing it.

By Word of Mouth

In actual practice, both Smṛti and Śruti texts depended upon a more immediate source, as the texts themselves often acknowledge. That source was the living knowledge of an individual teacher, who used the texts to pass the knowledge on.

As the terms 'śruti' (hearing) and 'smṛti' (memory) show, this was primarily an oral tradition. The emphasis was not, as it is today, on reading and writing; but instead on listening, reciting and remembering. A teacher would recite some passage of text; the students would listen carefully and recite after. And the recitation would be repeated, until it was committed to memory. In the course of such education, a student's memory would get more and more trained, so that less and less recitation would be needed to remember.

For the Śruti texts, there was a traditional ban on using any written texts when passing them on. They were meant to be learned entirely by hearing and recitation, without reading or referring to anything written. For the Smṛtis, written texts could be used, but they were so hard to come by and so cumbersome that they were used for occasional reference only. So, for both Śruti and Smṛti texts, by far the greater part of learning was through hearing and recitation.

In short, the traditional method of education was predominantly oral. It did not depend upon written texts or printed publications or audio or video recordings or electronic and computer media, to anything like the same extent as the modern education that we take for granted today. In traditional education, there was far less use of libraries and publications media. And hence, there was far less use of organized institutions — to collect and maintain libraries, and to prepare and distribute publications through various kinds of media.

With far less use of media and institutions, traditional learning depended more intensively on person to person contact. Methods and systems of learning were suited for passing on from individual teacher to individual student, with relatively little use of written texts or libraries or academic organizations. For a traditional student, the individual teacher loomed far larger than we are used to today. A very large part of the student's horizon was filled by the texts that the teacher recited and by the explanations and instructions that the teacher gave. There wasn't much alternative to learn from. There was far less to read, far less available information, far less contact with people from other places, far less access to other teachings and teachers than we take for granted now.

This emphasis, on oral learning and the individual teacher, is generally found in many traditions before the widespread use of printing. It is found not only in India, but also in Europe and elsewhere. In Europe, printing took root in the fifteenth century and went on growing after that. So its impact on the European and Western tradition is more than 500 years old. In India, it was only in the nineteenth century that printing began to have a significant effect upon the Hindu tradition. So here, the impact of printing is much more recent. It is somewhere around a century and a half old.

In the late nineteenth century, modern schools began to be developed by Hindus, teaching in their own languages and making use of printed books. The traditional system — of oral reciting — continued alongside the developing modern system, until after the middle of the twentieth century. Till then, many Hindus were still traditionally educated, either as an alternative or as a supplement to the new kind of education that was spreading fast through modern schools and colleges.

Traditional Authority

Thus, in the Hindu tradition, the old ways of learning are much less in the past than in Europe and the West. This has the advantage that we can look at these old ways more closely. They went along with old attitudes and manners of expression that are no longer appropriate, to the rather different way in which we learn and understand things today. So we also have a problem. The Hindu tradition is still expressed in unfamiliar ways that confuse us and are difficult to understand. The old texts and teachings need reinterpretation in familiar, modern terms whose meaning we can understand more clearly.

In particular, the old texts were expressed in a rather condensed way — so that more could be said, with less labour of recitation and memorization. Such a condensed expression was often didactic and cryptic. It often took the didactic form of short and bare assertions, which were not immediately understood. They had to be accepted on authority — without, at first, much explanation why or how.

That required an attitude of faith and obedience, to undertake the labour of memorizing long passages of incomprehensible text whose value had to be taken on trust. The attitude was: 'First do as you are told. Keep on reciting the texts. When explanations are given to you, listen very carefully. Then keep reflecting, on what has been said. Recite, listen and reflect, over and over again. Keep on repeating this, without giving up. Eventually, little by little, the riches of meaning will dawn.'

In the modern world, we take quite a different approach. Because information and explanations are so freely available, we can encourage questioning right from the start. Our approach is to ask immediately for the meaning of what we read or hear, and to remember it for the sense that it makes to us. We try to make sense of things, and our memories follow after that. In short, we first ask and then remember.

The traditional approach was just the reverse. It was: 'First remember, repeat and listen, intensively. Then, when you are ready for it, reflect and ask.' Traditional learning was a highly repetitive and laborious affair. The repetition and the labour were needed to pass on the texts, from person to person, with minimal use of written books and records. For, before printing, such books and records were too cumbersome to reproduce and to use extensively.

Of course, both modern and traditional education have the same final goal, of investigating and understanding. But in modern education, the approach is *extensive*: by reproducing and spreading information widely, through the mechanized use of external media. In traditional education, the approach was *intensive*: through the personal labours of teacher and student. The texts described and represented the formal components of learning, as encapsulated in highly condensed forms of expression. They were passed on, explained and brought to life by the individual teacher, who embodied the informal essence of knowledge.

An Individual Emphasis

However great the authority ascribed to the texts, it was always external. In actual practice, all texts depended upon their use and interpretation by a living teacher. The teacher's individuality was the immediate centre of the tradition, for each student. And that remains the same, very much so, today.

Through this individual emphasis, the Hindu tradition can be seen as many-centred. It has many versions — each of which may be seen as the best, for those who have taken to it. For someone who makes use of a particular version, that version is central and the others are peripheral. Such an attitude, of cultural relativism, runs through the Hindu tradition. It is found in many texts, starting with the earliest that we know, the *Ṛg-veda*. And the same relativism is acknowledged as a basic ideal by a great many Hindus today.

According to this ideal, different views — and differing cultures — provide us with alternative and complementary approaches. One needs to be fully committed, to the approach that one currently takes, in order to take it seriously. Such a full commitment is needed, for each particular approach, in order to make a proper use of it. But as a particular approach is made, that approach becomes central. So each approach results in a particular centre — which seems different from other centres, resulting from other approaches.

A question then arises, of how these different centres are to be reconciled. This question runs through the Hindu tradition, along with the ideal of cultural relativism.

Society and Caste

Social Classes — Jāti and Varṇa

In Hindu society, there was a coalition of different groups, called 'jātis'. A jāti was a hereditary group — a group into which a person was born and then remained for life, till death or excommunication or voluntary renunciation (sannyāsa) of normal worldly society. Generally, one inherited one's jāti from one's parents, sometimes from one parent only.

Each jāti had its special customs and conventions, its special myths and beliefs, its special rituals and gods — which set it apart from other jātis. But, among different jātis, culture was also shared in common, to a greater or lesser degree. There was thus a sensitive balance — between keeping the jātis apart and relating them into a common society of shared interests, in villages, towns, kingdoms and broader cultural regions.

In early myths from the *Ṛg-veda,* three social classes are mentioned, each with its place in human society:

- First, there were the priests, who chanted the sacred verses and performed the rituals, so as to mediate between human beings and the divine.
- Second, there were warriors and nobles, who took to arms and ruled, for the sake of honour and justice. They were described by the word 'kṣatriya', which means 'sovereign' or 'ruling'.
- Third, there were the common people, who came under the protection of kṣatriya rule. This third class — of commoners — was described by the word 'viś', which has many implications. It means 'entering' or 'pervading', and hence 'being common'. It also means 'settling down onto', and hence it implies 'property' or 'wealth'. In early Vedic society, the majority of common people were probably farmers, artisans and traders. Evidently, the ideal was that they should produce goods and services, in settled lives of growing wealth and prosperity, under the protection of a just kṣatriya rule.

In a late hymn from the *Ṛg-veda* (10.90), a fourth class was added to the previous three. The hymn describes a universal spirit, called 'Puruṣa'. The word 'puruṣa' means a 'man' or a 'person'. In particular, it refers to an essential spirit which is expressed in each of our personalities. In this hymn, a universal 'Puruṣa' or 'Person' is mythically described. Here, 'Puruṣa' is an undying spirit whose body is the whole universe, and whose actions are everything that happens:

> Puruṣa is truly all of this:
> whatever has been, whatever will be.
> That is the Lord of deathlessness – from which,
> through food, it grows beyond [expressed outside,
> here in the world of change and death]. *– 10.90.2*

The hymn goes on to describe the cosmos in its various aspects: the regions of space, the cycle of seasons, human society and culture, celestial bodies and gods. Each aspect is described as a cosmic sacrifice of the one Puruṣa, thus creating divisions and differences. For the aspect of human society, Puruṣa is pictured as a human body, which was sacrificed by dividing it into parts. The hymn says:

> Its mouth was the brahmin.
> Of the arms, the ruler was made.
> Of its thighs, the vaiśya.
> From the feet, the śūdra was born. *– 10.90.12*

This stanza describes a division of society into four classes. They are clearly ranked according to status, from high to low. The first three have already been mentioned in the early part of the *Ṛg-veda*. The priests are called by the name 'brahmin' ('brāhmaṇa' in Sanskrit). Next come the ruling kṣatriyas. The third class is called 'vaiśya', which is a different form of the word 'viś'. But this is no longer the lowest class. So there is a shift of emphasis — away from the implication of 'common' people, towards a higher status that came to be associated with wealth and commerce.

The fourth group, called 'śūdra', is not mentioned in the early Veda. In this late Vedic hymn, the śūdras are pictured metaphorically — as the 'feet' of society, thus implying an ideal of service and support. There is of course a dark side to the metaphor. It indicates that the śūdras were in a 'fallen' state, of servitude to the classes above them. What sort of servitude was it? How far was it like the subjugation and exploitation that we have recently seen, in nineteenth and twentieth century India? It is all too easy to jump to conclusions. But for ancient India, particularly for the Vedic period, we can only guess and surmise. We do not have the historical records to give us a reliable picture.

We do not even know how far these four classes were jātis (or hereditary groups), at the time of the Vedas and the early Upaniṣads. We know of jātis only later, when we have more records. In classical times — when Hindu kingdoms and empires flourished — we have a few, rather sketchy indications. In the medieval period — when Hindu society continued developing under the political supremacy of Islamic conquerors from the Middle East — we learn a little more. But fuller records, which flesh out the picture, come only with modern communications — during British rule and Indian independence — in the nineteenth and twentieth centuries.

As Hinduism grew and spread, a great many jātis were formed, in a variety of different ways. Some jātis were formed by warrior tribes and peoples, who adopted Hindu ideas and accepted the ritual authority of brahmin priests. For example, in north-western India, many invaders and conquerors were assimilated, to form the Rājpūt clans. And, in southern India, brahmins from the north were welcomed by local rulers and martial tribes, who took to Hindu ways. They used brahmin rituals to legitimate their power, they acquired Sanskrit learning, and they formed jātis of their own.

Some jātis were formed by migration; as, for example, various brahmin jātis were established in southern India by migration from the north. Some jātis were formed by trade and occupation, as for example the various jātis of traders and artisans and other specialists that are found all over India. The lower jātis were of course regarded as degraded peoples — who had fallen into subjugation and servitude, through a combination of human failing, military conquest and economic exploitation.

Many jātis were ethnically formed — as various local and regional groups adopted classical Hindu ideas and Sanskrit forms, on top of their ethnic customs, their folk culture and their vernacular languages. Some jātis, like the Liṅgāyats in Karnataka, were formed by religious affiliation: as the followers of a particular teacher or religious sect.

There were a great many jātis, in a social system that could be very complex. On the one hand, different jātis depended on one another, in an overall exchange of goods and services. On the other hand, over the generations, there was a natural drive for each jāti to claim more power and status, in competition with other jātis. In this long-term competition, power and status were acknowledged through the old idea of the four classes, which took its authority from an ancient, mythological past.

In Sanskrit, the four classes were called 'varṇas'. In English, the word 'varṇa' is usually translated as 'caste'. Thus, we speak of the 'four castes'. A reader may wonder why the word 'caste' has been avoided. The problem is that the Sanskrit word 'jāti' is also translated as 'caste'. So, when applied to Hindu society, the word 'caste' can mean either 'varṇa' or 'jāti'. The two meanings are quite different:

- There were an indefinite number of jātis. They were social groups into which people were born. Each jāti had its own history, which gave it an ethnic flavour of its own. In traditional Hindu society, a person's jāti provided the intimate cultural environment of family life and upbringing. And it also provided a network of community relationships. Through this combination of family culture and communal networking, the jāti was — for its various members — the effective base from which they conducted their social and worldly affairs.

- Unlike the jātis, the number of varṇas was essentially fixed. According to ancient tradition, fixed by the authority of the Vedas, there were just four varṇas. This was not a plainly historical description, of actual social groups. Nor was it a straightforward code of conduct, to anything like the same extent as the legal and institutional codes that govern a modern society.

Instead, the fourfold varṇas were a highly mythical set of ideals, which had to be interpreted in very flexible and delicate ways.

As Hindu society developed, it became more and more complex; so that its mythical ideals required a more and more flexible interpretation. In course of time, the society gradually outgrew its traditional ideals and conventions. They became increasingly artificial, and were threatened by the very flexibility that was needed to apply them. To protect themselves, they developed artificial rigidities, in proportion to their increasingly complex and often devious application.

The caste system is a prime example of how the tradition outgrew some of its ancient ideals. We have our usual problem here, with the history of Hindu society. Until the nineteenth century, when Hindus began keeping more plainly historical records, our information is very patchy. So, for a fuller knowledge of ancient and medieval history, we have to do a lot of interpreting back, from the nineteenth and twentieth centuries. But, by the nineteenth century, Hindu society was in a rather decadent state — at the end of a long medieval period in which the classical systems had been decaying for over a thousand years.

In the caste system, there was a somewhat corrupt and hypocritical disjunction between the current practice of jātis (hereditary groups) and the ancient varṇa ideal of a fourfold hierarchy. In its details, the situation differed considerably, from one part of India to another. But the basic pattern was similar, stemming from a shared tradition. So, for a concrete example, let us consider the social system in southern Kerala, in the princely states of Ṭravancore and Cochin — which remained under a traditional and well-administered Hindu rule, until Indian independence in 1947.

In ritual status, the highest group were the Nambūdiri brahmins. Next were other groups of brahmins, in particular the Tamil-speaking brahmins from the neighbouring state of Tamiḷ Nāḍu. Though these different groups were all ranked ritually as brahmins, they were separate jātis, who did not marry amongst each other.

Below the brahmins, there were a variety of 'temple-servant' castes. As their name implied, they were traditionally occupied in relation to the temples, and they sometimes had priestly functions.

But they were not ranked as brahmins. In fact, they were not acknowledged as any one of the four varṇas. Ritually, they had an intermediate status: below the brahmins, but above the next group, who were the Nāyars (Nairs).

The Nāyars were the warrior class, from whom the kings and the ruling nobility came. They were educated in Sanskrit and followed kṣatriya ideals; but they were not given the ritual status of kṣatriyas. For the brahmins ranked them as śūdras.

Below the Nāyars came a group called the 'Īravas' (Īzhavas). As their name implies, their traditional occupation was to tap toddy. From this association with an intoxicating drink, their ritual status was low and polluting. They were not even ranked as śūdras. Instead, they were ranked below all four varṇas: as outcastes and untouchables. And yet, there were families among them who had prospered: who engaged in trade and commerce, owned reasonably prosperous estates, contributed warriors to the army, and were educated in Sanskrit.

Besides the Īravas, there were a great variety of groups who were ritual outcastes and untouchables, ranked below the four varṇas. But, in actual practice, these 'outcaste' groups were often integrated into Hindu society. They depended on the society; and the society depended on them, all too often at the cost of their exploitation.

Moreover there were non-Hindu groups. In particular, there were various sects of Syrian Christians, who had been established in Kerala for well over a millennium and a half, since the early centuries of the Common Era. They were well integrated into the social system, as respected members of society. They had some education in Sanskrit; and they were often part of the landed aristocracy, with the same sort of rank as similarly landed Nāyars.

This is only a general and rather simplified picture; but it is enough to show an obvious disjunction between the varṇa ideal and the social practice that it was supposed to regulate. Ritually, only two of the four varṇas were recognized. The Nambūdiris and some other groups were recognized as brahmins. But no groups of warrior nobility were recognized as true kṣatriyas. No commercial and professional groups were recognized as vaiśyas, though the actual society of Kerala was thriving in trade and in professional skills. Besides the brahmins, the only varṇa recognized was that of the śūdras. According to the varṇa ideal, this was the class of uneducated labourers. And in this menial class was placed the Nāyar aristocracy — including the highest nobility and even the kings of the realm, despite the historical fact that the nobles and kings were highly cultured and educated.

In fact, there was a glaring discrepancy between ritual and social status. Though the Nāyars had a low ritual status as śūdras (or menial labourers), they had a high social status as warriors and nobles and kings. It was in regard to this social status that they followed kṣatriya ideals.

Moreover, there were some Tamil brahmins who were traditionally employed as cooks by the aristocracy, because their high ritual status meant that the food they cooked would not be polluting to any caste. But then, as employees and cooks, their social status was lowered — beneath that of their employers, who could be of lower ritual status.

In practice, even the Nambūdiri brahmins acknowledged the social status of the Nāyar aristocracy, through a curious custom called 'sambandham' or 'relationship'. The relationship was between a Nambūdiri gentleman and a Nāyar lady. It was not quite a full-fledged marriage, but it was accepted as a respectable relationship. The Nāyar lady would stay in her joint family home, which would become a sort of second home for the Nambūdiri. The children were perfectly legitimate, and belonged to the Nāyar family. But neither the Nāyar lady, nor the children, could visit the Nambūdiri at his joint family home. Nor could they associate with his family. For that would be polluting to the Nambūdiris.

In this quasi-marital relationship, the Nambūdiri gentleman would have to visit his Nāyar wife and children at their home. And when he did so, he was ritually polluted by his contact with them. Before performing any rituals or before returning to his ancestral home, he had to take a ritual bath, to cleanse himself of the pollution. There was thus a ritual divide — between the father on the one side, and the mother and children on the other. This could of course be cruel, on both sides. It made the mother and children feel inferior and unwanted. And it made the father feel coldly distanced — as he remained something of an outsider, among those who could otherwise have been his closest family.

But this custom had two important functions, in Kerala society. On the one hand, it helped the Nambūdiris to maintain their excellence in culture and learning, by preventing the break-up of their ancestral estates. In Nambūdiri families, it was customary that only the eldest son should take a Nambūdiri wife and have Nambūdiri children. The other sons would enter into relationships with Nāyar women, so that they would not produce a potentially divisive proliferation of Nambūdiri offspring.

And, on the other hand, these same relationships helped to pass on classical learning from brahmins to Nāyars. Over the generations, this was one of the ways in which the Nāyar nobility had become so highly educated, and had come to the position of joint partners in learning with the brahmins. Some brahmins even entered into such quasi-marital relationships with the more prosperous of Īrava families, thus helping to pass on classical education to them as well.

To a modern reader, the caste system can seem merely awful and inhuman. It raises barriers between different classes of people; and it gives those barriers a supposedly divine sanction, by ritualizing them. Then, to get past the same barriers, it adopts devious means, like the quasi-marital relationships described above.

However, the ideals of caste had also a positive side. At their own historical time, they played a useful and necessary part in the functioning of Hindu society. This was a time when learning could not be passed on extensively, through mechanized media like printing. Texts and pictures could not be reproduced by automatic machines and widely distributed through society. Information and learning were conveyed through intensive personal labour — from person to person, from teacher to student. So education required an attitude of reverence and obedience, in order to undertake the intense and sustained effort that was involved in personally reproducing and learning the traditional forms of expression. And such an education could only be passed on to a favoured few.

In that historical situation, knowledge was pursued esoterically, in restricted and revered groups of people, who were kept specially free from distracting intrusions. Barriers of ritual purity, and of social class, were maintained in order to keep special areas free for the pursuit of knowledge and excellence, in personal and social life. Such barriers had their costs; but they also brought returns, both to individuals and to society as a whole.

Today, the negative side of caste has naturally come into focus — as an outdated social system that is now giving way to something more democratic. But, to understand Indian history, it helps to get past one's modern prejudices; and thus to look also at the positive side of caste ideals. For each of the four varṇas was associated with a positive ideal which Hindus have looked up to, for some thousands of years.

Brahmins

The brahmanical ideal was one of sacred knowledge. First and foremost, the brahmins were priests, who cultivated a sacred knowledge of the divine. A brahmin boy was trained to recite the sacred chants. In particular, he was trained to recite one or more of the four Vedas. That entitled him to receive the initiation which made him a full-fledged brahmin. Only after that was he instructed in classical Sanskrit, so as to receive an intellectual education.

But the brahmins were not quite like Christian priests, who belong to some instituted church. Nor, like Jain or Buddhist monks, did they belong to monastic organizations. Brahmanical traditions did not centre primarily upon broadly organized institutions, but rather upon particular lineages of learning.

In Sanskrit, such a lineage is called a 'paramparā'. It is a line of teachers who have handed learning down, in an unbroken chain of direct personal contact. Each teacher has received learning directly, face to face, as the student of a previous teacher. This kind of lineage was emphasized because it represented the unwritten essence of knowledge. It represented the informal part of learning — the part that requires a subtle and delicate communication from person to person, beneath the gross forms of words and other external expressions.

There is of course an inbuilt limitation here. The traditional paramparā (or teaching lineage) was a formalized representation of something that is essentially informal. Thus, inevitably, it had its limitations and its biases. In particular, it had a tendency to stay restricted within particular families and ethnic groups; and it discouraged the brahmins from forming more universal organizations — in the way that Jain and Buddhist monks formed saṅghas, and that Christian priests formed church communities. In this sense, the brahmins were priests without a church.

In the absence of a universal church or saṅgha, brahmins continued to formalize learning through myths and legends that were idiosyncratic to particular lineages. This is one evident reason for the lack of historical writing in the Hindu tradition. When different kinds of people join together, to form broader organizations like a church or a saṅgha, that is a major incentive for writing historical records. There is a certain self-consciousness about such an organization; so it is encouraged to write down how it was founded, what its constitution is, and how it grows. Moreover, as such records are written, they require agreement from the different groups who are being organized together; so there is a tendency to strip away the idiosyncrasies of myth and legend, and thus to write plainer history.

Such a development, of historical recording, took place in Christian Europe, in the Islamic Middle East, and among Jains and Buddhists in India. It took place rather less among Hindus, whose written records are somewhat less plainly historical than Jain and Buddhist records in the same country. For Hindu accounts of the past were written by brahmins — who had a tendency to stay centred upon their particular lineages, instead of forming more universal organizations.

This tendency gave the brahmins a special flexibility, which was crucial to Hindu society and politics. They did not band together politically, to form a centralized body like the Christian church. Their political connections were highly decentralized, with local rulers and nobility. Instead of forming a separate political body, they served as priests and advisers to the ruling nobility. Here, the ideal was that the brahmin's sacred knowledge should educate those who ruled, and should thus ground the rulers' decisions in the underlying justice of a divine order.

Kṣatriyas

The kṣatriya ideal was one of true justice. At the centre of this ideal, there is a basic question. In a world of conflicting powers and mixed interests, how can what is true and right be told apart from what is false and wrong? Thus the question of true knowledge was fundamental to brahmin and kṣatriya alike.

But where a brahmin was trained in sacred chants and rituals, a kṣatriya was trained in courage and skill at arms and in determination and judgement at statesmanship. So, while the brahmin was inclined towards formal learning and symbolic religion, the kṣatriya was inclined to a more practical and direct engagement with the secular world of ordinary affairs. These two approaches were complementary; and they led to an inherent partnership of brahmin and kṣatriya.

In the political sphere, the partnership is obvious. The brahmin provided religious legitimacy and learned advice, for the military force of the kṣatriya. In return, the kṣatriya provided patronage and protection, for the brahmanical development of learning and culture.

But the partnership went much further than that. It was intimately involved in the pursuit of knowledge. The brahmins composed most of the texts in which the tradition has been recorded. However, a tradition is not just an accumulation of texts and records carried passively along, like some ceremonial procession of mummified corpses and relics carried by mourners in remembrance of their dead. More vitally, a tradition lives and grows through face to face teaching and discussion — as situations and issues arise, and as questions are asked and answered in the course of current life.

Here, through living discussions and teachings, the kṣatriyas played a major role — as partners who had much to contribute, in the tradition of learning that the brahmins were codifying and recording. In the Vedas, with their religious and ritual emphasis, this kṣatriya role is not much described. But it is prominent in the Upaniṣads, which turn towards philosophical enquiry. Here, there are many discussions between kṣatriyas and brahmins; and the discussions are by no means one-sided. The brahmins are supposed to know more, but the discussions often show that they do not. Surprisingly often, it is a kṣatriya who teaches the highest truth, and a brahmin who learns.

The Upaniṣads thus show an ideal of true knowledge in which both brahmin and kṣatriya share. The same ideal is shown in the *Rāmāyaṇa* and *Mahābhārata* epics, and in the more mythological Purāṇas. It has continued into modern history, as for example in the princely states of Travancore and Cochin. There, in the nineteenth and twentieth centuries, the ruling nobility were fine scholars and poets. In response to the changing times, they collaborated with both brahmins and Christian missionaries, to lay the foundations of a modern educational system that has proved remarkably successful.

Vaiśyas

The vaiśya ideal was one of productive enterprise. So the vaiśyas were wealth creators, engaged in a variety of highly skilled professions. They produced goods, through agriculture and craft; and they traded for profit. Part of that profit was taxed by the state; but enough was left for many to amass commercial fortunes — as landowners, merchants and financiers. To promote their interests, they organized themselves across family and communal divisions, in professional and commercial guilds (called 'śreṇis').

Like brahmins and kṣatriyas, the vaiśyas were greatly concerned with skill and knowledge. But their approach was pragmatic, through the achievement of profit and its accumulation into lasting wealth. This vaiśya aim of profit was decidedly ranked lower than kṣatriya and brahmin aims of just power and sacred truth. But it had several advantages.

Economically, the vaiśyas made money — which could be contributed as patronage to brahmins, or to Buddhist or Jain monasteries, or to any cause that the giver found appropriate. Politically, the vaiśyas could leverage position and power, by acting as financiers for the projects and the treasuries of ruling governments. And socially, the vaiśyas developed extensive networks of trade and industry; thus opening up contacts between different regions and peoples, with their differing cultures.

Beyond these economic, political and social factors, how far were the vaiśyas directly involved in the pursuit of knowledge? Again, there is the problem of recording, even more so than with the kṣatriyas. Since the vaiśyas were more distanced from the brahmin recorders of tradition, their association with learning is further in the background of recorded descriptions. But there is an indication that this association may run a little deeper than is immediately apparent.

In the Hindu social system, the theory of karma was crucial. It enabled people to accept their very unequal positions. But its whole approach is one of profit and loss — resulting from a person's actions and accruing over the course of time. This approach is clearly connected with the vaiśya ideal; and it does show a tradition of learning in which there was room for those who practised the ideal.

In recent history, no less a person than Mahatma Gandhi was of vaiśya stock. He was a Baniyā from Gujarat, famous for his pragmatic intelligence and practical ethics, which bore the clear stamp of his social origins. In his own way, he was very much a man of knowledge, as can be seen from the title of his autobiography: *My Experiments with Truth.*

Śūdras

The śūdra ideal was one of faithful service. A śūdra was supposed to labour, in service to those of higher station. And the higher classes were supposed to have the resources and the judgement to reward that labour with an appropriate return. It was not for the śūdra to demand; but to serve in a spirit of obedience and faith, towards those who were fit to be served.

Of course, such an attitude can seem quite repugnant, to a modern, democratic view. It can seem no more than self-serving hypocrisy that the upper classes should have insisted on such undemanding obedience, towards themselves. And it can seem no less than inhuman that the lower classes should have been forced into a grovelling acceptance of their inferiority and their loss of personal freedom.

But it would be wrong to conclude that the śūdra ideal was only negative. What upsets us is its acceptance of personal dependence. Today, we have come to develop a new kind of society, which is centred upon an ideal of individual freedom. But traditional societies were different. They were unable to provide the growth of individual opportunity that we take for granted today. So they had a tendency to emphasize an ideal of acceptance and personal surrender. In its proper context, that surely is a positive ideal, at the centre of traditional religion.

In Hindu society, of classical and medieval times, that positive ideal was exemplified by the lowly status of the śūdra. In fact, the ideal was not restricted to śūdras, but was central to personal relationships throughout society. In an ideal sense, each person was in a relationship of trusting obedience towards someone higher. A child was in such a relationship with a parent or elder, a student with a teacher, a wife with her husband, a vassal with his lord, a subject with the king, a devotee with God. In the traditional hierarchy, everyone was meant to serve with faith and devotion. Each lord served overlords; and in the end each king, like every subject, was the mere servant of a divine principle that transcended all social distinctions.

Over the last two thousand years or more, the religion of the Purāṇas has developed progressively, as a popular movement of religious devotion. Here, the lower classes were not excluded; but played a vital and increasing part, as saints and devotees. Traditionally, this is a way to truth that has been open to everyone, regardless of caste.

And in modern times, closely connected ideals of devoted service have inspired a great variety of social organizations, religious and secular, to work for the uplift of disadvantaged communities.

Outcastes

Taken together, the four varṇas made up an ideal model of human society, as sanctioned by the authority of Vedic tradition. Of course the ideal did not quite fit. There was society outside the tradition and its mythically stylized ideals.

First, there were foreigners with different languages and cultures, associated with distant lands. There was a certain prejudice against them, indicated by calling them 'mlecchas' or 'barbarians'.[2] But there was also a constructive engagement with foreigners: both through trade and travel abroad and through the assimilation of foreign communities in India. Sometimes, like the Rājpūts, such communities could become assimilated to the extent of forming Hindu jātis that accepted Vedic authority. Or, like many Greek, Christian, Islamic, Parsi, Jewish and Chinese communities, there could be an accommodation that gave the community an effective status of social and cultural respect; though ritually its position remained alien, outside the sanction of the varṇa hierarchy.

Second, there were highly civilized communities, like Jains and Buddhists, who were of local origin but who did not accept Vedic authority. They shared with Hindus a common tradition of language and regional culture; but they followed different teachings and they recognized the authority of different texts and teachers. The result was a vigorous interaction, including both competition and co-operation; so that Buddhists, Jains and Hindus all played a vital part in developing a common tradition that each could draw upon. Buddhists and Jains did not follow the ritual hierarchy of varṇa, but they did manage to live with Hindus — in a common society that gave them a respected place, as active participants in it.

Third, even within the Hindu fold, most groups of people were not adequately described by merely identifying them with one of the four varṇas. This problem was often approached (as in the codes of conduct recorded in the Dharma-śāstras) by elaborating the four-

---

[2] In Sanskrit, the word 'mleccha' means 'indistinct' or 'unintelligible', and it is associated with a 'mlecch' sound that Indian ears still tend to hear in foreign tongues. Similarly, the Sanskrit 'barbara' means 'stammering', and it is associated with an unintelligible 'bar-bar' sound — like the cognate Greek word 'barbaros', from which the English 'barbarian' is derived.

varṇa ideal. Thus, sub-castes could be considered, as subdivisions of each varṇa. And there could be intermediate castes, with a status somewhere in between two varṇas. Then there was the problem of different castes getting mixed, by intermarriage or adultery. Such indiscriminate mixing was regarded with some horror — as subversive to the whole hierarchy, and to the purity that it was supposed to maintain. So the children of mixed unions were supposed to have a low status, often below the level of śūdras. In this and other ways, by virtue of defiling origin or actions, a number of groups were considered outcastes. They were lower than the lowest varṇa, beyond the margins of civilized society; though that society made use of them, to perform the most defiling tasks.

And fourth, there were tribal peoples, deep in untamed jungles or far out in wild mountains and deserts, quite independent of civilization. Towards such tribal peoples, there was a curious ambivalence. On the one hand, they could be subjugated and exploited inhumanly, as little better than animals. Then they were seen as subhuman, and reduced to the status of outcastes. But on the other hand, they could be respected for their wild independence, as expressing a divine spirit beyond all the conditioned refinements of culture and civilization.

Thus, in the *Rāmāyaṇa* epic, much emphasis is laid on the independent spirit of a monkey people who ally themselves with Rāma, the human incarnation of God. One of the monkey chiefs, Hanumān, is often worshipped as Rāma's great devotee, and hence as a form of God in his own right.

Or, to take an example from the *Mahābhārata* epic, when the hero Arjuna is meditating in the depths of a secluded jungle, the great God Śiva comes to him in the form of a tribal hunter. At first, Arjuna's attitude is one of arrogant dismissal. But then there is a fight; in which Arjuna is thoroughly humbled, despite his great resources of strength and courage. Eventually, from the depths of utter defeat, Arjuna realizes his mistake and sees the hunter more truly: as manifesting that one spirit which is the source of all respect.

Renunciation

There was one special kind of outcaste, who was greatly respected and who played a major part in the tradition. This was the sannyāsī — who had renounced ordinary life and society, in order to focus energy and attention upon the search for truth.

Sannyāsa (or renunciation) was the last of four stages in life, which were prescribed for individuals of all classes. The prescription was again a highly stylized ideal, very flexibly applied in practice. The first stage (called 'brahmacarya') was one of education as a student, with ideals of innocence and simplicity. The second stage (called 'gārhasthya') was one of engagement in the world as a householder, with ideals of practical responsibility. The third stage (called 'vānaprastha') was one of retirement into a gentle forest retreat, with ideals of harmonious tranquillity. And the fourth stage (called 'sannyāsa') was one of full-fledged renunciation, with a radical ideal of complete freedom from all restraints and conditions.

A sannyāsī (or renouncer) was thus a voluntary outcaste, seeking to break free from all social and personal conditioning. In an obvious sense, this was a negative approach, which rejected the conditioned aims and wishes of ordinary people. But, beneath the obvious rejection, there was a positive aim. It was to clarify knowledge, beneath the obscuring prejudices of social and personal belief.

A sannyāsī's outward renunciation, of normal customs and beliefs, was meant to be symbolic. It was meant to express a deeper detachment, from the sannyāsī's own culture and personality. Thus, the basic aim was an unconditioned depth of experience — where knowledge is impartial and unlimited, in everyone.

From that depth, a sannyāsī could return to interact again with society — as a guide or a teacher or as a founder of tradition. In the history of Hinduism, we hear story after story in which sannyāsīs play that sort of role. And the stories tell us of an intimate connection between such highly regarded sannyāsīs and other kinds of outcastes who were regarded in quite the opposite way.

One great sannyāsī was Śrī Śaṅkara, a central figure in the philosophy of Advaita Vedānta. Despite his importance and the many works attributed to him, we do not know quite when he lived and taught. Many modern scholars place him somewhere towards the end of the classical period, usually in the eighth or ninth centuries CE (though more traditional datings are earlier). From legendary biographies and from a poem (*Manīṣa-pañcakam*) attributed to him, we hear of an encounter that he had with a particularly polluting kind of outcaste, called a 'Caṇḍāla'.

Śrī Śaṅkara was walking with some disciples in the city of Kāśī (Benares), when they saw the Caṇḍāla approach. There were four dogs with him, and he carried a pot of toddy on his head. For Śrī Śaṅkara and his disciples, this was a picture of defiling pollution — not only from the Caṇḍāla, but also from the dogs and the intoxicating toddy. According to custom, the Caṇḍāla should have stepped off the path and remained at some considerable distance from it, in order to avoid polluting Śrī Śaṅkara and his party as they passed. But this Caṇḍāla kept coming at them. Śrī Śaṅkara was a Nambūdiri brahmin by birth and upbringing. As the threat of pollution loomed closer, his social conditioning made him cry out: 'Move off! Move off!'

The Caṇḍāla's reply is reported in *Manīṣa-pañcakam*:

> Sir, when you say 'Move off! Move off!',
> is it matter that you wish
> to distance from matter,
> or consciousness from consciousness? *– 1*
>
> Is the sun any different,
> reflected in the river Gaṅgā,
> or in a stream that flows
> through a Caṇḍāla settlement?
>
> And is pure space made different
> because it's not just in a pot
> of clay, but in a vase of gold?
>
> In truth itself, found in the
> waveless ocean of uncaused joy
> inherent in experience,

what is this big discrimination
spinning drunkenly around?

'This here,' it says, 'is born a brahmin,
high and wise. But this, here born
to feed on dogs, is mean and low.' – 2

These words made it clear that the Caṇḍāla was a knower of truth. Immediately, Śrī Śaṅkara put aside his social conditioning and bowed before the Caṇḍāla, in a traditional gesture of the utmost respect. For caste did not apply to truth. In the sphere of truth, the Caṇḍāla was a teacher, and Śrī Śaṅkara treated him as such. The stories go on to report a further discussion between the two, with Śrī Śaṅkara receiving some useful advice about his future work.

In recent times, sannyāsī ideals and institutions have played a major role in the process of modernization. Many movements, of self-respect and social uplift, have been inspired and led by sannyāsīs: like Caṭṭambi-svāmī among the Nāyars of Kerala state, and Narayana Guru among the Īravas. Moreover, sannyāsīs have been modernizing their own organizations, with an increasing emphasis on active social service and democratic reform.

CHANGING VIEWS OF EARLY INDIA[3]

When and Where?

As we try to make sense of India's old traditions, we have to negotiate a rather tricky contrast. On the one hand, there is a vast accumulation of old texts, which continue to be interpreted by a vigorous proliferation of living teachings and retellings. But, on the other hand, it is difficult to place the texts historically, in an external context of physical space and time. In sharp contrast to the rich profusion of texts and teachings and stories, we are rather short on plain historical facts.

When were the texts composed and written? Who were their authors? Where were they composed? In what historical societies and circumstances? To what actual events do their myths and legends refer? To these questions, our answers are remarkably uncertain. In particular, for early Indian history, as its ancient and classical traditions formed, our basic picture is very much in doubt.

Among many modern scholars, there is a currently established picture that the Hindu tradition was formed by an immigration of 'Aryan' peoples into India, somewhere around 1500 BCE. According to this picture, the immigrants came over the mountains of Afghanistan, into the north-western plains of the Indian subcontinent. Here, they came upon the remains of the Indus valley civilization, which had rather suddenly declined a few centuries before, around 1800 BCE.

As the Aryans settled in India, they established their dominance, while assimilating many elements that were inherited from the old Indus civilization. During this period of settlement and assimilation, the Vedas and subsequent texts were composed. So the Hindu tradition was formed through a process of cultural fusion, between

---

[3] Much of this chapter is adapted from an internet article (*Vedic Aryans: Horse-Borne Immigrants or Ancient Educators?*) written by the author and published by Sulekha.com on 8 May 2003.

the immigrant Aryans and the remains of an older civilization. In India, our first major written records are Aśoka's edicts, inscribed on stone in the third century BCE. That was a little more than a millennium after the Aryans are said to have immigrated into India. By then, the resulting fusion of cultures had developed into a classical civilization that had spread through north India.

However, there is a growing unease about this picture of an Aryan immigration. Some scholars are proposing an alternative picture, that the Vedas were composed by inhabitants of the Indus civilization. But that would push back the dating of the Vedas, by many thousands of years.

Horses and Immigrations

One major reason for an Aryan immigration theory is the importance of horses in the Vedic texts. There is a wealth of archaeological evidence to show that horses were native to Central Asia, and were domesticated there from very early times. By contrast, there is far less evidence of horses and their domestication in the Indus valley civilization. The evidence for horses becomes more certain and more plentiful rather later on, when the Vedas had already been composed in their present form.

So it is evident that horses were far fewer in early India than elsewhere; and their Vedic importance does evidently show a cultural influence that came into India from outside. But here, there is a tricky question, which can be answered in rather different ways. How did that influence from horse-centred cultures come into a geographical region where horses were not quite so commonly available and so much used?

Before the current immigration theory, there was an older version of it, which said that the Aryans invaded India with devastating force, overwhelming whatever civilization they found here. This is a rather crude answer to the question of cultural influence. It tells us that the Vedic tradition was carried in as a foreign import, imposed by invading conquerors upon the lands they came to dominate. This invasion theory was extensively developed by some two hundred years of modern academic scholarship, since William Jones pointed out our common Indo-European heritage, at the end of the eighteenth century.

But recently, in the last few decades, archaeology has shown that the invasion theory does not properly account for the decline of the Indus civilization. Its cities were not destroyed by invading conquest, but instead abandoned by their inhabitants. So, what used to be an Aryan *invasion* theory is now being refined into a more complex picture that cultural influences came into India through a number of horse-borne *immigrations*, perhaps in small groups of people, perhaps over an extended period of time. This refinement is clearly an improvement, taking a closer look at the process of cultural influence; and it is natural to expect that quite a bit of influence did come in thus, through immigrating groups.

Knowledge and Travel

But immigration is still a rather crude way of accounting for cultural influence. If we think that the Vedic tradition was to a large extent brought in by immigrants, we are still thinking of it as a possessed commodity, which is ethnically owned and carried and transacted by immigrating groups. Cultural influence does of course take place at this level of ethnic immigration and transaction, but there is also a further and deeper level that needs to be considered as well. That further level is concerned with knowledge, and its communication between those individuals who are interested in it.

Such a concern, with knowledge and education, is fundamental to the Vedic tradition. The very word 'veda' means 'knowledge'. And the knowledge meant is very definitely *not* a possessed commodity, transacted between persons or groups. Instead, it is an impersonal concern — intimately shared by different people, across personal and community differences. Here, an educated knowledge is meant to be conveyed in a spirit of impersonal dispassion, through a direct learning that is communicated face to face, from individual to individual. The Vedic tradition tells us that it is essentially 'apauruṣeya' or 'impersonal'. And it essentially implies a direct, face to face communication, between individuals who share a special interest in the impersonality of knowledge.

So, for the history of the Vedic tradition, it is only reasonable to look beyond invasions and immigrations, so as to consider individual journeys as well. In the ancient world, travelling to distant lands took far more time of course than it does today; but it did take place, both for the sake of trade and for the communication and learning of knowledge.

During the classical period of Indian civilization, we know that individual travels, by knowledge specialists, played a major, long-term part in the movement of cultural influence: as for example in the spread of Buddhism northwards to China, and in the southern and eastward spread of Sanskrit learning into south India, Sri Lanka and South-East Asia. These influences were not mainly carried through military or political invasion, nor through the social immigration of ethnic peoples, but rather more through monks and brahmins making individual journeys for the sake of conveying or learning knowledge.

And this communication had a two-way effect. It stimulated journeys in the reverse direction as well: in particular the famous journeys of Chinese travellers to India. It is from a few of these journeys that we get some of our best chronicles of classical India.

There is no good reason for us to rule out such individual journeys between India and the West, and at earlier times that included the Harappan and Vedic periods. In fact, we do have indications that such journeys did take place. In the New Testament, there is of course the story of wise men from the east. From classical Greece, we have old accounts of India and of Indian philosophers who had travelled west. In pre-classical Greece, there may well be indications of an Indian connection, shown by Pythagorean and Orphic conceptions that are strikingly similar to corresponding ideas in India. And for the ancient civilizations of the Middle East and Egypt, there is both archaeological and cultural evidence of a flourishing trade and a mutual communication of ideas and learning with India.

Thus, it may not have needed ethnic invasions or immigrations to bring information and culture into ancient India. It may well have been through individual travellers that the composers of the Vedas were open to cultural influences from beyond their immediate circumstances. From what the Vedas tell us, their composers were individuals of deep insight and powerful imagination. The Vedas are highly imaginative documents: using symbols primarily for their imaginative appeal and for an esoteric or spiritual significance, much more so than for any factual description of external events.

So, when we consider that the Vedas give a special significance to the horse, mythically and ritually, this does not have to mean that there were many horses in the society where the Vedas were composed and handed down. Strictly, it only tells us of a keen imaginative interest and conceptual knowledge concerning horses, and it only requires the presence of a few horses used in special Vedic rituals. In fact, it is quite possible that a scarcity of horses in ordinary life and common usage should actually increase their imaginative and ritual interest. It is even possible that horse-like substitutes were used in Vedic rituals at places and times where actual horses were not available. Such are the often paradoxical ways of mythic imagination and ritual practice.

Energy and Inner Light

In the Vedas, the horse is a symbol of moving and forceful energy, associated with the wind-god, Vāyu. The horse is thus treated with some awe, as a special animal with an extraordinary potency. But there is a complementary conception, represented by another animal, which is described with a much gentler sense of loving and familiar homeliness.

Where the horse stands for dynamic and disruptive power, the cow represents a life-giving nourishment that comes from underlying knowledge. In particular, the cow is a symbol of awakening light, associated with the dawn-goddess Uṣas and the sun-god Sūrya. The 'herds of dawn' are metaphorically conceived as the emergent stirrings of awakening rays that come forth from primal light.[4]

---

[4] See Aurobindo 1999 (in the *Bibliographic References* at the end of this book).

This poetic metaphor shows a fundamental conception — of knowledge as an inner ground of self-illuminating light, inspiring all stirrings and changes of manifested life and energy. That subjective ground is essentially native and familiar, for everyone. It is a home ground of continuity and settlement, from which all disruptions of motive energy arise and where they are all taken in. They are its outward and changing expressions. It is their home ground of intimate and ever-present light, remaining always close at hand.

Vedic Texts and Archaeology

Thus, if we look closely at the meaning of the Vedas, the horse could be associated with a sense of awe and wonder, at something relatively foreign and unfamiliar. And the cow could be associated with a sense of loving fondness, for something closer to home. Then it would not be unreasonable that the Vedas could have been composed and compiled in the Indus civilization, for which the horse was a relatively uncommon and exotic animal.

The early Vedic Saṁhitās (the mythic and poetic texts before the ritualistic Brāhmaṇas and the philosophical Upaniṣads) look rather more pastoral than urban in their character; so their composition would then be associated with the pre-urban phase of Indus civilization, before the mature Harappan period.

Of course, the dating and geographical location of the Vedas is a physical question, which properly belongs to quite a different level from philosophical considerations of what the Vedas mean. But, while such considerations can't directly determine dating and location, they can help indirectly, by giving us some indications about the nature of Vedic language and education. That language and education were both rather special. They were not meant for ordinary usage at the popular level of everyday life, but only for the special use of those with a particular interest in knowledge.

Vedic language does use what at first seem to be ordinary words, like 'cow' or 'horse' or 'sun' or 'dawn' or 'wind'. But the words are used in a metaphorical and often cryptic way, which enables them to encode special kinds of knowledge and learning. The Vedas are thus composed in a very special language of education, which rather cryptically condenses knowledge and learning into its chanted texts.

This was, however, a rather different kind of education from what we are used to now. The Vedas were not written down in any early documents that could help us to date or to locate them. Instead, we have inherited them through a living tradition that has been reciting and memorizing them from generation to generation, for several thousand years. Amazingly, this memorized recitation has been so careful, with such rigorous safeguards against misremembering, that their textual accuracy is not seriously in doubt. There is very little variation in different versions of Vedic Saṁhitās that have been passed down through different lines of tradition, in widely different localities that were not organized to create an artificial concordance by checking with each other.

So we are pretty sure that the Vedas have been accurately transmitted to us. But it is far less clear when or where they were composed and compiled in their present form. The problem here is the essential character of the Vedic texts. They are centred upon a spiritual and philosophical teaching that is somewhat esoterically removed from the material level of outward life and culture. Since our archaeological records consist essentially of material remains, we cannot reasonably expect them to reflect such a spiritual and philosophical knowledge in some simply literal and direct way.

It is true that the Vedas were associated with special rituals, which are described in the Brāhmaṇa texts and which come down to us in the living religion of Hinduism today. But, such Vedic rituals are not those of any temple or monumental religion. They do not involve temples and statues and idols and other material monuments or artefacts of a kind that may be expected to leave much by way of easily identifiable and conclusive remains in the archaeological record. (It is reported that some remains in Harappan sites could have been ancient Vedic altars[5], but the interpretations here are not indisputably conclusive.)

---

[5] See Klostermaier 1998.

In this respect, the Vedic tradition fits in rather well with the Indus civilization. We know of them rather differently: the Vedic tradition through orally transmitted texts and the Indus civilization through archaeological remains. And yet, in either case, there is an evident sophistication of knowledge combined with a curious lack of material monuments and written records.

From remaining artefacts of the Indus civilization, in particular from the Indus seals, we do have evidence that writing was known and used, and we also have rather fragmented indications of what seems to be a popular iconic religion. As archaeologists point out, such an iconic religion is rather different from the animistic way in which Vedic deities are conceived. So, if the Vedic tradition were present in the Indus civilization, it would have to be interpreted more deeply, beneath the iconic level of popular religion; just as the idol worship of modern Hinduism has to be interpreted more deeply today, beneath the merely popular level, in order to see the Vedic principles that still underlie it.

In the end, archaeology alone cannot be expected to determine the dating and location of the Vedic tradition. It also matters crucially how we interpret the knowledge that the Vedas express. And since that kind of interpretation is rather open to question, we need somehow to account for our different historical pictures and our uncertainties about them. Currently, the uncertainties are huge, with a rather heated dispute between two broad pictures that are very different.

The Current Immigration Picture

The first picture is the one of Aryan immigrations into India, envisioned to be mainly after (and perhaps also during) a major decline in the cities and towns of the Indus civilization. Archaeological evidence tells us that by about 1800 BCE, major Indus cities had substantially declined. And the current immigration theory says that the Vedic tradition resulted from an invigorating mixture of Aryan immigrant culture with what continued from the decline of Indus civilization.

In this theory, the distribution of Indo-European languages, through Europe and Asia, is explained to have been brought about by language-carrying migrations whose southern branches passed from Central Asia into Iran and India. From Turkey and north Syria, south of the Black Sea, we have written records on clay tablets which refer to 'Mitra', 'Indara' and 'Aruna' as gods of the Mitanni kingdom, and which use Sanskrit-related words like 'aika' (one) and 'satta' (seven) in connection with the training of chariot horses. A link with Vedic deities and language is too clear to be ignored.

These tablets are reliably dated by archaeologists to around 1400 BCE; and their evident linkage with the Vedic tradition is explained as the result of branching migrations which had first come southwards together, from Central Asia. One branch had then gone west, through Iran, to have an effect upon the Mitanni kingdom in north Syria. And another branch had proceeded eastwards into the Indus region. By working backwards from the Mitanni dating, the migrations before the split are estimated to be earlier than 1600 BCE. That, in turn, gives an estimate that the earliest Vedic text, the *Ṛg-veda,* was composed in the period between 1500 and 1000 BCE; by which time the eastward-branching migrations would have come to India, and the process of interaction and assimilation with the indigenous inhabitants would have been taking place.[6]

As this use of the Mitanni dating shows, the immigration picture is derived in a very indirect and complicated way, interpreting a vast range of highly circumstantial evidence and involving many assumptions about the spread and development of language and culture. So, while an immigration picture clearly has its uses and may rightly tell us many things, its conclusions on their own can hardly be so certain and so definite as to rule out a consideration of other pictures that arise from different points of view.

---

[6] For how the Mitanni evidence gives a *Ṛg-veda* dating, see Ratnagar 1996 and 2000. Particular thanks are due to Ms Ratnagar for very generously sharing information with someone whose views are rather different from hers.

The immigration picture is an external one, viewing culture as an ethnic commodity made up of external objects and behaviours that are carried physically from place to place, by migrating communities. But, for a tradition of living knowledge, there is another point of view that needs to be considered as well. As a tradition expresses knowledge, it tells us something about itself and thus gives us a picture of its own history. In particular, the Vedic tradition very definitely gives us a picture of its past, in many ways. And currently, there is a major problem here. As the Aryan immigration theory stands at present, it still flatly contradicts the view that we get from within the Vedic tradition. That internal view is still largely ignored and dismissed by many academics who favour the current immigration picture.

Such a dismissal is of course a problem for those of us who take the tradition seriously, as one of living knowledge. The problem is not basically a nationalistic one, of which region or which people can lay claim to have composed the Vedas. For a tradition that views its true authorship as 'apauruṣeya' or 'impersonal', geographical location and racial or ethnic possession must necessarily be incidental and peripheral. What's more significant are the continuity of traditional learning and the time-scale of its development.

Time-scales of History

All major traditions in ancient India — Buddhist, Jain and Hindu — describe a continuity of culture that has been developing over very long periods of time. In particular, the Hindu tradition gives us a historic time-scale that would date the compilation of the four Vedas at somewhere around 3000 BCE, along with the Mahābhārata war. (This Vedic compilation and the *Mahābhārata* epic are both associated with a sage whose name is 'Vyāsa', meaning the 'arranger' or the 'compiler'.) And going further back, several thousand years before the *Mahābhārata* events, we are told also of a preceding epic age — when Lord Rāma was king of Ayodhyā, as described in the *Rāmāyaṇa*. This time-scale is much longer than most modern academic datings, and it is often dismissed as completely fanciful. But do we have to dismiss it in this way?

Not necessarily. True, we should not take this time-scale too literally, since it is described in the Purāṇas and other such texts that are largely mythical. But the epics and the Purāṇas were most definitely intended to tell history, even though that history was dramatized by mythical elaboration and imagination. So there may well be a framework of historic fact, fleshed out by dramatic imagination. And the factual framework might well include much of the genealogy and dating and the story outlines, while spectacular descriptions of horses and chariots and amazing weapons and palaces and cities might belong to the mythical dramatization.

Thus, it is possible that the *Rāmāyaṇa* and *Mahābhārata* events could have occurred historically at very early times, when horses and chariots were not actually used; though these and other elements were later added on, imaginatively, for the dramatic appeal of epic and mythical storytelling. It may even be significant here that in the epics and the myths, mention of horses and chariots is largely confined to war and fighting, with little mention of them in connection with travel and ordinary life, to an extent that one would not expect from a culture which actually used horses very much. It may well be that it is horses and chariots which tend to be the fanciful elements of Hindu myths and legends, while the genealogies and time-scales are more historical.

In fact, there is some good evidence to indicate that there may be something in the longer time-scales described in the Purāṇas. In the Vedas, and in Hindu astrological texts and tables, there are references to astronomical constellations going back to 4300 BCE and perhaps even earlier. Such constellations depend in a somewhat complex way upon the various orbits of the planets and the moon, and also upon the gradual wobbling of the earth (whose axis wobbles as it rotates, like a spinning top). Through modern physics and mathematics, we can easily calculate when particular constellations occurred. Traditional astronomy was able to calculate a little, but not nearly well enough to calculate the constellations to which the texts refer. Accordingly, the constellations must have been actually observed and somehow recorded or remembered, so as to pass down into the texts.[7]

This is clear evidence that there was continuity on a time-scale that goes back, as the Purāṇas suggest, to a period long before the Indus cities and any subsequent immigrations. And this continuity is very much part of the Vedic tradition, however it may have been assimilated.

Another Picture, from Old Riverbeds

Moreover, there is some geographical and geological evidence which strongly reinforces the indications of a long-term and substantial continuity extending well back into the history of the Indus civilization.

In general, the Vedas describe a geography that corresponds quite well to the north Indian plains. Nearly all the major rivers are named identifiably — including those that flow south-east, through the Indus plain, and those that flow south-west, through the adjoining Gaṅgā plain. But there is a striking exception to this geographical fit. The Vedas give great prominence to a major river called the Sarasvatī, which isn't found in north India today.

Instead, we find the dried beds of a great river that once flowed down the eastern side of the Indus plain into the gulf of Kutch. In course of time, over some thousands of years, tectonic changes altered the levels of the earth's crust so as to deflect the river westwards, towards the Indus. Thus deflected, it kept changing its beds and then joined the Indus, of which it became a tributary. Eventually it lost its own tributaries, which were deflected towards other rivers; and it was reduced to what is now the river Ghaggar. This is today a very minor, seasonal river that does not reach anywhere near the sea. Instead, it dries up in the Rajasthan desert, far inland. But it is a river that has been traditionally identified with the Vedic Sarasvatī; and it was once a major river, with many

---

[7] Elst 1992.

tributaries and an abundant, perennial flow of water from the Himalayas down to the Arabian sea.

Accordingly, there is a quite reasonable and plausible theory that this once great river was indeed the Sarasvatī. Along its dried beds, there are many archaeological sites, showing that it was an important part of the Indus civilization. And it is pretty clear that this great river dried up substantially at about the time when the Indus cities declined. In the aftermath of the Indus civilization, it was no longer the abundantly flowing river that the Vedas describe.[8] So, if the Sarasvatī theory is correct, it associates the Vedas with the long continuity of the Indus civilization, which dates back archaeologically to early settlements in 6000 BCE or maybe even earlier.

The Sarasvatī theory thus provides a second picture of early Indian history. In this second picture, the dating of the Vedic tradition is pushed back by several thousand years, a huge increase that accords rather better with the time-scale that the Purāṇas describe. Instead of the *Ṛg-veda* being composed in 1500–1000 BCE, through a hybridization of immigrant and native cultures in the aftermath of Harappan decline, the roots of Vedic composition are conceived as extending back at least to the beginnings of Indus civilization, currently dated at around 6000 BCE.

Encoded Knowledge

But why this fuss about Vedic civilization and early dating? Is it just a chauvinistic wish to prove that Indian texts belong to India, or that they are older and better than other texts? Again, not essentially. Beneath the obvious chauvinist appeal, there is a more basic concern that applies to ancient and sacred texts in general, not just to Indian texts like the Vedas or the Purāṇas. That deeper and broader concern is to understand such texts as encoding and expressing knowledge, not just as poetic and fanciful formulations of archaic superstition, speculation and belief.

---

[8] Frawley 1993.

The fact is that ancient texts and chants were able to encode some quite sophisticated and far reaching knowledge in a very condensed way. For example, the ancient syllable 'om' has long been analysed into three component sounds: 'a', 'u', and 'm'. These three sound-elements are taken to represent three states of experience, corresponding to three levels in our perception of reality. 'A' is the state of waking: where reality is seen through our external senses, at an outer and superficial level of material objects. 'U' is the dream state: where reality is seen through mind, at an intermediate level of conceiving thoughts. And 'm' is the state of deep sleep: where reality is seen through pure insight, at an underlying level of quiet, unaffected consciousness. Thus, in a single syllable, there was encoded a deeply reasoned philosophical enquiry — which came to be explained and elaborated later on, in many subtle and complex systems of analytic and practical investigation.

This kind of coding greatly complicates the way that ancient texts are interpreted and understood. The syllable 'om' is a fairly clear example, because there is so much discussion of it in subsequent texts and in the living tradition of Indian philosophy today. Naturally, we cannot expect that all such coding would be similarly well explained; but traditional scholars tell us that this kind of coding is quite common in Vedic texts, which thus express a wealth of scientific and technical and artistic knowledge.

Much of the encoded knowledge may now be lost, and the encoding difficult to interpret; so more work is clearly needed to investigate this aspect of ancient learning, in the context of modern science and education. Some work has begun in this direction; and it does give initial indications of a highly sophisticated and long-evolved ancient knowledge that needs to be taken more seriously, particularly in the fields of philosophy, linguistics, psychology, biology, astrology, astronomy[9] and mathematics[10].

---

[9] Kak 1994.

[10] See Klostermaier 1998. He says: 'One of the reasons for considering the Indus civilization "Vedic" is the evidence of town-planning and architec-

footnote continued on next page ...

There is thus a fresh consideration of an ancient view that early knowledge is not essentially less true and more ignorant, but rather that its expression tends to be more condensed and less explained. In this view, knowledge is knowledge, no matter when or where expressed. What differs and changes is only the expression of knowledge, in different, long-evolving traditions.

Uncertain Pictures

In the history of early texts like the Vedas, the importance of long continuity is to allow time for the evolution and development of their encoded knowledge. If there is a wealth of knowledge encoded in them, that would imply both time and continuity for such a cultural development. Moreover, since the continuity is one of knowledge, it would also have extended across different traditions, through individuals travelling and communicating between different places. Though such communications were slow, they could well have been important in long-term developments of culture, across extensive regions.

To an immigration picture of ancient history, these considerations of knowledge add two complicating factors: first, the sophisticated encoding of ancient texts; and second, the communication of cultural influence through travelling specialists. The complications could be major, to the extent that their admission might seem to open a Pandora's box of loose speculations and ill-considered claims; thus hopelessly confusing the scientific study of linguistic and cultural

---

... footnote continued from previous page

tural design that required a fairly advanced algebraic geometry — of the type preserved in the Vedic *Śulva-sūtras*. The widely respected historian of mathematics A. Seidenberg came to the conclusion, after studying the geometry used in building the Egyptian pyramids and the Mesopotamian citadels, that it reflected a derivative geometry — a geometry derived from the Vedic *Śulva-sūtras*. If that is so, then the knowledge ("Veda") on which the construction of Harappa and Mohenjo Daro is based, cannot be later than that civilization itself.' (References to Seidenberg's work are given as in Seidenberg 1978 and 1983.)

behaviour that ethnic communities develop and carry along with their migrations. This is clearly a useful level of consideration in which much careful research has been systematically invested, with obvious benefits and contributions which have their place and which are not to be dismissed without good reason.

However, there is also a place for considering a more subtle level of investigated knowledge and educated learning, not only today but in the ancient world as well. For ancient India in particular, such considerations of knowledge do not fit well with the current Aryan immigration picture; so that an alternative is being attempted, with quite a different time-frame and quite a different interpretation of ancient texts and learning. The implications are not just particular to India, but apply to ancient traditions in general, on a global scale.

There are thus two very different pictures of early Indian history, neither of them proved conclusively. Their contradictions leave us with a huge uncertainty, amounting to several thousand years in our datings of early texts and of legendary events that may be more or less historical.

To a great extent, the different pictures arise through different approaches and presumptions, from which the same evidence gets differently interpreted. On both sides, the presumptions are of a kind that do not readily and simply get disproved by external evidence. So the dispute may well continue for quite some time.

Meanwhile, it is only fair that each picture should be dispassionately described, in its own right, with an open admission of our uncertainty about how far either of them may or may not be right.

History and Living Knowledge

Our major uncertainty in early Indian history, with its two very different pictures, has a knock-on effect. It doesn't just affect the Vedas, but also the dating and the context of later texts, like the epics and the Purāṇas, and the various treatises and commentaries of the śāstras (the traditional sciences and intellectual systems). Their dates and their historical circumstances may also turn out to be somewhat different from our recent estimates.

How far does this uncertainty affect our interpretation of the texts? It greatly affects the kind of modern scholarship that focuses on linking texts to the particular circumstances of their history. This kind of scholarship is obviously useful: to build an accurate picture of the past, and to help us take into account the various historical contexts in which the texts were composed and handed down.

But here we must come back to the fact that the Hindu tradition was not centrally interested in handing down an externally accurate picture of its historical circumstances. That is not what the tradition has to tell us, not at least from its own point of view. For a very long time, its focus has not been on past circumstances, but instead on the current knowledge that it keeps handing down. And that remains its focus, very much so, today. In this sense, it is rather like a modern science, in particular like modern physics. It keeps throwing away its past, to reinvent itself in the present.

How does one understand such a tradition? As with modern physics, two approaches are involved. And they complement each other:

- On the one hand, there is a past, from which the tradition has come. To understand that, we examine old records and improve our historical pictures. The pictures provide a context in which past knowledge is understood, as belonging to another age.
- On the other hand, there is the current knowledge that the tradition presents to us today. As we understand this, our reconstructions of the past must retreat into the background. In this approach, one is not describing what other people did or thought or believed in the past. Instead, one is asking what we can learn from the tradition now. This is a more direct approach: of listening to a tradition for what it has to say in the present.

For a tradition of living knowledge, like modern physics, the historical approach can of course be useful; but in the end it is peripheral to a more direct understanding of current knowledge. If one studies some subject in the history of physics, then clearly that study is going to be centred (implicitly or explicitly) upon one's present understanding of physics. In so far as that understanding is mistaken, it will surely compromise one's historical study.

It is the same with the Hindu tradition. Though a historical approach is clearly useful, it is in the end peripheral. Hindu texts are not centred upon history, but upon a human and philosophical knowledge that is very much alive and current today. In so far as that knowledge is misunderstood, the misunderstanding must inevitably compromise our historical studies of the tradition.

So, alongside a historical approach, which reconstructs the past, we also need a more direct investigation of traditional ideas: to ask what knowledge they have to teach us, in modern terms. In this kind of investigation, we are looking for a knowledge that is common to past and present. We are looking for a continuing knowledge that is differently expressed in differing circumstances. Here, we are interested in the historical context only to allow for its idiosyncrasies; and hence to look beyond it, for a knowledge that is independent of historical and cultural differences.

Like modern physics, the Hindu tradition is centred upon a search for independent knowledge, beyond the idiosyncratic circumstances of history and culture. So, to get past our uncertainties about Indian history, it may help to ask how Hindus have looked for such independent knowledge, just as they continue to look for it today.

Four Aims

In the Hindu tradition, there is an analysis of four main aims that motivate human beings. They are called 'kāma' or 'desire', 'artha' or 'wealth', 'dharma' or 'well-founded order', and 'mokṣa' or 'freedom'. They form a progression that leads to the independent knowledge of mokṣa. And this progression can be interpreted as uncovering a series of levels that go down to the basis of human motivation. An illustration is given in figure 1.

Figure 1

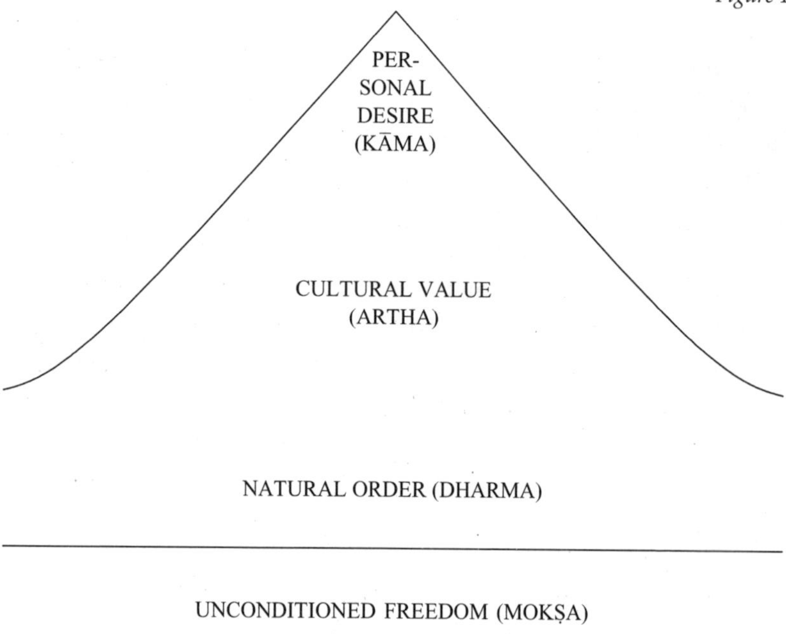

Kāma — Desire

The word 'kāma' implies a personal desire for some object of passing fancy. This is the most superficial level of motivation. It refers to a person's desire for some narrow object which gets to be fancied at some particular moment of experience. Such personal, narrowed desire is essentially variable and unstable. For the narrowness of personally desired objects means that different persons desire different things; and each person's objectives change in the course of time, as desire turns from one narrow object to another.

Artha — Wealth

The word 'artha' implies achievement in general. In particular, it implies the kind of achievement that accumulates into a store of meaningful wealth. This wealth may be a store of material goods; or it may be a store of more subtle merit: such as fame and honour, or learning and skill, or good habits and virtuous character.

Such a store of wealth is not just personal. It has a broader, cultural value — which gives it meaning and enables its merit to accumulate. Because of its cultural value, it is a broader and more lasting aim than the immediate satisfaction of personal desire.

Accordingly, the achievement of artha is an intermediate level of motivation. It refers to the culturally conditioned values through which personal desire is formed. Such cultural values have a relative degree of breadth and stability. They are broader and more enduring than personal desires; because they are shared in common by different people, in a community that continues, while particular persons come and go.

In the course of community life, cultural values are developed; by attributing them to various objects of continued use: like money, or property of various kinds, or works of art, or observed phenomena, or ideas. Thus, personal desires are based on systems of cultural value, which define the physical and mental 'wealth' of a relatively enduring community.

Dharma — Well-founded Order

The word 'dharma' is usually translated as 'duty', 'virtue', 'morality', 'justice', 'law', 'religion'. These various translations can be useful in particular situations, but they unfortunately mask an essential core of meaning that is common to them all.

Literally, 'dharma' means 'supported' or 'held' (from the root 'dhṛ' — meaning to 'support' or to 'hold'). It is etymologically akin to the English word 'firm'. As this derivation suggests, the concept of 'dharma' refers essentially to something that is properly supported or well-founded. When the performance of a duty is described as 'according to dharma', it is implied that the performed duty is well-founded, upon firmly established principles. And the same is true when the word 'dharma' is used to describe a quality of virtue, or an ethical injunction, or a dispensation of justice, or an articulated law, or an act of religious faith.

Thus, the concept of 'dharma' is inherently reflective. It implies a reflection back to the root level of motivation, going down beneath the relativity of cultural conditioning. When any object is desired or valued, it implies a question of 'What for?'. Because an object is only an incomplete piece of a larger world, any desire or value for it implies a larger, more basic function or purpose, through which the object fits in with other things. Such a broader function or purpose is what makes a particular desire or value 'well-founded', by supporting it in a more stable order of things.

In this sense, the word 'dharma' refers to a universal order of nature, through which are supported all particular objects and relationships, all particular actions and motivations.

The trouble with cultural systems is that they are all limited constructions, built artificially from limiting names and forms and qualities. Each cultural system provides only a partial and one-sided view — with something always left out, to be seen through other views. Within such a limited system, the question 'What for?' can never be fully answered. Any answer can only describe some larger objective, but the limitations of description prevent the objective described from being complete. And the incompleteness gives rise to another 'What for?'.

Despite the limitations of cultural description, people do have the sense of a 'natural order' that is somehow complete and is shared universally in common, beneath our partial and differing views of it. When a particular object or action is perceived, there is naturally inborn with it a sense of its place in a common order that relates it to other things. This underlying sense — of a common, natural order — is expressed in all our cultural systems: of science, or management, or art, or ethics, or religion. When we perceive how objects are related or how actions are motivated, we understand these relationships and motivations as part of a natural order that we somehow sense, beneath our limited cultural expressions of it.

In traditional times, this 'natural order' was usually conceived in terms of religious metaphor, as a 'divine harmony'. Here is a characteristic description from Shakespeare's *Merchant of Venice* (act 5, scene 1):

> Sit, Jessica. Look how the floor of heaven
> Is thick inlaid with patens of bright gold.
> There's not the smallest orb which thou behold'st
> But in his motion like an angel sings,
> Still quiring to the young-eyed cherubims;
> Such harmony is in immortal souls,
> But whilest this muddy vesture of decay
> Doth grossly close it in, we cannot hear it.

In the modern world, through the growth of science, emphasis has shifted from religious metaphor to a more direct, analytic enquiry. But the sense of an underlying harmony in nature remains fundamental. As Albert Einstein put it:

> You will hardly find one among the profounder sort of scientific minds without a religious feeling of his own. But it is different from the religiosity of the naive man. For the latter, God is a being from whose care one hopes to benefit and whose punishment one fears; a sublimation of a feeling similar to that of a child for its father, a being to whom one stands, so to speak, in a personal relation, however deeply it may be tinged with awe.
>
> But the scientist is possessed by the sense of universal causation. The future, to him, is every whit as necessary and determined as the past. There is nothing divine about morality; it is a purely human affair. His religious feeling takes the form of a rapturous amazement at the harmony of natural law, which reveals an intelligence of such superiority that,

> compared with it, all the systematic thinking and acting of human beings is an utterly insignificant reflection. This feeling is the guiding principle of his life and work, in so far as he succeeds in keeping himself from the shackles of selfish desire. It is beyond question closely akin to that which has possessed the religious geniuses of all ages.[11]

The above quotations are of course from the European tradition. But they aptly show the Hindu sense of 'dharma': as a universal harmony that is naturally expressed in the world outside and in our bodies and minds as well. The problem is that our bodies and minds are incomplete. As we see the world through them, they produce a superficial show that doesn't tell us everything. This leaves us uncertain and confused, in our physical and mental perceptions of the world. So we do not rightly see the harmony that is expressed. And we often get out of touch with it.

Through duty, ethics, virtue and religion, the aim of dharma is to get back in touch. This aim is inherently reflective, as can be seen from the English word 'religion'. It comes from the Latin 'religāre', which means to 'bind back'. It implies a reversal of direction: from the divided and passing aims of cultural value and personal desire, towards a secure grounding in the natural order of some more fundamental principle that different motivations share in common.

Mokṣa — Freedom

The word 'mokṣa' implies a complete freedom from all the limited and uncertain conditions that affect our bodies and minds. That freedom is sought at the ground level of motivation: where the roots of conditioned manifestation have been followed back, into the unconditioned and unmanifest ground. In the spiritual search that follows back down the roots, a distinction is sometimes made between 'dharma' and 'dharmī':

---

[11] Einstein 1989.

- 'Dharma' means 'that which is supported'. It refers to the whole order of nature, at the roots of changing manifestation.
- 'Dharmī' means 'that which supports'. It refers to the supporting ground — from where all aims originate, and where they must eventually return.

Thus mokṣa (as pure freedom) is both goal and source. As the aim of mokṣa is attained, all desires and values are returned to that originating ground from which they come. In that one origin, there are no divisions, no constraints. There are no partialities that cloud pure knowledge and obscure plain truth. There, knowledge is found free of ignorance, as unconditioned truth. And there is nothing further to desire or to value. That is the final aim: where unaffected freedom is realized, by returning back to source.

However, this is only one way of describing a final aim that is approached in many different ways. As the Hindu tradition developed, it did not focus on any one approach. Instead, it considered all actions, thoughts and feelings as intermediate steps that lead eventually to one, same truth. So, in the course of Hindu history, a whole range of differing approaches have been developed and passed down to us today. It is in these many approaches that the tradition consists. Their differences are manifest. Their unity is to be found, in what they each express and seek.

Part 2 — Authority and Power

Creation in the Vedas

Subjective and Impersonal

What gives the Vedas their traditional authority? In practice they were learned and used as ritual chants, valued for their power of chanted sound. In chanting them, or hearing them, the prime concern was not their intellectual meaning. Instead, it was an unseen benefit that was supposed to come from chanting them, and listening to them, in the right way.

And yet, the word 'veda' means 'knowledge', quite straightforwardly. It comes from the root 'vid', which means to 'know'. It is thus related to the English words 'wit' and 'wisdom'; and to words like 'vision' and 'video', which come from the Latin 'vidēre' — to 'see'. The knowledge implied is a direct, immediate seeing. It is the seeing of pure insight: beneath theoretical constructions and beyond abstract analysis.

In Sanskrit, 'veda' does not mean constructed theory or knowledge in the abstract. Grammatically, the word 'veda' is not just a noun. It is also the first person singular of the verb 'vid', in what is called the 'perfect' tense. In this sense, 'veda' means: 'I know.' And the perfect tense is significant, because a perfection of knowledge is very definitely implied.

According to traditional grammarians, the perfect tense is used to describe a completed fact that has not been witnessed by the person who is describing it. Thus, the word 'veda' may be interpreted to mean 'I know' as a complete fact of knowledge that has not been witnessed by the person who is speaking. This 'I know' is an essential fact of knowing that has never been *seen objectively*, as an observed action. Instead, it is *realized subjectively*, as an inner illumination. It is not seen as any kind of act; but only found by joining back within, beneath all acts and functions of outward personality.

Hence knowledge is conceived as both subjective (ātmīya) and impersonal (apauruṣeya). Its essence is an inmost ground of pure spirit, beyond all differences and variations of personality. From that unchanging ground, the Vedas draw their power and their authority. They are thus sacred speech: drawing from that ground and leading back to it. As it is said in the *Ṛg-veda* 1.164.45-46:[12]

> The word is measured out in four.
> Those steps of speech are known to them
> of broad and deep intelligence.
>
> Three are laid down concealed.
> These three are not articulated forth.
> Of speech, the fourth is what men speak. *– 45*
>
> They speak of 'Indra' (Chief of gods);
> of 'Mitra' (Friend); of 'Agni' (Fire);
> of 'Varuṇa' (the All-enveloping);
> and of fine-feathered 'Garutmān'
> (Celestial bird of prey).
>
> Of one same being, those who are
> inspired speak, in different ways.
>
> They call it 'Agni' (Burning fire),
> or 'Yama' (Death of changing things),
> or 'Mātariśvan' (Subtle energy). *– 46*

In a way, this passage summarizes what the Vedas do. They use myth and ritual to connect two aspects of experience: microcosmic and macrocosmic. Here, in the above passage, the microcosm of individual experience is analysed into four levels of expression: three of them laid down 'concealed', the fourth articulated into apparent form. The macrocosm of the outer universe is represented by mythic names of gods, who manifest the cosmic powers of nature. And we are told that all these manifesting powers are only ways of speech. They are only differing expressions of a single source. That is their

---

[12] The translations in this book are rather free, each showing only one among many possible interpretations.

common inspiration: in everyone's experience, and in the world outside.

As the Vedas are chanted, they are meant to inspire nature's powers — evoked by sounds of mythic incantation, and by ritually enacted forms. Such inspiration may be conceived to rise from deep within the chanter's or the listener's experience. It starts unseen, beneath the mind; and rises up into feelings, thoughts and perceptions, at the changing surface of physical and mental appearance.

In each individual's experience, it's at the changing surface that the world appears. In effect, for every individual, there is a microcosmic creation of the world's appearances, as they keep rising up into the surface of conception and perception in our minds and senses. Thus, when we speak of 'creation', we can use the word in two ways:

- On the one hand, we can speak of a *subjective* creation from within: expressing consciousness through living personality. This is the kind of creation that imagines pictures, tells stories, invents new ways of doing things.
- On the other hand, we speak of an *objective* creation in the world outside, through processes of interaction between external things. This is the kind of creation that forms stars and galaxies, solar systems, planets, clouds and storms, wind and rain, lightning, fire, rivers, oceans, land and mountains, rocks and earth.

In the modern world, we have developed very elaborate descriptions of the second kind of creation; and we tend to separate it from the first. In the Vedas, there is an opposite tendency: to describe both kinds of creation together, through an intimate connection that is seen between the inner microcosm of subjective experience and the outer macrocosm of the universe.

A Skeptical Creation Hymn

In the late *Ṛg-veda,* there are a number of creation hymns where mythical cosmology is used to ask some fundamental questions, about the nature of experience. In one of these hymns (*Ṛg-veda* 10.129), the questions asked are deeply skeptical:

Non-being then was not, nor being.
There was no changing atmosphere,
affected by conditioning;
nor any changeless sky beyond.

What was comprehended? Where?
On whose support? What depth of
potency was there, unmanifest? *– 1*

There was no death, nor deathlessness.
There was no sight of night or day,
no breath of wind-blown air.

The one lived by itself, desireless.
Beside it, there was nothing else. *– 2*

A driven blindness, from the start,
has been concealed, by driven blindness.

All this entire universe
has been an unseen, surging flood.
And that, as it has come to be,
has been superimposed, by empty
pettiness and vanity.

All that is just the one, born forth
through the unbounded energy
of thought intensified as power. *– 3*

Right from the start, upon that one
desire has turned entirely.
That has been mind's primal seed.

Searching heart with mind intent,
inspired seers, in non-being,
have found out the bond of being. *– 4*

Their radiance has spread out, across.
Has it been deep? Has it been high?

They have been deeply seminal,
and have transcended pettiness:
established in themselves beneath
and driving forcefully beyond. *– 5*

Who truly knows? Who speaks out here?
From what has this, seen world been born?
From what is it created forth?

The gods have come from its creation.
Then, who is it that knows
from where this has arisen? *– 6*

From where has this creation come to be?
Has it been established, or has it not?
Only its witness in the highest heaven
truly knows it, or knows if it is not. *– 7*

This hymn is part myth, part philosophy. It starts (in stanzas 1 and 2) with a story of the world's creation, at a mythical time of origin. At this time, the story goes, there was no non-existence, no existence, nor air or sky, no death, no deathlessness, no night or day. But, as the story is told, there is an immediate questioning. What was there at this time of origin? What supporting depth was there, before the world appeared? That depth is described as the 'one', living by itself.

As the story goes on (in stanza 3), it describes the process of creation. It all starts with a driven blindness (tamas), which gives rise to a surging flood (salila). But the flood is inherently undifferentiated and unmanifest (apraketa). As it surges forth unseen, it gets covered up, by pettiness and vanity (tucchya). All this, says the story, is the 'one': as it has been born forth, through the boundlessness (mahimā) of its intensity (tapas).

But this is not just a story, of some past process in time. It may also be interpreted as a philosophical description: of appearance and reality, in present experience. As we look at the world, we do not see it directly. Instead, we look through our limited senses and our fanciful minds, which produce a somewhat partial and distorted show of what they see. The show is not reality, but only a superficial covering, superimposed by the pettiness and vanity of our personal faculties.

Beneath the surface, there is a much greater world of unmanifest happening that is not apparent to our senses and minds. That unmanifest happening is like a surging flood — which carries along our little bodies and our minds, and all that they perceive. Beneath their petty and vain perceptions, they are just driven blind: pushed from somewhere else, like everything in the created world.

Thus, in the creation story, earlier stages of creation can be interpreted as deeper levels of manifestation, which are found to underlie the pictured surface of physical and mental perception. And the source of creation, called the 'one', can be interpreted as an underlying ground: of plain, uncompromised reality, beneath all differentiated picturing.

By thinking back in time, to an uncreated and timeless beginning, the story implies a reflection down, to an unconditioned and changeless ground of present experience. Since the 'one' is prior to time, it is unaffected by change. By trying to imagine such a prior unity, at the start of the world's creation, there is also a reflection down: to the same unity that now underlies one's own experience, in the immediate present.

Accordingly, the hymn turns next (in stanza 4) to our subjective experience of mind and desire, which are described as centred upon the 'one'. And we are told of inspired seers: who have searched intently back, from outward appearances, into the inner core of subjectivity. There, beneath the emptiness of outward show, they are said to have found out a common, central unity — which joins all different-seeming things together.

That common centre is at once subjective and impersonal. It can be found subjectively, by reflecting back within, beneath all outward show. As the reflection returns to source, it must transcend all seeming differences, of outward personality and world. The aim is thus an inmost centre that all experience shares in common: no matter in whose personality, nor at what time or place in the world.

It's from that inmost, common centre that the Vedas are supposed to draw their inspiration. They are conceived as the inspired sayings of authentic seers: who have found that centre and who stand established there. From there, seeing is direct, with the immediacy of pure insight. In the Vedas, such a seer is called a 'ṛṣi' or a 'kavi'.

A 'ṛṣi' is a pure see-er, with a direct insight into 'ṛta' or 'nature's underlying truth'. A 'kavi' is a 'poet': from the verb 'kū', whose meaning is associated with the 'coo'-ing cries of birds and the humming of bees. This implies a direct expression — which arises, quite spontaneously and naturally, from beneath the deliberations of thought. A 'kavi' is thus one who is inspired, from beyond the partial and biased promptings of mind and personal ego.

The hymn goes on (in stanza 5) to describe the effects of this inspiration, on culture and society. We are told of a subtle radiance that spreads out from the authentic vision of inspired seers, through their seminal creativity and their far-reaching capabilities. Here, another question is raised: of whether this radiance is deep or high, immanent or transcendent. And an answer is suggested that it can be seen both ways. On the one hand, it expresses an immanent potential: as it arises, of its own accord, from the underlying source in which the seers are established. On the other hand, it is transcendent: in the sense that it drives forcefully upwards, from within their personalities, to a far-reaching influence upon learning and tradition in the world outside.

Up to this point, the hymn has described the 'one' in a rather general way, as an underlying source that is shared in common, by everyone and everything. But then, how can this source be found? How can one look for it, in particular? The hymn ends (in stanzas 6 and 7) by suggesting such an enquiry, which questions how the world is known. It asks: 'Who truly knows?' And it points out that even the gods arise from creation. They are dependent parts of a created world; so we cannot look to them for an impartial knowledge of what is really true.

To understand this questioning, we need to take another look at the Vedic conception of a 'deva' or a 'god'. The word 'deva' is related to the English 'divine'. It implies a sacred light, shining out into the manifested world. In the Vedas, the gods are not just supernatural persons, ruling nature from outside. Instead, they are shining spirits, manifesting nature's varied powers and aspects, from within. In the macrocosm of the external world, the gods are personified descriptions of subtle energy: manifested in the natural phenomena of land, water, fire, atmosphere and sky. In the microcosm of individual experience, the gods shine out as our own living faculties: manifested in our feelings, thoughts, perceptions and our external acts.

So, when the gods are questioned in the Vedas, this isn't just a skepticism of some outmoded superstitions that are no longer taken seriously. The Vedas are quite serious about their gods. Thus, when the gods are questioned, the questioning is radical. It amounts to a complete skepticism of all belief in anything created in the world, or anything constructed and construed in anyone's experience.

This doubt applies to everything in the external world and to all our faculties of mind and sense. All objects and energies, all persons and all faculties arise from creation. No matter how subtle or powerful they may be, they are still dependent parts of a created world. They are thus compromised, by dependence and partiality. That leaves us inherently in doubt: about what they really are, and what they tell us.

With all creation thus in doubt, the hymn suggests a way out. It speaks of a transcending witness, in the highest heaven. Only that witness, it concludes, can know truly, whether the world exists or not.

What sort of conclusion is this? From the phrase 'in the highest heaven', it may be taken as an affirmation of religious belief. But it may also be interpreted as pressing on, beyond all mere belief, with a thoroughly skeptical questioning.

There is in fact a problem of translation. The English phrase 'in the highest heaven' is a translation of the Sanskrit 'parame vyoman'. 'Parama' means 'supreme' or 'furthest beyond'. 'Vyoma' means 'heaven' or 'pure space'. For both words, the essential sense is not physical height, but a more subtle transcendence. Most obviously, 'vyoma' is the sky above; but more essentially, it is the unaffected pervasion of pure space, through all the changes and differences of conditioned things.

When our eyes look up towards the sky, they see a variety of changing sights: like birds that fly, mists and clouds that gather and disperse, the sunlight that appears by day, the moon and stars that shine by night. These are sights that come and go, against the background of the sky. Looking up into the sky, we are struck by a vast background of space and time — which continues on and on, containing everything. The sky thus represents a background continuity, which transcends the changes that appear and disappear in it.

In the Vedic concept of 'vyoma', the sky is used as a cosmic symbol. It does not only represent the physical sky, seen through our eyes and senses. Nor does it only represent some pictured heaven, conceived on the basis of belief. More fundamentally, it directs attention in a search for truth, beyond all physical and mental pictures. In this search, 'vyoma' represents a transcendent background that continues through all experience: through all perceptions, thoughts and feelings of a physical or mental world.

What then is meant by 'parame vyoman' or 'in the highest heaven'? Through a little reflection, it can be seen to signify a background that is utterly beyond all change. That background is the same throughout experience, entirely detached from all changing actions in the world. By speaking of a witness there, in that changeless background, the Vedic hymn suggests an ultimate standpoint: of complete detachment from body and mind. It is only from there that knowledge can be true.

Looking In

Since our bodies and minds do not know fully, they inevitably introduce a confusing and distorting element of ignorance. So, to attain clear knowledge, one has to stand back from them and all their biased faculties. One has to stand as an unaffected witness: quite unprejudiced by all the partial feelings, thoughts, perceptions and activities through which the world appears.

Is such detachment possible? To know the world, each person depends upon a body and a mind that are called 'mine'. Without this body and mind, a person cannot do anything, nor even experience anything, in the physical and mental world. So, body and mind seem indispensable. Together, they make up one's personality, which thus appears at the centre of their physical and mental activities in a surrounding world. All of one's actions, observations and enjoyments are theirs. How then can one detach oneself from them and all their partialities?

An answer is suggested by the very word 'mine'. When a person speaks of 'my' body or 'my' mind, that implies a sense of self, to which both body and mind belong. In the Hindu tradition, that self is called 'ātman'. It is conceived as pure spirit, found at the inmost core of personal identity. In search of it, one's own identity comes into question: as one distinguishes an inner source, of pure seeing, from which all outward faculties arise. Such a search is described in the *Ṛg-veda* 1.164.37-39:

> I do not know this that it seems
> I am. Concealed, tied up
> by mind, I wander.
>
> When the first-born of nature's truth
> has come to me, then alone may I
> receive a rightful share of speech. *– 37*
>
> It goes turning back and forth,
> self-empowered from within:
> the undying issued forth
> together with the dying,
> from one common origin.
>
> Those that get diverted turn
> in different ways, continually.
> They always look at some one thing,
> and do not see some other thing. *– 38*
>
> All gods (and all the faculties
> they represent) are seated finally
> in that transcendent background which
> continues changeless through the chants.

What will someone, who does not
know that, do with the chants?
They who know it are themselves
at one, established here. *–39*

This passage is concerned with our experience of individuality. First (in stanza 37), it describes the appearance of a seeming ego. Entangled in mind, uncertain of itself, the ego wanders, somewhat helplessly. Its only rightful meaning is to share in the expression of nature's underlying truth.

Next (in stanza 38), the ego is described as a mixture of two parts, one deathless and the other dying: both issued forth together, from a single origin. The undying part is empowered from within, as it keeps reflecting back into its source and emerging forth again. As it emerges, it appears together with a dying personality: perceiving other dying things outside. Thus, in all appearances of personal ego, a self-empowered, deathless life is seen inevitably compromised: shown always mixed with driven, dying things. The mixture is unstable, made up from changing faculties which keep on getting diverted in different directions: producing partial views that each see something, but leave something else unseen.

Finally (in stanza 39), a common basis is identified. It is a transcending background, to which all Vedic chants aspire: the same, unchanging background where all powers and energies are seated. A knowledge of that background is essential to the chants. What use are they, it is asked, to 'someone who does not know that'? The purpose of the Vedas is thus made quite explicit. It is to know the changeless background from which all change arises. And, to know that background is to stand established in it: as one's own, true individuality, shared in common with all else. As the Veda says (at the end of stanza 39):

They who know it are themselves
at one, established here.

The Mantra 'Om'

In the Vedas and the Upaniṣads, the source and background of creation is described as 'akṣara' or 'changeless'. And the same word 'akṣara' can also mean a 'letter of the alphabet' or a 'syllable or word of spoken sound'.

Of course, as a person speaks, letters, syllables and words are heard as passing sounds, which keep on changing all the time. But, as such sounds of language pass, each represents a changeless something — which can later reappear, as a repetition of the same thing. We imply such a changeless something every time we recognize some sound as a letter or a syllable or a word that we have heard before. It is then the *same* letter or the *same* syllable or the *same* word that has already been heard — though spoken differently — on previous occasions. Thus, behind the passing sounds of speech, we somehow recognize particular letters, syllables and words that stay the same. This 'sameness' is essentially implied, whenever the word 'akṣara' is used.

One syllable, in particular, is described as 'akṣara'. It is *the* akṣara: the one, unchanging syllable that signifies all speech, all expression and creation, all experience. That syllable is 'om'. In the texts, the actual sound 'om' appears first in the early Upaniṣads; but traditional scholars say that the practice of reciting 'om' goes back much further than that. It is taken to be implied in many Vedic passages where the word 'akṣara' occurs (including the *Ṛg-veda* 1.164.39, the last stanza translated above).

What makes the word 'om' interesting is that its recitation is a living practice, very much in active use today. And this practice tells us forcefully how chanted sound has long been used to convey knowledge: in an extremely condensed, though rather cryptic way.

On religious occasions, 'om' is often used as an affirmation of faith, at the beginning or end of many chants. It is then a kind of ritual punctuation, showing where a chant arises into manifestation or returns to origin. In this ceremonial use, 'om' is somewhat similar to the Latin 'āmēn'.

However, there are also more intensive practices, where the sound 'om' is repeated by itself, over and over again. And here, the shape of sound is intimately linked to an encoded meaning.

Phonetically, the sound is analysed into three elements: 'a', 'u' and 'm'. 'A' is pronounced as '-er' in 'father' (without any 'r' sound). 'U' is pronounced as 'oo' in 'good'. 'M' is pronounced as a humming sound 'mmm...'. This analysis is not just theoretical. 'Om' can be pronounced in a prolonged way: with an initial 'a' sound merging gradually into an 'u' and then into an 'mmm...', which fades finally into silence. The 'a' and 'u' sounds coalesce to form an 'o' and then join into the 'mmm...', thus forming 'om'.

But, in pronouncing 'om', the coalescence of sound and silence is even more crucial. The initial 'a' emerges imperceptibly out of silence, as it merges with the subsequent 'u'; and the 'mmm...' is a gradually fading sound that carries on from the 'u', into an imperceptible merging with a final background of pure silence. The whole point is to emphasize a sense of background continuity, which carries on quite undisturbed, beneath the rising and falling of changing sound.

In this experience of progressing sound, the coalescing elements may be interpreted philosophically, as different states of experience:

- 'A' represents the waking state: where our minds and senses see objects, in an outside world. Here, experience has an outside and an inside. There is a world of space and time outside, perceived through a stream of perceptions, thoughts and feelings in each person's mind.
- 'U' represents the dream state: where our minds imagine an apparent world, made up of their own thoughts and feelings. Here, experience has an inside, but no outside. All objects in a dream are in the dreaming mind. There is no world of space and time outside, but only a succession of dream appearances that come and go in mind.

- 'Mmm...' represents the deep sleep state: where there are no appearances, neither in an outside world, nor within some inner mind. Here, there is no sense of outside or inside, no distribution of objects in space, no flow of happenings, no passing states of time. There's only pure experience, quite undivided and undisturbed by any seen activity.

Viewed from the waking state, deep sleep can be quite paradoxical. On the one hand, it seems to be quite blank and empty, and therefore negative. But on the other hand, there must be something positive in its quiet experience; because we keep returning there, to relax from physical and mental activity. As we fall into deep sleep, our thoughts and minds become dissolved in it; and we often wake refreshed, with a clearer and more settled understanding. That's why we sometimes talk of 'sleeping on' a problem, as a way of solving it.

Thus, despite the seeming blankness of deep sleep, it has an intimate connection with the absorption of perceptions, thoughts and feelings into settled understanding. Beneath its negative appearance, the deep sleep state has a profound capacity for assimilating mental activity into a quiet understanding that continues at the background of experience. From a subjective point of view, deep sleep is just that state where all changing activities become absorbed into their continuing background.

That is why, as 'om' is chanted, the deep sleep state is represented by the 'mmm...' sound, which merges into a background of quiet stillness. As the sound trails off and merges into stillness, attention is supposed to follow it and thus reflect into the changeless background.

Here, the syllable 'om' is being used as a 'mantra'. Literally, a 'mantra' is an 'instrument of thought' or a 'mental device'. In particular, when some chanted sound is called a 'mantra', it is implied that the shape of sound is being used as a device to direct attention and mental energy, in order to achieve some desired effect. The verses of the Vedas are thus called 'mantras', and so are other chants whose shapes of sound are valued for their special effects upon the chanting and the listening mind.

As a mantra, 'om' is called the 'praṇava'; from the verb 'praṇu' which means to 'reverberate' or to 'make a humming or droning sound'. In the chanting of 'om', the shape of sound has a precisely focused use. It is meant to draw attention through the initial 'a' and 'u' into the droning 'mmm…', and thus to take attention down from chanting mind into the underlying background of experience.

As the chanting is repeated, sound rises up from that same background and returns back there again. As the repetition is sustained, it is meant to emphasize a positive emphasis upon that background: through a repeated reflection that keeps returning back there. All sounds and all appearances are to be seen as mere expressions of that inner background, reverberating out from there. The mantra 'om' thus represents a dissolution back into a changeless source, from which new appearances are born.

This cycle, of dissolution and rebirth, is called 'saṁsāra'. It refers to any coherent experience of change, where different elements are joined together in transforming happenings. In the Hindu tradition, such experience is described as a repeating cycle: of emission and absorption, creation and dissolution, birth and death. All changing flow is conceived to manifest this cycle — continually repeated at different scales of time.

Krama Sṛṣṭi — Cyclic Cosmology

At a macrocosmic scale, many myths describe the universe as a vast process of pulsating emanation.

This process starts with an inherent paradox — as the passing of time and the differentiation of space have somehow to be born, from an undifferentiated timelessness that underlies them. But, once time and difference have paradoxically begun, there is a procession of macrocosmic ages in which we find ourselves now, seeing only a very small and limited part of the whole process.

Through our human personality and our resultant failings, we represent a destructive tendency that must eventually engulf the whole created universe. This destructive tendency proceeds through change and difference; but all its passing changes and its conflicting differences keep taking it inevitably on to an eventual dissolution, where it must get taken back into its timeless source. From there, the cosmic cycle of creation, development, destruction and dissolution will repeat; as it has been repeating in the past, before the universe we see today was born.

This kind of creation is called 'krama sṛṣṭi'. It represents a temporally ordered process (krama) of emanation (sṛṣṭi) through which the universe recurrently develops, towards a recurrent dissolution, in the course of repeating time. The process thus described is clearly meant to be quite universal: including all created beings and all events that anyone perceives, from any point of view. But here, as in all such descriptions of universality, there is a tricky problem. Though what's described is meant to be universal, the descriptions made of it are not. They have their idiosyncrasies, depending on their points of view.

In the Hindu tradition, this problem of idiosyncrasy is freely admitted, by presenting an extraordinary variety of macrocosmic myths. The myths are clearly idiosyncratic: meant for the various needs of different groups and individuals who use them. Their users recognize them as stories that are told and retold differently, in various versions. And in effect, through all the differences, the stories have a common purpose. They are each designed to encourage an expanded contemplation, beyond some current narrowness of personal and cultural perception.

As a religious myth describes the universe, it tells a story of some contemplated deity. The contemplation is designed to help transcend the narrow limitations of the audience for whom the myth is meant. But, for a myth to work effectively, it must appeal to its audience, through just those narrow limitations — of perception and insight — that it is trying to transcend. To make its broadening appeal, each myth is idiosyncratically described, to suit the particular needs of its intended audience. So, a mythic deity is represented in some idiosyncratic form: as playing some appealing part, in the manifestation of the universe.

In classical and medieval times (as represented in various Smṛti texts), Hinduism developed a broad pantheon of religious deities: who are conceived to play their various parts in the functioning of cosmic manifestation. The pantheon is headed by a trinity: of Brahmā (the Creator), Viṣṇu (the Preserver) and Śiva (the Destroyer). Represented thus, these gods are masculine; but they each have a feminine aspect, represented by female partners who are often worshipped and contemplated in their own right. Brahmā's partner is Sarasvatī, the goddess of creative inspiration and learning. Viṣṇu's partner is Lakṣmī, the goddess of prosperity. And Śiva's partner is both Śaktī and Kālī, the goddess of life-giving power and all-consuming death.

Beyond this trinity, further aspects of divinity are represented by a great number of associated gods and incarnations, which may in turn be worshipped and contemplated in their own right. There are thus many variations of worship and contemplation, and the variations can differ greatly from one another. They go along with many very different myths and stories, about the life cycle of the universe. The idiosyncrasies of human aspiration here take rather different paths, in these attempts to look beyond what sense and mind immediately perceive.

But, beneath these differences of cosmic myth, there is a common metaphor. Their description of the universe is biological. Each deity implies an underlying spirit, somehow expressed throughout the universe: and that expression makes the universe alive. All such myths describe the universe as a living organism, whose unity expresses an organic functioning of self-renewing life. Even when the universe is utterly destroyed, an essential principle of life remains, though it is then unmanifest.

In that unmanifested state, life is present, though unseen: just like the unseen essence of life within a tiny seed. This conception is described in a story from the *Chāndogya Upaniṣad*. Here, Śvetaketu is being taught by his father (who speaks first):

> 'Bring a fruit from this nyagrodha tree.'
>
> 'Here, Sir.'
>
> 'Break it.'
>
> 'It is broken, Sir.'

'What do you see in it?'

'These seeds, Sir, like tiny particles.'

'Well, break one of them.'

'It is broken, Sir.'

'What do you see in it?'

'Nothing at all, Sir.' *– 6.12.1*

Śvetaketu's father said to him:

'Truly, dear son, this subtlety
which you do not see,
truly dear son, of this subtlety
the great nyagrodha tree thus stands.
Be sure of this, dear son.' *– 6.12.2*

'That which is this subtlety
is that "this-itself"-ness
which is all this world.

'That is truth. That is self.
Śvetaketu, you are that.' *– from 6.12.3*

In this illustration, the tree represents the entire universe, as we see it grown today, with all its vast size and mind-blowing complexity. And it is said that like the tree, the manifested universe consists of nothing more than the unseen subtlety of life that's found within each tiny seed. Before the universe was born, it was this subtlety unmanifest. Now that the universe has grown, it is in essence this same subtlety of inner life, seen manifested into outward form.

According to the *Chāndogya Upaniṣad*, that essence is an inmost self — which lives throughout the universe, and in Śvetaketu's personality. That, in truth, is the life of all the universe, and Śvetaketu's life as well. It is from there that all renewal comes: throughout the manifested happenings of space and time, and in each individual's experience.

Karma — Transmigration and Psychology

At the scale of a person's lifetime, dissolution and rebirth are described by the theory of transmigration.

In this theory, a person's body is conceived as a physical rebirth, expressing a more subtle mind that is reborn in it. The mind has been through many previous births: in previous bodies that were born into the world, where they grew up, matured, decayed and died. A person's current mind and body are thus seen as the result of a long development, extending back through many previous cycles of bodily rebirth and death.

When a person's body dies, how can the mind continue to another birth? This question is answered by a sophisticated conception of action, as manifesting different levels: gross and subtle.

- The gross level is that of material bodies, seen by our physical senses. Through their material actions upon each other, gross bodies give rise to other bodies, at a material level of causation. It is at this level that the body of a child is born, from its material parents.
- However, as we understand the world, material bodies and their actions are interpreted to express more subtle levels that our minds conceive. Through such interpretation, we can find more meaning and coherence than our unaided senses see. It is at these more subtle levels that we understand a child's intelligence and aptitudes and character.

In Sanskrit, the general word for action is 'karma'. It comes from the root 'kṛ', meaning to 'do', to 'make' or to 'act'. When the word 'karma' is used, it carries two kinds of implication. On the one hand, it refers to an apparent act or an objective performance, like a ritual or a duty. But, on the other hand, it refers to a pervasive process of subtle causation — which is conceived to underlie our physical and mental acts and their continuing results, in the formation of our personalities and our experience of the world. A person's karma is the cumulative effect of previous actions, shaping how that person acts today and what that person will experience in the future.

As a child is born and grows, two levels of causation come together:

- At the gross objective level, a child receives an inheritance from its parental family. This inheritance is partly genetic, from the parents' bodies; partly social and economic, from the family's status and wealth; and partly cultural, from the behaviour learned through family upbringing.
- But, beneath the family inheritance, there are more subtle tendencies and aptitudes and dispositions with which a child is gifted (or sometimes burdened, as the case may be). These are conceived to be inherited from previous births: resulting from past actions and experiences in previous bodies, before the present child was born.

The second level of causation is purely mental. Here, cause does not work through the actions of one body upon another, in any physical space. Instead, it works essentially in mental time — through after-effects that have been left behind, by previous mental states.

The transmigrating mind is reborn in a new body. In this new state, effects remain from previous mental states that have now vanished. These effects are called 'saṁskāras' (trainings) or 'vāsanās' (residues). And they are conceived as seeds — which have been sown by previous actions. In the course of continuing experience, such seeds of karma keep on being sown, and then continue in the mind unmanifest: as unseen potencies that later on get activated into manifestation.

As a biological and psychological description, this conception of karma is just common sense. If we consider the process of our lives, as each of us experiences the world, then it is only common sense that our actions and experiences result in personal tendencies and inclinations which go into the make-up of each person's character. As we go about our lives, our actions take us through a succession of experiences — which keep on passing by, appearing and disappearing at the surface of our minds.

But, though they disappear at the surface, our experiences get somehow absorbed into longer lasting attitudes and traits of character and stores of memory, which continue underneath. Thus, as our experiences pass by, they leave their effects behind: in a subtle assimilation of experience that continues unmanifest, beneath the surface of our minds. Through that underlying assimilation, we develop a psychological and human potential — which is expressed in further actions, and takes us on to further experiences.

In short, the theory of karma is a description of living development. And the approach it takes is psychological. It says that living creatures develop through subtle inclinations that their actions leave behind. These subtle inclinations, called 'saṁskāras', are primarily mental. They are inclinations of intention, thought and feeling, which result from previous actions and experiences. In the course of our lives, as we pass through many different experiences, these subtle inclinations are assimilated at the depth of our minds, into a developed potential that manifests itself from there.

In this psychological description, our mental processes are not based on any brain or nervous system that manipulates information behind the scenes, like a computer making calculations behind a video screen. Nor are mental processes based finally on any language that uses particular symbols and symbolic structures to articulate ideas. Instead, all mental processes are based upon an underlying continuity that carries on through changing mental states. That continuity is a subjective ground: deep within our minds, beneath the changes of apparent objects that come and go at the surface.

It's at this underlying ground that actions and experiences leave their effects behind. And it is from this ground that future actions and experiences arise, to carry on the process of experience. Thus, when an action comes to end, its energy becomes absorbed into an unmanifested potency, which emerges in some later action, somewhere further on. This is a common psychological experience: of subtle influences coming from the past, to motivate some present action. From here, the theory of karma goes on to a more radical position. It says that the whole universe is driven by the same subtle energies and influences that we find within our minds. Just as subtle influences of feeling, thought and intention are found expressed in our living bodies and their actions, so too such subtle influences are expressed throughout the universe.

In this conception, the entire universe is a living organism with two aspects: gross and subtle. The gross aspect, consisting of material bodies, is only a crude and superficial appearance, seen by our gross senses. Material bodies are only crude coagulations of subtler flows of energy, which we can see more subtly by looking back into our minds. As we fall deeper back into our minds, gross bodies and their actions can be interpreted as expressions of a more subtle flow of influence and happening.

For example, when a child is born, not only its mental disposition but also its physical embodiment can be interpreted as showing the influence of its past lives. Thus, its capabilities of body, its genetic inheritance, its social and economic circumstances, the family in which it's born and the upbringing it receives can all be interpreted as manifesting a human potential that it has been developing through a succession of past births. This kind of interpretation is perhaps most famously illustrated in the story of the Buddha, whom Hindus revere along with Buddhists.

But on what basis can such an interpretation be made: of subtle energies and influences, behind the objects that our senses see? How can one find out more about the outer universe, by reflecting deeper back into one's own experience? If a reflection deeper in can help one find out more outside, then there must be some common ground which one's own experience shares with outside things.

In the Hindu conception of karma, it's from this common ground that all birth and all experiences arise. As Varuṇa tells his son Bhṛgu, in a story from the *Taittirīya Upaniṣad*, knowledge is attained by investigating back to that supporting origin:

> Truly, that from which these beings are born,
> that by which born beings live,
> that into which those who depart dissolve,
>
> that you must seek to know.
> That is all reality. —*from 3.1*

Yugapat Sṛṣṭi — Creation All at Once

In the experience of our minds, each succeeding moment may be conceived as an instantaneous rebirth, following upon the dissolution of the past.

At each present moment, previous moments have now passed, and future moments have not come. Only the present state of mind appears, as an instantaneous thought. In the immediate present, there is just this appearance — which we may call a single thought. If one considers only what is immediate in present mind, there is no time to analyse it and divide it into parts. So, in the present, what appears immediately can only be a single experience: of undivided thought that now appears in mind.

And yet, in this single thought that is now present, there is a sense of time — including an assimilation of many past experiences and an anticipation of many more experiences that are yet to come. How is this possible? How can the simple immediacy of the present be reconciled with the complexities that we perceive through passing time?

In Advaita (or non-dualist) philosophy, this question is answered by distinguishing two aspects of mental experience:

- On the one hand, there is a succession of passing states in time.
- On the other hand, if any state is examined as it immediately occurs, then it is found to be a single thought, arising by itself from an underlying background of experience.

In this mental experience, all sense of time depends upon the underlying background. It is there that the assimilation of past experiences is understood, as each present thought arises. And it is there, to the same background, that each thought returns, as it passes on and gets assimilated in its turn.[13]

---

[13] As it is said, in the *Yoga-vāsiṣṭha*:

> paramān nibhaso jātaḥ saṅkalpaḥ svottha ucyate
> jāyate svayam evā'sau svayam eva vilīyate

footnote continued on next page ...

As each state of mind arises, it produces an appearance — of some object at the forefront of attention. And in this attention is understood everything that is known about the object: its location, its relationship with other objects, and how it is part of a larger world. Thus, while the object is perceived at the front tip of attention, this narrowed perception is built upon a broader basis of understanding, at the background of experience.

For example, suppose a driver notices that his car is sounding a little odd. Many things go into this perception: like how the car sounded before, the various other things that have been happening with the car, what sort of car it is, the uses for which it is needed, the other people who are going to drive it, the driver's previous experiences with cars and machines and mechanics, and so on. All these things are understood at the background of experience, while attention is focused on the sound of the car. The background understanding provides a subjective basis, upon which the driver listens to the sound.

Figure 2

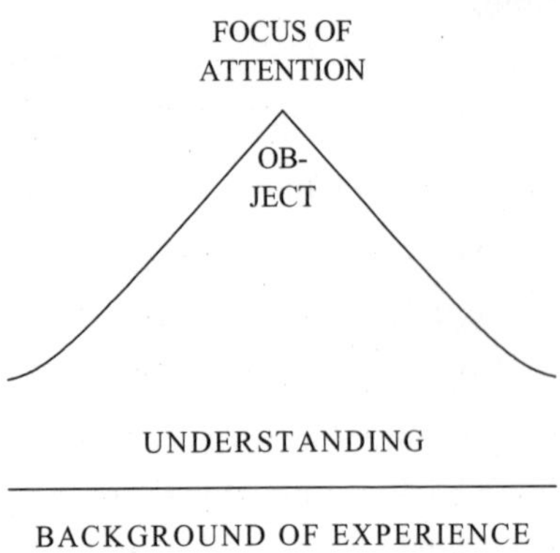

We have here a mental picture of experience: as rising from an underlying background to focus on a particular object. Figure 2 shows an illustration.

What is this subjective basis, at the background of experience? It is evidently the underlying depth of our minds, beneath the apparent surface of limited mental attention.

As attention turns to different

... footnote continued from previous page

> Born from the final background,
> Thought is called 'self-arising'.
> It is born just by itself.
> Just by itself, it is dissolved away. – 4.53.6

objects, they appear one after another at the surface of our minds, in a changing stream of limited perceptions. But we know more than this limited and changing surface. As we see an apparent object, we somehow take other things into account, in our understanding of what is seen. So we do not just *see* things at the front tip of the mind's attention. We also *understand* them, and thus take different things into account, at the background of experience.

Beneath the changing surface of appearance, there is a background knowledge that continues quietly, without distracting attention from the apparent objects which come and go at the surface. That quiet, continuing knowledge enables us to take into account what our minds do not make appear. Whatever may appear and disappear, that quiet background of knowledge carries on beneath. From underneath, it supports each appearance with our entire understanding of the world, including the understanding that we have of our perceiving faculties and of ourselves as perceivers in the world.

Whenever any object is perceived, its perception draws upon the background of experience, expressing a prior understanding that we have of the entire world and its perception. This prior understanding is built into each apparent object. In every mental state, we are presented with the whole of our experience: with some apparent object in the foreground, and the remainder understood behind. The object is a part perception of a larger world that it implies. Each mental state is thus conceived as a 'vṛtti' or a 'transformation', which modifies the mind's perception and interpretation of an implied totality.

As one state is replaced by another, the former state dissolves into the changeless background. Then there occurs a timeless interval, from which the latter state arises. The process of experience is thus conceived as a succession of momentary transformations, with timeless intervals in between.

At every moment, the world is instantaneously created and destroyed: in the perception of some passing object that is interpreted to show a larger world. This is called 'yugapat sṛṣṭi' or 'creation all at once'. Here, the perceived world is created together

Figure 3

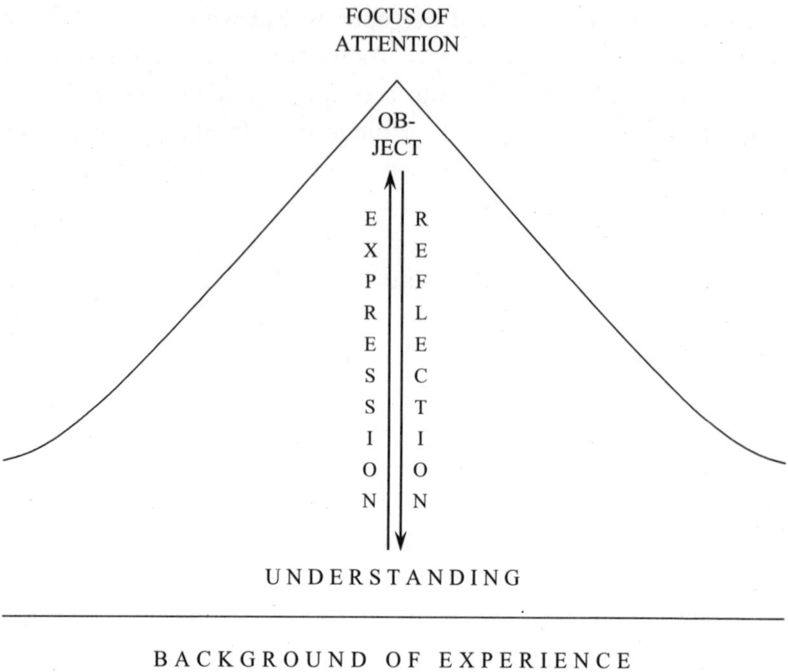

with its immediate perception and the person who is supposed to be perceiving it. But the same immediacy also destroys the world at once: as the perception is interpreted and taken in, reflecting back into the timeless ground from which it is expressed.

In the perception of each object, there is thus an expression of understanding from the background of experience; followed by a reflection that returns into the same underlying background, as the perception is interpreted and understood. This cycle of expression and reflection is illustrated in figure 3 (above), by a small addition to the preceding diagram.

Differing Accounts

What are we to make of such greatly differing accounts of rebirth and dissolution: from the rise and fall of chanted sound, through vast cosmic cycles, to the instantaneous appearances and disappearances of passing experience in the present moment?

They show an understanding that all experience is ultimately singular: pulsating always from a single source, at all scales of space and time; but never changed within, no matter how enormous or minute the fluctuations seem from the outside. Each experience, no matter how short or long, is another repetition of that one singularity, which thus connects all different-seeming things.

NATURE'S MANIFESTING LIFE

Personal Ego and Impartial Objectivity

Through cosmic myths and psychological analysis, the Hindu tradition presents us with very different accounts of how the things we see are found created. These differing accounts are reconciled through the concept of 'prakṛti' or 'nature'. For nature is taken to include the creative process of a perceiver's mind, along with everything else in the universe.

In the word 'prakṛti', there is an interesting ambiguity. 'Kṛti' means 'activity'; and the prefix 'pra-' has a double implication. It means 'forward', like the English prefix 'pro-'. And it also means 'before', like the English prefix 'pre-'. Thus prakṛti includes not only actions that go forward from change to change, but also a prior source from which the motivation arises. The ongoing actions are nature's changing manifestations, in physical and mental phenomena. The prior source is underlying nature, continuing unmanifest, at the changeless background of both inner and outer experience.

The underlying source is called 'pradhāna' or primal: thus conceiving it as a first principle, of which all things perceived are changing modifications. And it is also called 'mūla-prakṛti' or 'root nature': thus conceiving it as a support that draws up animating energy into a living manifestation. (Just as the root of a tree is a support that draws up nutrition into the living manifestation of branches and leaves and flowers.)

When nature is conceived like this, it is essentially complete, in itself. It is itself the source of all the actions that take place in it, of all the phenomena through which it manifests itself. It includes not only the environment, but also our personal and technological capabilities.

Why then do people think so often of their personalities and their technologies in opposition to nature, as though our actions could somehow go against the nature that they manifest? According to the *Bhagavad-gītā*, the reason is a false image that we have of ourselves: as personal, doing egos:

> Everywhere, all acts are done
> by nature's constituting qualities.
> Mistaking ego for the self,
> a person thinks: 'I am the doer.' *– 3.27*

Each particular doer is inevitably limited, by particular faculties and capabilities of action. If one identifies oneself as a doer, one's perception becomes inevitably limited, and therefore partial. There's no escape, the *Gītā* says, through technical sophistication; nor through personal restraint:

> One acts according to one's own nature.
> A learned, knowledgeable person
> is no exception. Beings follow nature.
> What will holding back achieve? *– 3.33*

Here, 'holding back' is treated as a negative action. Accordingly, the driven partiality of action cannot be avoided by doing or not doing anything, by any action or restraint towards some limited object. To attain impartiality, a deeper understanding is required, beyond our senses and our minds:

> Our senses are transcendent, it is said.
> Beyond the senses is the mind.
> Beyond the mind as well is understanding.
> Beyond the understanding is just *that*. *– 3.42*

At the depth of understanding, all faculties are known objectively, as nature's happenings:

> As truth is known, one who joins into it
> can understand: 'I don't do anything.
>
> 'Sight, hearing, touch, smell, eating,
> going here and there, sleeping, breathing,
> speaking, holding on and letting go,
> eyes opening and closing…
>
> 'these are just faculties, acting
> towards their various objects.' *– 5.8-9*

Thus, an unaffected knowing is utterly detached from doing faculties. That detachment is meant to uncover a pure impartiality of knowledge; as Kṛṣṇa tells Arjuna, in the last chapter of the *Gītā*:

> Pure knowledge is just that by which
> one changeless principle
> of undivided nature
> is seen in all divided things.
>
> That's what you need to know. *– 18.20*

In the approach taken here, knowledge is completed by detaching it from nature's manifesting actions. Through such a detachment, all objects and all faculties are left to nature: where they are seen objectively, as instruments of nature's happening. No faculty of body or of mind is then left out, to act on nature from outside. Thus nature is conceived to act spontaneously, moving of its own accord, from its own source within.

Illuminating Consciousness

Since our perceiving faculties belong to nature, it manifests itself through them. In everyone's experience, it produces the appearances that come and go, succeeding one another in the course of time. At each moment, what appears is lit by consciousness. That consciousness is pure illumination, witnessing what comes and goes. It is not a changing act, but just that silent knowing which illuminates the changing acts that nature manifests.

As changing acts and objects come and go, they are manifested 'noisily', competing for attention in a stream of clamouring replacement at the surface of appearance. Throughout this passing stream, consciousness continues quietly, at the underlying background of experience. There, consciousness is utterly detached, from the appearances that nature manifests before its light.

When consciousness is conceived like this, as a knowing principle before which nature acts, it is called 'puruṣa'. In Sanskrit, and in many modern Indian languages, the word 'puruṣa' is used in an everyday sense to mean a 'human being' or a 'person'. However, it has a philosophical usage which is quite different from the English word 'person'. The English word comes from the Latin 'persona' — which originally meant an actor's mask, and hence an actor's role. As this derivation shows, the word inherently implies an outward sense of manifesting action.

In the word 'puruṣa', there is an implication which is just the opposite. Philosophically used, 'puruṣa' implies an inner principle that is shared in common by all human beings, beneath their differences of outward personality. In this sense, 'puruṣa' is an inner 'humanness', as described in the *Bṛhadāraṇyaka Upaniṣad*:

> That, in truth, is this 'humanness'
> in all bodies: abiding here
> at rest within the body. *–from 2.5.18*

In this passage, the word used for body is 'pur', which literally means a 'rampart wall' or a 'fortified enclosure' or a 'walled town or city'. The body is conceived as mere outward fortification: within which the inner principle called 'puruṣa' lives at peace, undisturbed by the conflicts and destructions of the outside world. And, the Upaniṣad goes on to conclude, this inner principle is an unlimited self — which is present everywhere, comprehending everything within its own experience:

> This self is all reality,
> experiencing everything. *–from 2.5.19*

In the thirteenth chapter of the *Bhagavad-gītā*, this inner principle is more explicitly described as pure consciousness, completely independent of the changing faculties and qualities that it illuminates:

> It has no faculties; but shines
> illuminating every faculty
> and quality perceived.
>
> It is itself quite unattached,
> yet everything depends on it.

In it, there are no qualities,
as it experiences them all. – 13.14

It's said to be that light of lights
which is beyond obscurity.

As knowledge in itself, it's that
which should be known — which can be reached
as knowledge standing firmly back
within each heart, in everyone. – 13.17

Here, knowledge is described as that 'light of lights which is beyond obscurity'. In other words, it is that knowing light which never gets obscured. As other lights appear and disappear, it carries on throughout experience, illuminating all appearances. It is consciousness itself: the illuminating principle that is essential to all experience. It's that which knows: the knowing subject which is always present, no matter what appears or disappears. That pure subject is identified as puruṣa, the inner principle of consciousness which all persons share in common, beneath their physical and mental differences.

But, in this description, it must be understood that the word 'consciousness' is not being used in its mental sense. It does not refer to the changing stream of perceptions, thoughts and feelings in our minds. Here, that stream is not regarded as subjective knowledge, but as an objective production of nature. The stream is a succession of manifestations, objectively produced by nature. Each passing manifestation is illuminated by reflecting light from consciousness — which shines subjectively, ever-present and unmixed, from the inmost centre of experience. And there, within each person's heart, consciousness is found as self-illuminating light: the knowing ground of all experience.

Knowing and Doing

Side by side with consciousness, as the subjective principle, the *Gītā* speaks of nature, as the objective principle. In the following passage, 'puruṣa' is translated as 'consciousness':

You need to know that consciousness
and nature are both unbegun;
and that all changes and all
qualities are nature's happenings. *– 13.19*

In doing, doership and what
is done, the underlying principle
is spoken of as 'nature'.

In the experience of
enjoyments and dissatisfactions,
the underlying principle
is spoken of as 'consciousness'. *– 13.20*

In manifesting nature, it
is consciousness that stands within,
experiencing the qualities
born forth as nature manifests.

For good or ill, as wombs give rise
to passing births, in every case
the cause is an association
of some manifesting qualities
with consciousness itself. *– 13.21*

It is the witness, looking on,
confirming and supporting what
is seen. It is the subject of
experience, the boundless Lord
to whom all that's experienced
belongs. It is the truth of self,
with nothing to be found beyond.

But these are only ways of speech:
describing consciousness here in
the body, and yet quite beyond. *– 13.22*

This passage describes a paradox that is inherent in the notion of embodied life. Within our living bodies, we experience a consciousness that somehow knows a world beyond its immediate embodiment. Thus, paradoxically, consciousness is both *within* the body and *beyond* it (13.22 above).[14] Whenever a living person is born, that birth implies a compromising association, between a knowing consciousness and some qualities of personality in which it is supposed to be embodied (13.21 above). In the manifested world, consciousness is always seen associated with compromising qualities that nature manifests.

This manifest association, between consciousness and nature, is conceived in two ways: negative and positive.

- On the one hand, consciousness appears degraded by associating it with the limited qualities of a personal ego. In Sanskrit, 'ego' is called 'ahaṅkāra', which means literally: 'I-acting'. Each personal ego is thus conceived as a confused mixture of knowing self and acting personality. Through this confusion of knowing and acting, our minds and bodies appear to possess a qualified consciousness that gets degraded by dissatisfaction and limitation and passing pettiness.
- On the other hand, behind its degraded appearance in our personal egos, consciousness itself remains quite unaffected, in its pure illumination of what nature manifests. And the illumination is conceived as nature's inner inspiration. Thus inspired, nature's actions are essentially positive. They do not act from calculating how to gain some narrow object of egotistical desire. Instead,

---

[14] In the preceding translation, this stanza (13.22) is a little elaborated, to bring out the meaning of a string of Sanskrit epithets whose literal translation is rather lifeless. Here is a more literal translation (with apologies for an awkward opacity that is quite alien to the spirit of the original):

> The onlooker and confirmer,
> the supporter, experiencer,
> great Lord, ultimate self.
>
> And though thus spoken of
> in this body, consciousness beyond.

nature's acts are done spontaneously: inspired by an inner principle that lights them from within. They are done for its sake, not for objective gain.

Both these aspects are described in the *Sāṅkhya-kārikā*. Here (to allow for an approach that is a little different from the *Bhagavad-gītā*), the word 'puruṣa' is translated as 'inner principle':

> The inner principle is consciousness.
> But, in the world, it comes
> to suffering: created by
> degenerating change and death.
>
> Where subtle body does not cease,
> there suffering is natural.
> [For subtle body is the mind,
> which makes the inner principle
> seem brought into the world outside.] *– 55*
>
> As milk unknowingly performs
> a function nourishing the growth
> of a young child; so also
> primal nature serves the liberation
> of the inner principle. *– 57*
>
> Just as a dancer shows her dance
> on stage, and then retires from it;
> so also nature shows herself
> before the inner principle,
> and ceases then to manifest. *– 59*
>
> All qualities belong to nature,
> as she acts in many ways:
> not for the sake of objects gained,
>
> but serving only for the sake
> of that true inner principle
> which has no qualities itself
> and is not moved by any act. *– 60*

Expressive Energy

How is nature affected by consciousness? This question is answered by the concept of 'prāṇa', which means 'breath' or 'life' or 'living energy'. It comes from the root 'an', which means to 'breathe' or to 'live' or to 'move'. There is a sister root 'aṇ', which also means to 'breathe' and which is associated with both 'sound' and 'subtlety'. Thus 'ana' means 'breathing', 'living', 'moving'; and it carries an implication that our living actions are the meaningful expression of some subtle energy, just as our acts of speech are meaningful expressions of the subtle functioning of living breath.

In the word 'prāṇa', 'ana' is combined with the prefix 'pra-' — which means not only 'pro-' or 'onward', but also 'pre-' or 'prior'. Thus, as in the concept of 'prakṛti' or 'nature', there is a dual implication. 'Prāṇa' implies not only the ongoing actions of life, but also an underlying principle from which they rise.

As described in the *Kauṣītaki Upaniṣad*, the underlying principle of life is consciousness:

> But then, in truth, life in itself
> is consciousness, the real self:
> which holds this body all around
> and causes it to rise, alive. *–from 3.3*

It's from this underlying consciousness that life is expressed, in ongoing actions. And the expression is through mind. Here, a brief description is provided by the *Praśna Upaniṣad*:

> It is from self that life is born.
>
> But as, on consciousness, there's a
> reflected play of light and shade;
> so too, on self, there is this [play
> of life] that get's extended out.
>
> Through the activity of mind,
> it comes to be in body here. –3.3

In this passage, mind is conceived as a mediating process, between consciousness and objects. To understand the mediation in modern terms, it may be conceived as a repeating cycle: of expression and reflection.

- First, consciousness is expressed: through understanding, feeling, thought and action. But the expression has a limiting effect. It narrows down attention to some limited object — which then appears at the front tip of personal experience.
- As the object appears, it is perceived, interpreted, judged and understood. This is a reflection back: from the apparent object at the forefront of attention, to underlying consciousness, at the background of experience.

There is thus a movement up and down, through five levels that are illustrated in figure 4 (within the broken triangle formed by the three lines). At the uppermost level, objects keep appearing and disappearing, as attention turns to them and turns away from them. At the second level, actions take attention to objects and thus perceive

Figure 4

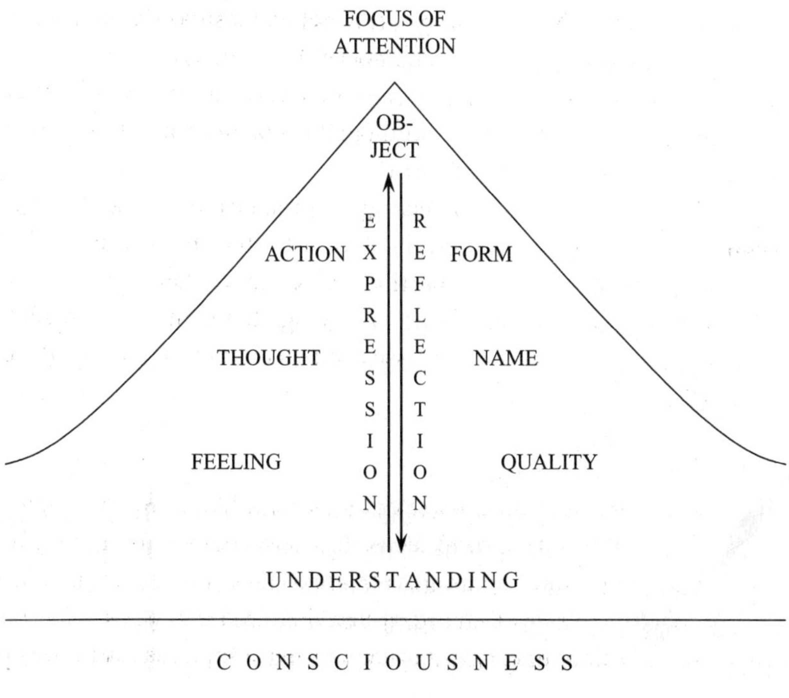

objective forms. At the third level, thoughts direct action and interpret names. At the fourth level, feelings motivate thought and judge qualities. At the fifth level, understanding co-ordinates our faculties and assimilates our changing experiences into continued knowledge.

All five levels are supported by consciousness, which is their final ground. All levels and all living faculties depend on it, but it does not depend on them.

By repeatedly expressing consciousness and returning back to it, we learn from experience. It is thus that misunderstandings can get exposed and clarified, and that our living faculties can get developed and adapted. But, throughout this process of learning, consciousness continues, quite unaffected by the achievements and failures of our dependent faculties. Beneath them, it is fully independent, on its own.

As our faculties perform their living functions — like feeling, thought, perception, speech — we experience in them a subtle sense of living energy, which expresses consciousness. This expressive energy is conceived as 'prāṇa'. It is not just a subordinate possession that belongs to objects, which knock it on — or project it on — to one another. Instead, it is an energy that rises up from its subjective source, in consciousness. And there it keeps returning to renew itself, and thus to rise again, refreshed.

Accordingly, the living energy of prāṇa cannot be reduced to the mutual interaction of perceived objects. It can only be described through a subjective reflection back, to a common ground of consciousness. To see an act as living, there must be a sense of kinship with it: that it expresses some common principle of life, in which one shares oneself.

Living Kinship

The sense of kinship is most obvious with like-minded people who share similar attitudes and ideas. It is less obvious with those whose ideas and habits are unfamiliar; but there is still some sense of kinship that enables us to recognize them as human, like us. There is even some rudimentary sense of kinship with living creatures of all kinds; though the more primitive they are the more rudimentary is the sense of kinship that enables us to recognize them as alive, like us.

Eventually, there are objects — like a table or a rock — that are not recognized to be alive at all. They do not have anything that even remotely resembles our sense faculties, and their behaviour does not show even the most rudimentary kind of purpose or intention that we experience in our minds.

So it seems that life is a special property belonging to living creatures, with faculties of sense and mind that look at least a little like ours. Outside the bodies of living creatures, there seems to be no reasonable basis for seeing nature as alive. Beyond the fanciful imaginings of myth and fiction, we fail to see a living kinship with most objects, like a table or a rock. We take consciousness to be an exclusive privilege, which belongs primarily to our minds and bodies; though we concede that it is also expressed, most often to a lesser extent, in some few bodies and minds that look to us like ours. Our view of life and consciousness is rather narrowly dependent upon our particular faculties, and so we can only see a very small and special part of nature as alive. We find no rational basis for seeing otherwise.

However, in a spiritual tradition like Hinduism, all nature is conceived to be alive. And the conception is not just a matter of religious faith or mystical intuition. It is also reasoned, very carefully, through a skeptical enquiry into the nature of experience. Here, the conclusion reached is that anything in the world may be perceived as alive. Or it may not. Whether something is alive or not depends on how one looks.

For example, take a person's body. When it is seen to be made up of physical parts, interacting with each other and the world outside, then it is 'jaḍa' or 'lifeless matter'. But when these interactions are seen to express an inner consciousness, then the body is taken to be alive, animated by the subtle energy of living faculties.

The same analysis applies to a person's mind. When it is seen as an objective process, with previous states producing later states, then it too is jaḍa or lifeless. Mental states may be more subtle than physical objects; but they too are lifeless matter, if we consider only the relationships between them. However, if they are seen to express a consciousness from which they rise, then the mind is taken to be alive. It is then a 'jīva' or a 'living psyche' — which experiences what happens, as it goes on living in the world.

A similar analysis applies to an object that seems merely physical, like a rock. As something made of interacting parts, or as itself an interacting part of world, it is lifeless matter. But if we see some further meaning in its interactions and relationships, then the rock says something to us; and we listen to what it has to say, thus treating it as an expression of life.

If a rock has been sculpted into some implement or work of art, then it obviously expresses the living consciousness of those who sculpted it. But what about a natural rock: where no person has interfered, to impose an artificial meaning from outside? Here also, there are two ways of looking at the rock. One can picture it and describe it, as an arrangement of objective features; or one can look at it more deeply, in a way that awakens one's intuitions. As one looks more deeply, mere pictures and descriptions are left behind. Alternately pushed and pulled, by feelings of puzzlement and beauty, one is led to find correspondences and symmetries — which show an underlying kinship and harmony, between the rock and other things.

Thus the rock is seen to express an inner meaning, as a manifestation of nature. And this inner meaning is understood by reflecting back into the depths of one's own experience, thereby implying a profound kinship between the rock and oneself. Here, the rock is understood on the basis of its kinship with oneself, and so is all of nature. But that reflective kinship is exactly what characterizes our understanding of living beings. In that sense, both rock and nature are being treated as alive.

What could be one's kinship with all of nature? In the Hindu tradition, that kinship is conceived as a common ground of consciousness, found everywhere expressed. In each particular creature, it is expressed through a particular mind and body, with limited faculties of mental and physical action. In the world as a whole, it is expressed through nature's underlying order, with all the meaning and intelligibility that enables our conceptions of the world. As consciousness continues through all experience, so also nature's order extends throughout the world.

The Self in Everyone

In this overall conception, everything — throughout the world — is an emanation of one ultimate principle: whose inner essence is consciousness. The emanation is produced by an all-creating principle of nature, whose living energy expresses consciousness. Consciousness (or puruṣa) is the subjective principle of knowing experience. Nature (or prakṛti) is the objective principle of creative action that produces the appearances of world. These two principles are thus described as a fundamental duality from which arises everything perceived. But the duality may be described and interpreted in a variety of different ways.

For example, in a story from the *Chāndogya Upaniṣad*, the subjective principle is described as 'ātman vaiśvānara' — which may be translated as the 'universal self', or as the 'self in everyone'. Six brahmin householders go to King Aśvapati, and ask him what this self might be. He asks them to say first what they think of it. They give six different answers: identifying it as 'heaven', 'sun', 'air', 'space', 'water' and 'earth'. In each case, he points out that the answer shows a partial aspect, insufficient in itself. And then he gives his answer to them all:

> You who are these indeed
> take in nourishment,
> knowing as if separate
> this self in everyone.
>
> But one who heeds
> the self in everyone
> as that final measuring
> which measures all directions,
>
> such a one draws nourishment

in all worlds, in all beings,
in all selves. *–from 5.18.1*

This passage is quite clearly open to two kinds of interpretation:

- One is to believe, on the basis of religious faith, that everything is guided by a cosmic consciousness, to be worshipped as a supreme Lord of all the world. That universal consciousness is then the self in everyone.
- The other kind of interpretation takes an individual approach. It looks for a true self that is one's own consciousness, found at the inmost core of individuality. That inmost centre is here described as shared in common, by all nature and by everyone.

In the *Kaṭha Upaniṣad*, the entire universe is described as made of living energy, whose fluctuations take the forms of changing things:

The universe of changing things –
whatever may be issued forth –
it is all made of living energy:
which moves and oscillates and shines.

That's a great terror, an uplifted
thunderbolt. But those who
realize this come to deathlessness. *– 6.2*

Here, a way to deathlessness is suggested: of overcoming fear, by realizing the passing nature of objective things. But again, there is an ambiguity: of whether nature's energy belongs to God, to whom it must be surrendered; or whether it expresses a ground of consciousness that can be found by turning back within, to one's own self.

In the *Bhagavad-gītā*, Kṛṣṇa speaks in the first person, as an unaffected self whose pure witnessing is the unmoved source of all nature's motivation. And here again there are differing interpretations: on the one hand that Kṛṣṇa is speaking as an incarnation of God; or on the other hand that he is speaking from an inner core of individuality, which he shares in common with his friend Arjuna and with everyone else as well:

Just from my own established nature,
I give rise, time after time,
to this entire multitude
of beings: motiveless itself.

All motivation is from nature. *– 9.8*

Actions thus arise, but they
do not restrict me, Arjuna.
While present in the midst of actions,
I am present there apart:
in that same unaffected state
where I am always unattached. *– 9.9*

As I look on, it's by this
witnessing that nature urges forth
what's made to move or stay in place.
This witnessing, Arjuna, is
the motivating cause by which
the changing world goes turning round. *– 9.10*

THREE QUALITIES

Natural Activity

Since our personalities are partial, their actions are driven from outside, through our bodily and mental partialities for narrow objects of desire.

But nature's phenomena work differently. They work through a natural activity whose functioning is somehow governed from within, spontaneously. Since nature contains within itself all physical and mental happenings, it can't be driven from elsewhere, by any happenings outside. It must function impartially, completely of its own accord, motivated from within, as it continues through a variety of partial objects and events that it relates more comprehensively together.

In the Indian tradition, this continued functioning of nature is analysed as an interweaving of three constituting qualities, called 'guṇas'. A 'guṇa' is literally a 'strand', of which a string or rope is made. The guṇas are thus conceived as three elemental strands of quality which are twisted or interwoven together — so as to form a continued string of experience and happening, in the course of time.

In a passage from the *Bhagavad-gītā,* the three guṇas are clearly described, in the process of our embodied experience. First, we are told that the living principle which is embodied stays the same, as unaffected consciousness. But changing limitations are superimposed upon its underlying changelessness, by the interweaving of differentiated qualities:

> In nature's happening, there are
> three constituting qualities:
> called *sattva, rajas, tamas.*
>
> In the body, Arjuna, they limit
> the embodied principle;
> though in itself it stays unchanged. *– 14.5*

Next, the three qualities are described as personal limitations. Sattva limits personality by attachment to embodied knowledge and well-being. Rajas colours and distorts experience by attachment to passion and achievement. And tamas gets life stuck in carelessness and ignorance:

> There, *sattva* is what shines: from
> purity, set free from ill and harm.
>
> This brings in limitation, Arjuna:
> by holding on to comfort,
> and to knowledge that is known. *– 14.6*
>
> You should know *rajas*, Arjuna,
> as made of passion: rising up
> inflamed with craving and attachment.
>
> That brings limitation onto
> the embodied principle,
> by holding on to what is done. *– 14.7*
>
> And *tamas* you must know as
> stupefying, born of ignorance.
>
> It limits all embodied
> beings, Arjuna: by blind
> intoxication, laziness and sleep. *– 14.8*
>
> From sattva comes attachment to
> well-being; and from rajas comes
> attachment to activity.
>
> But tamas covers knowledge, and
> thus makes for an attachment to
> intoxicated lack of care. *– 14.9*

Then, each quality is described as sometimes predominating over the other two, thus giving rise to a variety of changing effects:

> Predominating upon rajas
> and on tamas, sattva rises,
> Arjuna. So also rajas,
> upon sattva and on tamas.

And thus tamas in its turn,
upon sattva and on rajas. *– 14.10*

When light arises at all portals
in this body, then it may
be known that sattva has matured. *– 14.11*

Ambition, enterprise, exertion,
restlessness and zest: all these
arise in rajas growing forth. *– 14.12*

Obscurity, inertia, driven
madness and delusion: these
arise in tamas growing forth. *– 14.13*

Where action is well done, its fruit
is pure, called 'sāttvic'. But the fruit
of rajas is discomfort; and
of tamas, it is ignorance. *– 14.16*

From sattva, knowledge comes. From rajas,
eagerness and greed. From tamas,
madness and delusion come
about, along with ignorance. *– 14.17*

Transcending Ground

And finally, it is described how nature's qualities and all their limitations may be transcended:

When it is seen that there's no doer
other than these constituting
qualities, and when the see-er
knows beyond the qualities,

that see-er reaches my own state. *– 14.19*

Transcending these three qualities
through which the body has arisen,

one who is embodied finds
undying freedom: unconfined
by being born into a world
where life degenerates and dies. – *14.20*

For I am the supporting ground
of all reality: undying,
changeless, permanent, held always
good and true, in its own state
of unaffected happiness. – *14.27*

The transcendence here described is a pure seeing, utterly unqualified and thus completely free of all attachment. Even the clarity and goodness of sattva is a limitation, because it is only the relative clarity and goodness of *embodied* knowledge and well-being. Such a relative clarity or goodness is only clearer or better than less clear or worse things. Something of the opposite is still implied and thus inherently mixed in.

Such a confused mixture is inherent in embodiment, where knowledge and well-being can never be completely true or real. True knowledge and well-being can only be achieved by returning to the subjective principle of consciousness, which is at once the truth of self and the ground of all reality. There, sattva as a quality is utterly dissolved. As a quality, it belongs to a more superficial level of appearance.

This brings us to a further aspect of the three guṇas. They are not just interweaving strands of quality, but also a hierarchy of levels expressed from consciousness, as nature manifests the world:

- *Tamas* is the most superficial level, furthest away from underlying consciousness. At this level, nature is *acted upon*. It is characterized by the inertia and obscurity of driven objects in the world.

- *Rajas* is the intermediate level, where nature *acts upon* objects. It is characterized by the excitement and turbulence of moving energies, through which we may begin to transcend the inertia and the blind opacity of driven objects.

- *Sattva* is nature's underlying level, immediately expressed from consciousness. It provides the underlying motivations of resolution and clarity, which inspire the driving energies of nature's acts. This is the co-ordinating level at which nature is found everywhere alive, *acting for* the sake of consciousness.

This threefold hierarchy applies to all of nature, to all mental and physical actions, as illustrated in figure 5. The ground of consciousness may be achieved through transcendence, but it is immanent in everything.

Figure 5

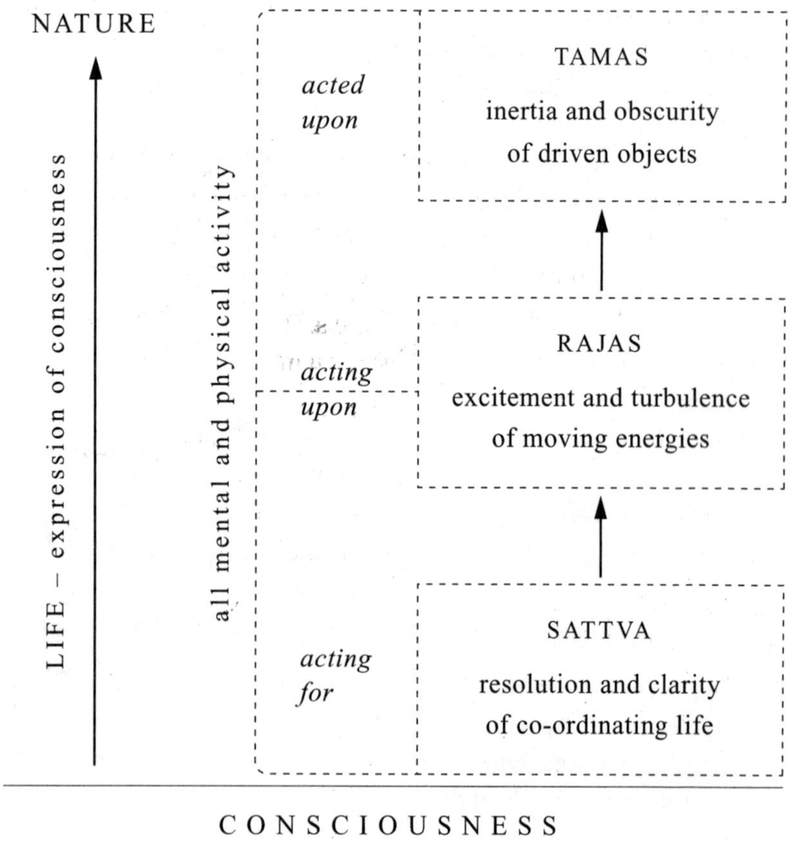

Arjuna's Fear

In the story of the *Bhagavad-gītā*, the delusion and evasiveness of tamas are shown to present us with a characteristic problem. Though the deluded evasions of tamas are driven by the dissatisfactions and conflicts of rajas, they pretend hypocritically to the well-being and resolution of sattva.

At the start of a great battle, when Arjuna sees the opposing army before him, he loses his nerve. He sees the great warriors on the other side, far more than on his, and he despairs of winning. Moreover, he is faced with an emotional dilemma. This is a battle against other members of his own family. In particular, he knows that he will have to fight and kill his great uncle Bhīṣma and his teacher Droṇa. Bhīṣma has brought him up as a father; and Droṇa has schooled him in the arts of war, since his early childhood. He greatly loves and respects these two men, and the feeling is reciprocated. He has their blessings to fight against them, because they know that he is fighting for a just cause. They are bound by warrior codes of allegiance to fight for a side whose injustice they realize. To that extent, they want him to win, even at the cost of their defeat and their physical deaths. But this will not prevent them from fighting to their utmost against him. And they expect him to fight to his utmost against them. Anything less would be a mark of disrespect to them and to the upbringing they have given him.

Arjuna is well aware of all this. The decision to fight has not been made lightly; and all these factors have been well considered, over a long period of time. But when he sees the formidable array of great warriors across the battlefield, including those he loves, he is struck by a moment of cowardice. He cannot face what he must rightly do. His mind is overtaken by confusion, his body trembles with fear, his weapons fall from his hands, and he delivers a bit of a sermon about the evils of war and family dissension. Better, he says, to renounce ambition for power and dominion than to commit the sin of killing his own kith and kin.

The sermon is delivered to Kṛṣṇa, who is acting as Arjuna's charioteer. Kṛṣṇa knows Arjuna very well, as a dear friend. He knows that this is no genuine renunciation, but just a hypocritical pretence: made from fear, in order to evade a difficult course of action. If Arjuna turns tail now, the basic problems will remain unresolved and will bring the warring parties to the battlefield again. Any genuine resolution would thus be delayed, with all the wasted effort and the added complications that such a delay must bring.

The problem is that Arjuna is caught in the driven weakness and confusion of tamas. What faces him is difficult, and he tries to avoid it by pretending to have attained the detached resolution of sattva. But such an evasion keeps him stuck in the driven inertia of tamas. The only way out of this inertia is through the moving energy of rajas, with all the forceful effort and the unsettled turbulence that it involves.

So Arjuna is told that he must fight. What's needed, Kṛṣṇa says, is not evasion; but a clear understanding, in the face of what is done. The *Bhagavad-gītā* is Kṛṣṇa's advice about the ways in which this understanding may be attained.

FIVE LEVELS OF EXPERIENCE

The Traditional Five Elements

What is the world that nature manifests? This question is answered by the traditional conception of 'five elements', shared largely in common by Indian and European traditions.

In the *Bṛhadāraṇyaka Upaniṣad,* there is an early account of these five elements. A lady called Gārgī points out that the entire world of earthly things is actually made of the element 'water', just as a cloth is woven from thread. What then, she asks, about the element 'water'? If all things of 'earth' turn out to be made of 'water', then what is 'water' made of?

She is questioning Yājñavalkya, who replies that 'water' is made of the underlying element 'fire'. And what about 'fire'? In its turn, 'fire' is reduced to the underlying element 'air'. Similarly, 'air' is reduced to underlying 'ether'.

Even by a modern academic dating that may have grossly underestimated the age of ancient traditions, the *Bṛhadāraṇyaka Upaniṣad* is over two and a half thousand years old. It describes the five elements as a conception that was then already established by ancient custom, handed down from the distant past. For thousands of years, in India and Europe, this conception has been used to progress from the gross particularity of earthly things to the ethereal pervasiveness of space and light throughout the universe. In India, traditionally-minded people still use this conception today.

Like many ancient conceptions, this one is metaphorical. It uses the metaphor of certain physical substances to suggest a subtler and more basic analysis of our experience. But what does the metaphor mean? How might it be interpreted in more abstract, modern terms? Since it is a metaphor that has been used over thousands of years, by many different people, we must expect that it can be interpreted in different ways. In the discussion that follows, one such interpretation is suggested. It is summarized in figure 6 (next page).

Through our limited senses and minds, we do not see everything at once. Instead, we see particular objects; and we conceive a

Figure 6

Traditional element	***A modern interpretation***	***Level of modern physics***
'Earth'	Matter	Material objects
'Water'	Energy	Changing configurations
'Fire'	Information	Relative observations
'Air'	Conditioning	Conditioned fields
'Ether'	Continuity	Space-time continuum

material world that is made up of many such objects. Each object is a particular piece of matter, divided from other objects by boundaries in space and time. This divisible *matter* corresponds fairly obviously to the traditional element 'earth'. In a classical Indian metaphor, the particular objects of the world are conceived to be formed from the element 'earth' as pots are formed from clay.

At first, the world of particular objects seems solid. But, upon further investigation, it is not so. As objects interact, they are caught in a constant process of formation and transformation. When changing time is taken into account, our solid-seeming world is shown to be only an instant snapshot: a momentary picture taken at a particular instant of time. As time flows, the objects of the world keep changing. Each moment that we look, what we have seen keeps vanishing, transformed into something else.

Through this examination, the seeming solidity of objects gives way to a fluidity of changing forms. It is then clear that matter is not the only element in our experience of the world. In addition to the concrete particularity of matter, we experience a second, more fundamental element — which may be called 'energy'. This second element, of *energy*, is manifested in moving activity; and it thus produces the changing forms of objects in the world. It is associated with the fluidity of change, which makes it correspond to the traditional element called 'water'.

Through the changing flow of energetic activity, information travels from place to place. This enables us to observe the world. Each observer receives information that represents other things. These represented things are then illuminated by observing them, from a particular point of view.

So, beyond matter and energy, *information* is a third element of our experience. By representing other things, it throws a particular light on them; and it thus corresponds to the traditional element called 'fire'.

We do not directly observe the matter and energy in the world outside our bodies and our measuring instruments. External matter and energy are only observed through the representations of information that our instruments have received. In this sense, information is more fundamental than matter and energy.

In its turn, information depends on something further still. In order to represent anything, information depends upon a comparison of represented conditioning. For example, a map shows some places closer together and other places further apart. Or it may show how various places are cooler or hotter: by comparative shades of colour, or by numbers that spell out the comparison in a more calculated way.

Thus, beneath the information through which the world appears to us, there is a fourth element: of relative *conditioning*. It shows the world as conditioned by varying characteristics and qualities, in much the same way that the atmosphere is conditioned by climate. So there is another correspondence here, with the traditional element called 'air'.

In order to compare the differing characteristics of different places, there has to be an underlying continuity, which extends through space and time. This continuity is understood in a way that is rather different from our perceptions of matter. Where matter is perceived, space and time are distances that *separate* particular objects and events. Where continuity is understood, space and time are not what separates, but what *connects*. Here, distance is not separation, but a connection in between. It is the intervening connection between parts of a world that has been made to seem divided, by our limited and narrow perceptions.

Thus, beneath the differentiated conditioning of the world, there is a fifth element, of pervading *continuity*. This evidently corresponds to the traditional element called 'ether'. It is described as the subtlest element, pervading the entire world.

A Comparison with Modern Physics

In this kind of way, the 'five elements' can be interpreted as different levels, which get mixed up, in our experience of the world. These same five levels can be seen in modern physics. (See figure 6 on page 104.)

At the first level, we have Newtonian physics, where the world is described as made up from pieces of matter, which act upon one another through force.

At the second level, physical objects are described as configurations of energy. Here, we have Einstein's principle that matter is only a concentrated form of energy. And we have quantum systems: as configurations of co-ordinated activity, which get disturbed by observation and other actions from outside.

At the third level, mass, energy, time and space are seen as relative measurements that depend upon the observer. They are not absolute things in themselves. Instead, they are interdependent components, in the process by which an observer receives and interprets information.

At the fourth level, there are various theories of fields. In physics, the word 'field' refers to a 'conditioned space'. The conditioning is described by attributing a mathematical value to each point of space and time. The idea is to explain phenomena, and to predict occurrences, on the basis of such mathematical descriptions of field conditioning. Relativity and quantum theory have gone a long way in this direction. They use field calculations to describe physical phenomena, in a far more accurate and systematic way than our common sense ideas. And, in building these more accurate descriptions, modern physicists have shown that our common sense assumptions are often wrong. In particular, our notions of separated matter are only approximations, and misleading ones at that. For many everyday purposes, our habitual assumptions work well enough to make us think that they are right. But, upon closer examination, they break down. Then they have to be replaced by rather different ideas, which look deeper into our experience of the world.

At the fifth level of modern physics, there is the space-time continuum. At the end of the nineteenth century, physicists had a somewhat degraded notion of the traditional element 'ether'. They were puzzled as to how electromagnetic waves, like light, could travel through empty space. So they thought of the 'ether' as a special kind of material substance, which invisibly filled all space. Electromagnetic waves were supposed to be carried by material vibrations in this invisible substance, like sound waves travel through vibrations in physical air.

But, as a material substance, the 'ether' was rather mystifying. To account for the tremendous speed of light, it had to vibrate extremely fast, like a very hard solid. On the other hand, it was like a very thin fluid, which penetrates through everything. To enable the passage of light, the 'ether' had to permeate the vast emptiness of outer space, between the earth and the stars. Similarly, the 'ether' had to be present in the empty space of a vacuum tube; and it had to permeate air and water and other substances in which light travels and electromagnetic phenomena take place.

Moreover, as our planet earth moves around the sun, it must move through the 'ether', like a ball moves through physical air. Thus, on planet earth, there must be an 'ether wind'; and this must affect the speed of light, depending on whether the light travels with the wind or against it or across it. But the Michelson-Morley experiment showed that there was no such wind. So something was badly wrong.

Albert Einstein took a rather different approach. He did not think of light and electromagnetism as the result of any material substance that is somehow *added on* to space. Instead, he saw that the transmission of light is an essential property of space itself. Light and electromagnetism are not transmitted through any material substance, but through the essential continuity that relates together the different points of space and time. Thus, in place of a material 'ether', Einstein developed the conception of a 'space-time continuum'.

In Einstein's conception, the mechanics of matter is replaced by a geometry of space and time. The world is no longer pictured through material objects and substances, mechanically acting upon each other in three-dimensional space. Instead, the world is conceived through events — which are related to each other by geometry, in four-dimensional space and time. The geometry connects events, into a space-time continuum. All occurrences and happenings are partial manifestations of this continuum, as it is seen differently by the different observers who travel through it.

This space-time continuum is much truer to the ancient concept of 'ether'. In India, the word for 'ether' is 'ākāśa'. It is an old Sanskrit word, which means 'pervading space'. On the one hand, it is commonly used for the overarching space of sky, beyond the atmosphere. And on the other hand, it is philosophically used for the pervasion of space and time within particular objects and locations: as for example when talking of the 'ākāśa' within a pot, or within a person's body and mind.

There is, however, a significant difference between modern physics and traditional conceptions of the universe:

- In modern physics, the field of study is restricted to a physical aspect of experience. This physical aspect is described through mathematical calculations; and the calculations are applied through the development of external technologies, which fabricate instruments and machines for use by our physical bodies.
- Traditional conceptions are broader and more comprehensive. They describe both physical and mental aspects of experience. Their descriptions are not restricted to mathematical calculation; and their application is not concerned so much with external instruments as with the cultivation and clarification of human faculties.

In short, traditional conceptions of the world are less dependent than modern physics upon the achievement of external objectives. They are more directly concerned with the education of our living faculties: through a reflection back to an underlying, subjective ground.[15]

Reflecting Back to Ground

For an illustration of such a reflection, let us return to the *Bṛhadāraṇyaka Upaniṣad,* where Gārgī questions Yājñavalkya about the five elements. When she asks what underlies the fifth element, 'ether', he gives her various mythological replies: about worlds of celestial spirits; about further worlds of the sun and moon and stars; about worlds of Indra (chief of gods) and Prajāpati (the divine creator); and finally about the world of Brahman, which is all totality. When she goes on to ask what underlies this world of Brahman, he points out that she has asked an illegitimate question (since there is nothing left to question, beyond the totality of everything).

For the moment, he has won the argument; so she falls silent, as he is questioned by other people. But she is not satisfied with the

---

[15] In Sanskrit, the word for 'field' is 'kṣetra'. And, as in modern physics, the word does not refer only to an agricultural field, but also to a subtle conditioning of space and time, underlying the manifestation of the world to our senses and minds. In the *Chāndogya Upaniṣad* 8.3.2, it is said:

> Those who do not rightly know
> a field where golden treasure lies
> keep passing over it, but may not find it.
>
> So also all these creatures entered here, day after day,
> in this world where all completeness is both shining goal
> and ever-present ground. They do not discover it;
> for they are kept distracted, by unreality.

In this passage, the distracting 'unreality' may be interpreted as the changing manifestation of the field — like the changing contours, plants, flowers and fruits of an agricultural field. The shining treasure is the changeless reality of the underlying ground — which is entirely complete, immediately underfoot. Each creature seen moving in the field is not a true knower of the field, but only a changing manifestation of the known field. The only true knower is the ground itself, supporting each creature and everything else in the field.

mythology; so she thinks a bit and comes back a little later to the argument, with a more careful question. She asks:

> Consider all that's said to be:
> above the heavens, below the earth,
> in heaven and earth and in between;
>
> including all there ever was,
> is now, and will in future be.
>
> In what is all that woven, warp and woof? *– 3.8.3*

Yājñavalkya replies:

> All of that is woven,
> warp and woof, in 'ether'. *– from 3.8.4*

What is going on here, in this argument? What could it mean to say that all the world is 'woven, warp and woof, in "ether"'? If the word 'ether' describes an underlying continuity of space and time, then it clearly implies that different parts of the world are essentially interconnected, beneath their seeming separation. But what is the nature of this interconnection? What does it finally show? That is the drift of Gārgī's last question, as she goes on to ask:

> In what is 'ether'
> woven, warp and woof? *– from 3.8.4*

Then, at last, Yājñavalkya gives Gārgī a direct reply, which settles her persistent questioning:

> Those who investigate reality
> describe it as the 'changeless'.
>
> It is not coarse, nor yet refined;
> it is not long or short.
>
> No flame of passion colours it;
> no fond affection is involved.
> In it, no shadow brings obscurity;
> there's no obstruction to be cleared.

It is not 'air', nor 'ether'.
Connection and relationship
do not apply to it. Nor do
any qualities, like taste and smell.

It has no eyes, no ears, no speech,
no mind; it is not sharp, nor has it
vital energy, nor any face, nor measure.

Nor does it consume, nor is consumed.
It has no outside, no inside. *–3.8.8*

This same changeless principle
is not the seen. It is the see-er.
It is not heard; it is the hearer.
It is not thought; it is the thinker.
It is not known; it is the knower.

Apart from it, there is no see-er.
Apart from it, there is no hearer.
Apart from it, there is no thinker.
Apart from it, there is no knower.

In just this unchanging principle,
the [all-pervading] 'ether'
is woven, warp and woof. *–3.8.11*

Thus, underlying the universal continuity of 'ether', Yājñavalkya identifies a changeless principle of pure subjectivity. He says that it is not what's seen or heard or thought or known. It is not an object of any kind. In particular: 'It is not known; it is the knower'. And: 'Apart from it, there is no knower.' In other words, it is a common principle of consciousness, underlying all experience of the world. From that underlying consciousness, the five elements arise, as a succession of levels in the appearance of the world.

World and Personality

Accordingly, in traditional cosmologies, the whole world's creation may be described as an arising of the five elements — from an underlying subjectivity. Such a description is given in the *Taittirīya Upaniṣad*:

> From this same self,
> 'ether' has arisen;
> from 'ether', 'air';
> from 'air', 'fire';
> from 'fire', 'water';
> from 'water', 'earth'.
>
> *–from 2.1*

How can we interpret this subjective arising of the world, in modern terms? One such interpretation is summarized in figure 7:

- At the level of 'earth', reality appears through pieces of matter, perceived by our physical bodies. This is the level specifically studied in physical sciences: like physics, chemistry, geology and astronomy. As modern physics shows, even these sciences uncover deeper levels which require a reflection back into the minds of investigating scientists.

Figure 7

Appearance of reality	***Perceiving instrument***	***Examining disciplines***	***Level of physics***
Pieces of matter	Physical body	Physical sciences	Material objects
Patterns of energy	Living organism	Biological sciences	Transforming configurations
Meaningful information	Conceiving intellect	Cultural sciences	Relative descriptions
Conditioned character	Intuitive judgement	Psychological sciences	Field conditioning
Continuing existence	Reflective reason	Philosophical enquiry	Space-time continuum

Non-dual consciousness

- At the level of 'water', reality appears through patterns of energy: observed by us as living organisms, who share in the patterns of energy that we observe. This organic level of experience is studied in 'life' sciences: like biology and medicine.
- At the level of 'fire', reality appears through meaningful information, interpreted through our conceiving intellects. This conceptual level of experience is studied in cultural and symbolic sciences: like the history of thought, the anthropology of culture and many of the humanities.
- At the level of 'air', reality appears through conditioned character and quality, contrasted and compared by our intuitive judgements. This level of comparative conditioning is studied in psychological sciences: like ethics and psychotherapy and sciences of meditation and mind-development.
- At the level of 'ether', reality appears through the continuity of common existence, discerned and clarified through reflective reason. This is a comprehensive level of experience, where common principles are understood beneath the variations of particular instances and differing phenomena. This comprehensive level is specifically studied in philosophical disciplines, through their skeptical questioning of superficial appearances and accepted beliefs that are usually taken for granted. But philosophical enquiry is not restricted to any particular discipline or group of disciplines. It occurs essentially in all disciplines: whenever something is found not to fit into current ideas, so that there is a questioning of underlying principles.
- Underlying all levels of appearance, the Hindu tradition identifies an unchanging ground of consciousness. This is not a level of appearance, but reality itself — where all appearances are found dissolved.

Thus, the five elements are treated as showing a division of apparent experience, supported by an underlying ground. The division is called 'pañcī-karaṇa' or 'making five'. When this division is applied to the manifested universe as a whole, it results in the five elements (called the 'pañca-mahābhūtas'). But the same division may also be applied to other fields of experience.

In particular, when applied to the personality that perceives the world, this fivefold division gives rise to the 'pañca-kośas' or 'five coverings' of personality:[16]

- The outermost covering is the 'annamaya-kośa', or the 'covering of food'. It is the material body: made of the element 'earth', and perceiving a world of material objects outside.
- Proceeding inwards, the second covering is the 'prāṇamaya-kośa', or the 'covering of living energy'. This describes a layer of personality that may be conceived as a living organism, functioning through purposeful activity. It is made of the element 'water', and it observes a functioning world of purposeful energy and activity.
- The third covering is the 'manomaya-kośa', or the 'covering of mind'. It is the conceiving intellect: made of the element 'fire', and interpreting an intelligible world of meaningful information.
- The fourth covering is the 'vijñānamaya-kośa' or the 'covering of discernment'. This describes the discerning sensibility of intuitive judgement. It is made of the element 'air', and it carries out the contrasts and comparisons that show a qualitative world of motivating value.
- The innermost covering is the 'ānandamaya-kośa', or the 'covering of happiness'. It is made of the element 'ether', and it enables an integrated understanding of common and continuing principles.

---

[16] For a diagrammatic representation, the reader may turn back to figure 4 on page 89. In this figure, five levels are shown within the broken triangle formed by the three lines.

These levels are: (1) Objects; (2) Action and form; (3) Thought and name; (4) Feeling and quality; and (5) Understanding.

They correspond both to the five coverings of personality and to the five elements of world.

- Within these five coverings of personality, there is the pure consciousness of knowing self — which is at once each person's inmost centre and the supporting ground of everything perceived in the objective world.

Similarly, there is a fivefold division of mind: into ahaṅkāra or ego, citta or will, buddhi or intellect, manas or sensibility, and antaḥkaraṇa or understanding. (Literally, 'antaḥkaraṇa' is the 'inner faculty'.) Further, there are five prāṇas or vital functions (prāṇa or forward functioning, apāna or reactive functioning, udāna or aspirational functioning, vyāna or disseminating functioning, and samāna or assimilative functioning). There are five senses of perception (smell, taste, sight, touch and sound: corresponding in that order to 'earth', 'water', 'fire', 'air' and 'ether'). And there are five faculties of action (upastha or reproduction, pāyu or expulsion, vāk or expression, pāda or movement, and pāṇi or holding — the order is rather uncertain).

These fivefold divisions are used — together with the threefold division of nature's constituting qualities — in various cosmological and psychological descriptions. But it is understood that they all arise from a subjective ground to which they must keep on returning, continually, in order to resolve their differences.

Yogic Discipline

Control of Mind

Traditional conceptions of world and mind are applied through the technology of Yoga.

This is, essentially, a technology of life. It is a technology of physical and mental practices — designed to return back from outward expressions of life, to an inmost source from which they are expressed. It thus prescribes a variety of exercises — which are meant to return from physical expressions of body, through mental expressions of intention, thought and feeling, to an underlying ground of pure, unchanging consciousness.

The word 'yoga' comes from the root 'yuj', meaning to 'harness, join, unite'. It is etymologically connected with the English word 'yoke'. Thus 'yoga' means 'harnessing' or 'joining' or 'union'. In particular, it describes a spiritual discipline that harnesses and controls our faculties: towards a final joining back, into an inner unity.

Central to the discipline is the control of mind, as described in Patañjali's *Yoga-sūtras*:

> atha yogā-'nuśāsanam
>
> Here described is the teaching of Yoga. *– 1.1*

In this first sūtra, Patañjali makes it clear that he is describing a living teaching, which must be taught by an individual teacher to an individual student. Patañjali's description is made through extremely brief and condensed statements called 'sūtras', which set out the basic principles of Yoga. There are of course many commentaries, which explain and interpret further; but the commentaries too are only texts, which get to be chosen and interpreted in various different ways, in the individual practice of teaching and learning:

> yogaś citta-vṛtti-nirodhaḥ
>
> Yoga is the restraint of mental turning. *– 1.2*

This second sūtra is Patañjali's basic definition of 'yoga': as the 'control of mind'. In the translation above, two concepts need to be explained further.

First, the phrase 'mental turning' translates the Sanskrit 'citta-vṛtti'. It describes the turning of mind from one object of attention to another. As the mind turns, it takes on the shapes and forms of different objects; and thus it enters into the changing modifications of perception, thought and feeling that keep appearing and disappearing in the process of mental experience. In effect, the turnings of mind are these modifications of mental appearance. From a mental point of view, the mind does not merely turn *towards* objects, it also turns *into* the objects that it perceives and thinks about and feels. Hence the word 'vṛtti' or 'turning' also implies a 'modification'.

Second, the word 'restraint' translates the Sanskrit 'nirodha' — which also means 'prevention, control, stilling, calming'. The essential idea here is not one of a forced suppression, imposed from outside. Rather, as the word 'yoga' (or 'union') implies, the basic aim is towards a natural and spontaneous governance, inspired from an unchanging unity within. Such an inwardly inspired governance is achieved by relaxing the mind from its outward turnings and modifications, so that attention may join back into a common inner unity from which our outward turnings rise. In the modern Bihar School of Yoga, a story is told of how wild horses are not trained just by rope and bridle; but, more essentially, by watching them carefully and sympathetically, living patiently in unison with them, and thus winning their friendship and trust. Faculties of body and mind are meant to be trained in the same way: on the basis of a shared unity that enables both detachment and empathy.

That underlying unity is identified in the next sūtra:

> tadā draṣṭuḥ svarūpe'vasthānam
>
> Then, there is stability,
> in the true nature of the see-er. *– 1.3*

This sūtra says that when the turnings of the mind have been stilled, it comes back to a supporting ground of stability and peace. That ground is essentially subjective, identified as 'the true nature of the see-er'. It is pure, unchanging consciousness: where unity and peace are found, beneath the differing and changing objects of mental turning.

That pure subjectivity — of the true see-er — is contrasted with everything else, in the fourth sūtra:

> vṛtti-sārūpyam itaratra
>
> Elsewhere, there is conformity with the turning. *– 1.4*

Only the true see-er is self-supporting and independent in itself. Everything else is driven and dependent, along with the tossings and turnings of body and mind. It is only by standing back, in the stability of the unchanging see-er, that control and harmony can be achieved.

Thus, at its very outset, the method of Yoga implies a sharp distinction: between the see-er and the seen, or in other words between a knowing self and the objects that it knows. In the second chapter of the *Yoga-sūtras*, the distinction is made more explicit:

> In its true nature, self is pure,
> unchanging happiness. When it's
> conceived as something else — which is
> impure, which suffers change and
> misery — then that is ignorance. *– 2.5*
>
> Egotism is the seeming identity
> of that which sees
> with the capability of sight. *– 2.6*
>
> The mixing up together
> of the see-er and the seen
> is the cause of what's to be avoided. *– 2.17*
>
> It's the seen that is habitually conditioned:
> by qualities of light, activity and state.
> It is made up of elements and faculties.

All this for the sake of enjoyed
experience, and for the freedom of release. *– 2.18*

The see-er is pure seeing, in itself.
But it's perceived [mixed up]
with supposition and conception. *– 2.20*

Of that [mixing up together]
ignorance is the cause. *– 2.24*

By removing that ignorance,
the mixing up is removed.
That is the absolute release
of seeing in itself. *– 2.25*

The means of that release
is to make discernment
unwaveringly known. *– 2.26*

In these sūtras, egotism is described as a seeming identity of the pure see-er with the capability of sight (2.6). This is a false identity, a 'mixing up together of the see-er and the seen' (2.17). The capability of sight belongs to what is seen. As such, it is 'habitually conditioned ... made up of elements and faculties' (2.18). The see-er is quite different. It is 'pure seeing, in itself' (2.20), quite unmixed with any conditioned elements and faculties.

The seemingly conditioned ego is thus a mixing up of different things, a mistaken confusion that results from ignorance (2.5 and 2.24). The final aim of Yoga is to remove that ignorance and confusion: thereby attaining to pure freedom, to 'the absolute release of seeing in itself' (2.25).

As Yoga practises control of mind, it does so as a preparation for truth. At base, it is the confusion of ego that causes disharmony and thus needs to be controlled. Where knowing self is falsely identified as a personal ego, the self's pure knowledge is confused with ego's limited perceptions, thoughts and feelings — which are thus given undue importance. From there arises conflict and disruption: as various inflated and distorted claims act one against the other, each trying to run away with a mind that gets pushed and pulled in many different directions.

In this confusion, trying to control the mind presents a basic paradox. Yoga seeks a final harmony and unity, through a controlled development and harnessing of one's personal faculties. But such control requires a detached knowing or seeing, free from the biased partiality and the disturbed confusion of our limited and driven faculties. Only by achieving an impartial and unmixed detachment can unity be known and harmony be reached. There is thus an inherent paradox: of seeking harmony and unity through detachment and separation.

In the discipline of Yoga, this paradox is brought into a sharp focus, by seeking control and unity through the separation of a pure see-er from everything that's seen. The see-er is sought as seeing in itself: entirely free and unaffected, completely unmixed with all the mental and physical activities that are controlled and co-ordinated from it. Where such an unmixed seeing has not been attained, all talk of harmony, control and unity is compromised.

This paradox, of seeking unity through separation, is sought to be resolved by achieving a complete separation. That separation is meant to bring detachment from the confusions of ego, which make the paradox so troublesome. The trouble arises wherever ego is involved. By its involvement, it subverts any attempt to achieve control of mind. That is why a complete separation is needed, to remove all trace of egotistical involvement.

For the inherent confusion of a personal ego makes it lay claim to controlling powers that arise more truly as an unpossessed inspiration from the true see-er. Even the smallest trace of ego thus inflates itself, with a mistakenly possessive claim that limits and distorts all of its efforts to achieve control and harmony. Such efforts go largely into an inflation of the very ego that obstructs the goal they seek.

There is of course a vicious circle here, which somehow needs to be negotiated and got past. The methods and practices of Yoga are designed to do just that: by carefully and patiently intensifying effort in a way that leads eventually beyond all effort, to a final relaxation.

Training of Character

Through its many techniques of control, Yoga is a discipline of purification — which is meant to attain a pure and complete self, free from its apparent mixture with the distortions and partialities of personal ego. In the *Yoga-sūtras*, this purifying discipline is described as an overall system: with eight 'limbs' or 'branches'. They are yama (or rule), niyama (or observance), āsana (or sitting), prāṇāyāma (or living energy control), pratyāhāra (or withdrawal), dhāraṇā (or concentration), dhyāna (or meditation) and samādhi (or absorption). These eight branches are meant to work together, each contributing towards a comprehensive training of character, on the way to a long-term goal of final purity and truth.

The first two branches, yama and niyama, are somewhat similar (as their names suggest). A '***yama***' is a 'rule of conduct', to be observed in general: throughout one's behaviour in the world. Five main yamas are prescribed:

- First, 'ahiṁsā' or 'non-violence'. This is an ethical injunction: asking for a balanced moderation, and cultivating an attitude of respect towards living creatures and nature's ordered harmony.
- Second, 'satya' or 'truthfulness'. This is a more intellectual injunction: insisting upon a straightforward accuracy of speech, expression and thought.
- Third, 'asteya' or 'not stealing'. This is a social injunction: pointing at the limits of personal entitlement, and demanding a respect for the rights of others.
- Fourth, 'brahmacarya' or 'continence'. This is a psychological injunction: restraining the dissipation of energy through sexual and other distractions. Literally, 'brahmacarya' means the 'practice of expansion' (from 'brahma' meaning 'expansion' and 'carya' meaning 'practice'). The idea is to avoid outward dissipation: so that attention and energy may be sublimated inward, towards an expansion of mind and understanding.
- Fifth, 'aparigraha' or 'not taking'. This is an economic injunction:

discouraging the taking of payments and gifts and other outward gains that compromise one's sense of inner independence.

After these five yamas comes ***niyama***. A 'niyama' is a prescribed 'rule' or 'observance': rather like a yama, except that the niyamas tend to be more specialized towards the practice of spiritual discipline. As with the yamas, there are five main niyamas:

- First, 'śauca' or 'purity': consisting of washing and rituals and other cleansing practices which keep special areas of experience relatively free from unwanted and distracting influences.
- Second, 'santoṣa' or 'contentment': so as not to be distracted by remaining irritations, but to go ahead positively with the actual practice of discipline.
- Third, 'tapas' or 'intensifying effort and energy': undeterred by discomfort and cost, in the achievement of what has been undertaken.
- Fourth, 'svādhyāya', which is both 'studying for oneself' and 'self-study': by carefully examining what is actually achieved and experienced.
- Fifth, 'Īśvara-praṇidhāna' or 'surrender to the Lord' of what may be achieved. Here, the word 'Īśvara' or 'Lord' does not have to be interpreted as a personal God, worshipped through conventional religion. It may refer to any transcendent source of power and value, beyond the driven pettiness of personal ego.

After yama and niyama comes the third branch, called '***āsana***' or 'sitting'. This is usually interpreted in a physical sense; and then it refers to a whole range of bodily postures that are used to control and develop various functions of the practitioner's body. The idea here is to prepare the body, with capabilities that are useful for further practices leading beyond the physical. In particular, there are special postures like 'padmāsana' (the cross-legged 'lotus position') which are developed for the purpose of sitting long hours in undistracted meditation.

But this same word 'āsana', or 'sitting', may be interpreted in a more fundamental sense. It is not just the physical adoption of special bodily postures. More essentially, it implies a 'sitting down' or 'settling back', upon an inner ground of natural, unwavering support. It is only from such a natural and steady seat that firm control and sustained development are possible. Thus, through all its many practices — from general rules of daily conduct to the highest flights of meditation — the discipline of Yoga cultivates an attitude of steady 'seatedness' that is at once its final aim and underlying base.

After āsana comes the fourth branch, called ***'prāṇāyāma'***. In its physical aspect, 'prāṇāyāma' is 'breath control': carried out through various bodily exercises of inhaling and exhaling air. But again, there is far more to it than that. The word 'prāṇāyāma' is a compound of two elements: 'prāṇa' and 'āyāma'. Each needs a little further explanation:

- 'Prāṇa' means 'breath' or 'life' or 'living energy'. This concept is a little metaphorical. It uses the metaphor of bodily breath to describe the ebb and flow of a subtle energy that underlies our living activities. The material body is thus conceived to be a gross and somewhat misleading appearance, produced by our crude senses. When further examined, taking mind into account, our living activities are more accurately described as made of fluid energy: whose currents form coagulated patterns that our senses see, with a very rough approximation, as materially interacting bodies.
- 'Āyāma' is related to the previous words 'yama' (rule) and 'niyama' (observance). They all come from the root 'yam' — which means to 'sustain', to 'expand', and to 'govern'. From this derivation, 'āyāma' means 'control', implying a supportive governance that develops an expansion of capability and power.

The discipline of prāṇāyāma combines these two elements: of 'prāṇa' or 'living energy' and 'āyāma' or 'expansive control'. The aim is to effect a radical expansion — in our habitually limited capabilities — through a carefully sustained channelling of psychosomatic power. This channelling, and its progressive effects, are described through the metaphor of a serpent called 'kuṇḍalinī'.

'Kuṇḍa' is a 'round hole or cavity', and 'kuṇḍalinī' means 'circular' or 'coiled'. The infinite energy of all creation, throughout the universe, is here conceived as latent within each body, coiled up like a serpent asleep in an interior hole. In the human body, this inner hole is located at the bottom of the spine, in what is called the 'mūlādhāra cakra'. But it must be understood that this is not a material hole in the gross body that is visible through our outer senses. Instead, it is an energy hole, from where currents of subtle energy are pulsated out and in. In other words, it is a nodal point for the pulsating flow of subtle, living energy.

In Yoga, the material body (the 'annamaya kośa' or 'covering of food') is conceived as manifesting an organic system of energy currents (the 'prāṇamaya kośa' or 'covering of living energy'). These currents of energy are called 'nāḍīs' or 'channels', and their nodal points are called 'cakras' or 'localized centres'. (A 'cakra' is literally a 'wheel', but it is used here as a place where energy currents are centred, like spokes at the hub of a wheel.)

At the bottom of the spine is the 'mūlādhāra cakra' or the 'root-support centre'. As conceived by Yoga, it is here that the infinite energy of kuṇḍalinī is usually latent, like a coiled up snake sleeping in a covered hole. Even in this latent state, small amounts of energy are drawn from the dormant kuṇḍalinī, thus producing the body's limited life and activities in the world.

There are two kinds of bodily energy: effective and affective. *Effective* energy moves the body's limbs and organs, thus bringing contact with particular objects. Such objective contact is taken in through an *affective* energy, which thus perceives and interprets a world outside. These two kinds of energy are conceived to flow in two main channels — which run along the spine, connecting the base of the spine to the head. But they are only limited channels, conditioned by bodily habit to carry very limited amounts of energy.

Such energy gets carried off by a host of branching channels, which dissipate it in different directions that lack co-ordination and harmony. Through that lack of co-ordination, the infinite energy of kuṇḍalinī counteracts itself, thus producing the appearance of limited bodily energy.

The two main channels of limited bodily energy are called 'piṅgalā' (or 'tawny' — for the effective energy that drives movement) and 'iḍā' (or 'refreshing' — for the affective energy that carries perception). Between them, a further channel is conceived, running up the centre of the spinal column. This central channel is called 'suṣumnā' or 'truly gracious'. The name is significant, because it is a channel of divine grace, through which the infinite energy of kuṇḍalinī may flow unlimited.

In most people, the central channel is habitually unused: blocked off by the disharmony and dissipation that makes energy seem limited, in our habituated bodies. However, it is possible for body and mind to get better tuned and harmonized: through purity of ethical conduct and character, through practices of properly balanced posture and breath control, through concentration of attention, through clarity of thought and depth of feeling. And, in the course of such psychosomatic tuning, the central channel can be opened up: so that the energy of kuṇḍalinī starts to uncoil itself, emerges from its hole at the base of the spine, and rises up the spinal column.

As the kuṇḍalinī rises, it passes through seven 'cakras' or 'centres':

- First is the 'mūlādhāra cakra' or the 'root-support centre', which has already been described as located at the bottom of the spine. This is where kuṇḍalinī arises from 'underground': at the 'earth' level, so to speak. This centre is thus associated with the element 'earth'.
- Second, two fingers width above the bottom of the spine, is the 'svādhiṣṭhāna cakra' or the 'centre of self-arising'. This centre is associated with the sexual organs, with regeneration, creativity and change, and thus with the element 'water'.
- Third, at the level of the navel, is the 'maṇipūra cakra' or the 'centre of the jewelled city'. It is associated with the solar plexus, with physical and mental digestion, and thus with the element 'fire'.

- Fourth, at the level of the physical heart, is the 'anāhata cakra' or the 'unstruck centre'. This is the centre of feeling and emotion. It is associated with sound or expression that is not just an effect of material objects striking against each other. Such sound is, more essentially, an effect of 'field' vibrations that travel through a surrounding medium of subtle conditioning. The association here is thus with the element 'air'.
- Fifth, at the throat, is the 'viśuddhi cakra' or the 'centre of purification'. This is the centre of pure speech or expression that is not attached to physical or mental objects, but inspired from the pervasion of pure consciousness throughout all space and time. Hence, there is an association here with the pervasive element 'ether'.
- Sixth, at the top of the spinal column (behind the spot between the eyebrows) is the 'ājñā cakra' or the 'centre of authority and command'. This represents the controlling aspect of consciousness: as the inner source from which all acts are inspired.
- Seventh, at the topmost point of the head, is the 'sahasrāra cakra' or the 'thousand-spoked centre'. In reaching this highest centre, kuṇḍalinī is conceived to pass entirely beyond all psychosomatic mixtures of body and mind, to the purely spiritual. There, multiplicity is reconciled with unity; as all activities and energies of nature are found to express no more or less than pure, unmoving consciousness.

What are we to make of this elaborate system of 'cakras' or 'centres': located along an ascending passage of psychosomatic energy, between the bottom of the spine and the top of the head? There is an obvious correspondence here with the gross physiology of the human nervous system: centred upon the brain and spinal cord, and extending through various branching nerves into the body's other organs and limbs.

Accordingly, there is a temptation to think that this traditional conception — of energy channels and centres — is just a fanciful account of the physical nervous system that modern science more accurately describes. Succumbing to such a temptation, the traditional nāḍīs or channels would be considered nothing more than bundles or pathways of physical nerves, and the energy carried would be no more than the electro-chemical impulses which physical nerves transmit. But that would be a rather ignorant misinterpretation of the traditional conception; no less ignorant than interpreting relativity theory and quantum physics as mere elaborations of Newtonian mechanics, without any reworking of basic principles.

Like relativity and quantum theories, the traditional conception of psychosomatic energy does not directly describe the gross matter that is seen by our external senses. Instead it makes an underlying description: of subtle kinds of energy beneath the material appearances perceived through our gross senses. Conceived thus, our physical nerves and nervous pathways are not themselves the nāḍīs or channels of psychosomatic energy. That flow of energy is not the nervous transmission of electro-chemical impulses, but something more fundamental. Our physical nerves and their electro-chemical transmissions are only very crude and superficial appearances of underlying energy currents that we may access more directly through a suitable training of mind and body.

The more fundamental the energy that is channelled, the less adequately may we expect it to be represented, in our physical nerves. This applies in particular to the infinite kuṇḍalinī energy, in its rise up the suṣumnā channel. Though that rise is conceived to be up the centre of the spine to the top of the head, it would be quite wrong to identify the suṣumnā channel with any pathway of physical nerves in the spinal cord and brain. As Svāmī Vivekānanda points out (in *Rāja-yoga*, chapter 4), the suṣumnā is just that energy channel which is not limited by association with 'any nerve fibres to act as wires'.

According to yogīs, the suṣumnā channel can be opened up in actual practice; and when that happens, the kuṇḍalinī energy rises upwards through its seven cakras. As it passes through each cakra, two things happen:

- First, and most obviously, there is a resonation of energy in the branching channels and nerves which originate or pass near the cakra: so that special experiences are triggered off in the personality (like feeling extraordinary sensations, seeing profoundly moving and beautiful visions, or developing mysterious powers of perception and expression).

- Second, and more significantly, there is a progressive sublimation of energy. At each cakra, the kuṇḍalinī energy is sublimated into a subtler and more inward form. Thus, from the 'earth'-bound energy of mūlādhāra (at the bottom of the spine), there is a progression of seven stages, culminating finally in the sahasrāra cakra (at the top of the head): where all powers and energies are completely sublimated into the pure illumination of an utterly impersonal consciousness.

The accuracy of this conception can only be tested by those who carry it out in practice; just as the accuracy of relativity and quantum theories can only be tested by relativistic and quantum physicists.

Altered States

The first four branches of Yoga are psychosomatic, concerned with both mind and body. But then, after the psychosomatic cultivation of prāṇāyāma, comes the fifth branch: called '***pratyāhāra***' or 'withdrawal'. The withdrawal is from the senses, which take attention out towards the physical world. So, from here on, the discipline of Yoga leaves the body behind and turns inward, towards the mind and its underlying depth.

The *Bhagavad-gītā* provides us with a classic description:

> When someone draws all senses in,
> back from their objects — like a tortoise
> drawing back its limbs — then
> knowledge is found there established, for
> that someone thus returned within. *– 2.58*

The limbs that the tortoise withdraws are counted as six: comprising the four limbs, the tail and the head. The legs and the tail are interpreted as the five bodily senses, and the head is interpreted as the mind. The inclusion of the mind is significant. What the analogy describes is not just a negative withdrawal; but a positive reflection of attention back to an unassailable source of pure life and truth, beneath the outward turnings of our restless minds.

In this sense — of turning positively back to truth within — the withdrawal of pratyāhāra is central to all yogic discipline. On the one hand, it does have its own particular techniques, as for example:

- 'yoga nidrā' or 'unifying sleep' — which is a deliberate relaxation of mind into a sort of voluntary sleep, with a remaining awareness of physical and mental quiescence;
- 'antar mauna' or 'inner silence' — which is a cultivated stilling of speech and thought and feeling, at times when they are not needed;
- 'ajapā japa' or 'unchanted chanting' — which starts from chanting out loud with the physical voice, then goes on to mentally chanting the shapes of sound in unspoken thought, and continues to progress through an increasing subtlety of mental chanting — until no shapes of sound remain, but only an awareness of the essence of the chant, without any physical or mental activity.

On the other hand, as these techniques suggest, pratyāhāra aims generally at a fundamental relaxation from the distractions of superficial appearance. As such, the first four branches of Yoga lead up to the reflective withdrawal of pratyāhāra; and it is implicit in the last three branches, which are further ways of putting it into practice.

After pratyāhāra comes the sixth branch, called '***dhāraṇā***' or 'holding on'. The aim here is to hold the mind to some absorbing object of attention. A suitable object is chosen and attention is turned towards it. As attention keeps wandering and turning away, it is brought repeatedly back: so as to focus again and again onto the chosen object, and to make it the centre of a prolonged stream of thought. Thus the mind's habitual tendency towards distraction and dissipation is meant to be relaxed, in a progressive concentration of energy and attention upon a single object.

As attention is progressively focused upon a particular object, it is perceived and thought about and felt more deeply. Superficial appearances and impressions give way to a deeper contemplation of the object's inner meaning and its more essential nature. Such deeper contemplation is called '***dhyāna***' or 'meditation'. It implies a falling back into the deeper nature of the practitioner's own experience. This is the seventh branch of Yoga. It effects a progressive detachment of watchful awareness: from the superficiality of passing experiences that come and go.

As meditation deepens, it results in special states of '***samādhi***' or 'absorption'. This is the eighth and last branch of Patañjali's Yoga. In a state of samādhi, the mind is powerfully drawn back in. There is an intense awareness, but not of outward things. The wandering mind becomes absorbed in an intensity of inner experience, which somehow knows more deeply and truly than before.

Broadly speaking, there are two kinds of samādhi. On the one hand, a samādhi may be '*sa*vikalpa': meaning that it contains some 'vikalpa' or 'differentiated perception'. Alternatively, a samādhi may be '*nir*vikalpa': meaning that no differentiated perception is contained in it.

In a savikalpa samādhi, attention is absorbed in some particular perception: like the sound of a mantra, or a vision of God or of some spirit. A classic example occurs in the *Bhagavad-gītā,* when Arjuna is granted a vision of the universal form of God. In Arjuna's vision, the body of God contains the entire universe, of moving and unmoving things. There is thus an intense perception, which contains everything in itself. This is characteristic of a savikalpa samādhi. It is a state of such intense perception that everything becomes absorbed in it. Then the world of external objects disappears. There is nothing but perception, containing everything perceived, just like a dream.

In its content, a savikalpa samādhi is an intense dream. There is only pure perception, with nothing seen outside. Perception is no longer directed outward, to external objects. Attention has been turned back in: so that perception is absorbed within the mind.

In a nirvikalpa samādhi, the absorption proceeds further. Not only is perception absorbed into the perceiving mind, but the mind becomes absorbed as well: in a state where no perceptions appear at all.

In its content, a nirvikalpa samādhi is exactly the same as deep sleep. There are no differentiated perceptions in it. There is no sense of passing time, in which appearances could come and go. There's only pure experience: unmixed with any physical or mental things that are perceived in space or time.

In short, a savikalpa samādhi is a special kind of dream; and a nirvikalpa samādhi is a special kind of deep sleep. But then, what makes these samādhi states so special and intense? The answer does not really lie in their content, but in the way that they are approached and regarded, from the waking state. Our everyday states of dream and deep sleep are entered involuntarily; and we take them largely for granted, without paying much attention to them. But, in Yoga and other such spiritual disciplines, special states of samādhi are cultivated through intensive practices that require a tremendous effort, sustained over a very long period of time. And when such samādhi states are attained, they are regarded with a corresponding degree of intense interest and respect. For they are conceived as specially altered states of experience: through which the perceptions and powers of a person's mind can be expanded, far beyond its habitual limitations.

This expansion is described by the name 'saṁyama' or 'integrated control'. It is a collective name for the last three branches of Yoga: dhāraṇā or concentration, dhyāna or meditation, and samādhi or absorption. By concentrating upon an object, meditating upon its meaning and becoming inwardly absorbed into its essential nature, a practitioner of saṁyama is supposed to attain control over the powers of nature that the object manifests. Thus, in association with the altered states of samādhi, extraordinary powers are also conceived to develop and appear.

But both the altered states and their associated powers are said to be double-edged. On the one hand, they show the inner source that is the true goal of spiritual discipline. On the other hand, they also present a temptation: to get attached to them, as goals in themselves. And any such attachment must of course obscure the real goal.

Undying Truth

The trouble with all altered states is their own alteration. Having come, they also go. As the results of change, they too get changed and pass away. In particular, the states of samādhi are experienced in isolation from the everyday world. When these states of isolation pass, the everyday world returns, with all its troubles and difficulties. What of value then remains from such samādhi states?

According to its own conception, Yoga is a very long term discipline. It does not work in the course of just one lifetime, but in the course of many. And it requires a sustained renunciation of other activities, so as to sublimate their energies into its special states of samādhi.

What is the purpose of this extraordinary cultivation of sublimated energy? It is a training of mental control, supposed to bring an extraordinary development of mental states and powers and faculties. But Yoga warns us that its special states and powers are not ends in themselves. They are only passing means to a more fundamental goal: of returning finally to an unaltered, lasting truth.

The purpose of samādhi states is to focus on that truth, in isolation from the external appearances which habitually obscure it for us, in the ordinary world. But it isn't enough to see that truth in isolation from the world. For it is the same truth that's shown by all appearances. It is their truth as well. It is the truth of all the world, including each one of our worldly lives and personalities.

Thus, in the end, the discipline of Yoga serves as a preparation. It prepares our dying personalities to look for an undying truth that each of them has always been. And the preparation is inevitably paradoxical. For it prepares a person to find out an utterly impersonal truth. And to become established there, where not the slightest trace of change or personality is ever found.

Detachment from Personality

Karma Yoga

Where knowledge is attained through any personal discipline, a problematic compromise is always left behind. For, to the extent that the discipline is personal, what it achieves is not strictly knowledge, but only an altered state of personality.

And such a state is inevitably changing, as it is experienced through a degree of personal isolation from the normally apparent world. How can this altered state lead on to lasting knowledge? Only by using it to see an impartial truth that is common to the altered state and the ordinary world. When the state passes and the ordinary world appears again, truth must be seen in this ordinary world as well, while the perceiving personality is fully engaged in it.

This requires that the personality must be fully engaged in what it rightly does, facing squarely and honestly whatever confronts it in the world. And yet, at the same time, there must be a complete detachment from this engaged personality: so that nothing which happens to it can affect a clear understanding of truth. In particular, there must be no attachment to any results of personal work.

Thus, when faced by something to be done, it is best to do it wholeheartedly, to work with full commitment towards the intended aim; and yet without attachment to what may result. There must be an active dedication which gives up all personal effort and all personal wishes to the work that's undertaken. This approach, of active dedication, is called 'karma yoga' or the 'discipline of action'. Kṛṣṇa describes it to Arjuna, in the *Bhagavad-gītā*. (The translations below are rather free, sometimes a little interpreted and elaborated.)

> The inner principle does not
> get freed from acts by ceasing
> to originate what's done.
> Its freedom is just what it is.
>
> No person can attain that freedom,
> from the bonds that limit action,

by not undertaking actions
which remain yet to be done.

Rejection by itself is not
enough to reach what must be found. – *3.4*

Not even for a moment does
a person stand, not doing
anything. No personality
stands independent in itself,
and thus acts independently.

Each personality is driven
to its acts, impelled by
nature's constituting qualities. – *3.5*

If someone sits about, suppressing
faculties of action with
a mind that keeps returning to
the objects of those faculties,
that person is just self-deceived.

All that's achieved by this pretence
may well be called 'hypocrisy'. – *3.6*

But if, with faculties controlled
by mind, one then goes on to use
those faculties, quite unattached
to them; that discipline of action
is much better, Arjuna. – *3.7*

You need to do what's due from you;
for doing what you must is surely
better than paralysis.

The very journey of your body,
through its course from birth to death,
needs action. It can't be accomplished
by remaining paralysed. – *3.8*

Except for actions done just for
the sake of sacrifice, all of
this world is an entanglement
in partial actions, Arjuna.

So act wholeheartedly, just for
the sake of sacrifice, free
from attachment to all partial acts. *– 3.9*

You need to know that partial actions
rise from that which is complete;
and, in its turn, this same completeness
comes from that which does not change.

Arising thus from changelessness,
completeness is found everywhere,
continuing through everything.
And its impartiality
is always based on sacrifice:
of changing things to what remains. *– 3.15*

Thus all creation cycles round:
turned forth from where there is no change,
and there returned in sacrifice.

One who lives up to that lives there
unchanged, quite unaffected by
the acts that are inspired from there.

One who does not live up to that
lives wrongfully, enjoying only
doubtful pleasures which depend
on temporary faculties.
No real value is found here. *– 3.16*

When all enjoyment is in self,
when someone is content with self
and is completely satisfied

with self alone, then for that someone
there is nothing to be done. – *3.17*

For such a one, at peace with self,
there is no object to be gained
or lost: by doing anything,
or by not doing anything.

Though living here, among all beings,
such a one does not depend
on any object in the world. – *3.18*

Thus you must fully carry out
whatever work needs to be done,
remaining always unattached
to any object gained or lost.

Thus acting fully unattached,
the inner principle comes up
into a world that seems outside,
and through this inspiration takes
a person to the highest state. – *3.19*

But how is it possible to be fully engaged in work towards a desired result, and yet to be completely disengaged from the same result that the work attempts to bring about? Left unresolved, this apparent contradiction keeps on causing trouble and confusion, in the practice of any spiritual discipline.

In the end, the contradiction can only be resolved by a philosophical detachment: of an inner, true self from the personality which is engaged. Only by standing in that truth of self can there be a complete detachment, while the personality is engaged in the work to which it has been committed.

Personality and Self

In the second chapter of the *Bhagavad-gītā*, Kṛṣṇa starts his battlefield discourse by carefully distinguishing a changeless truth of self from changing and dying personality. And then he goes on to describe an establishment in that truth, by those who achieve 'sthita-prajñā' or 'steady wisdom'. Such an establishment, he says, is the final and complete aim of all spiritual discipline.

First (as shown below in 2.12-33,37-38) comes the distinction of a deathless self, and how it applies to Arjuna's current situation on the battlefield:

For you, for me, for all these rulers,
there has never been a time
when what we are did not exist.

Nor, after this, at any time,
will any one of us come to
a state when what we are is not. *– 2.12*

As, in this body, that which is
embodied carries on through passing
states of childhood, youth and age;

so also, when this body dies,
the embodied principle
carries on through other bodies
in the course of passing time.

Someone whose stand remains unshaken
does not get confused by this. *– 2.13*

But contacts with sense objects bring
on cold and heat, comfort and pain.
They come and go, impermanent.
You need to bear them, Arjuna. *– 2.14*

For they do not disturb that inner
principle of consciousness
which is unchangeably the same
in states of pleasure and of pain.
Just that amounts to deathlessness. *– 2.15*

What is unreal and untrue
can't come to be. What's true and real

is just that which does not pass.
The final essence of both these
is seen by those who see the truth. – 2.16

You need to know just that which does
not get to be destroyed. It's that
by which all this entire universe
is joined and woven through.

It's that which nothing can destroy,
which does not change and pass away. – 2.17

We speak about these finite bodies
each of which must come to end.

But they belong to that which they
embody: to a self that lives
in them, immeasurable,
undestroyed and permanent. Arjuna,
it's from there that you must fight. – 2.18

If self is taken to be that
which kills, or if it's taken to
be killed; whoever thinks like this
does not correctly understand.

Self does not kill, nor is it killed. – 2.19

Self is not born. Nor does it die.
Nor, after being for a while,
can it then ever go away.

Unborn, continuing unchanged,
it's always here, before all time.
It is not killed when body dies. – 2.20

That principle which knows itself
forever undestroyed, unborn
and undecayed, how can it kill?

Who is there here for it to kill?
How can it cause whom to be killed? – 2.21

As used-up clothes are thrown away
to put on others that are new,

so also the embodied self
throws off our used-up bodies, and
appears in others, seeming new. – 2.22

It is not cut by any blade.
It is not burned by any fire.
Water does not make it wet.
No wind can dry it in the least. – 2.23

Uncut, unburned, not wet, nor dry,
it's always here, goes everywhere;
and stands unmoved, before all time. – 2.24

Unmanifest to changing thought,
it's spoken of as that which stays
quite unaffected through all change.

Known thus, it can't give rise to grief. – 2.25

But even where it's thought to pass,
continually, through birth and death,
this is no real cause for grief. – 2.26

Death comes to that which has been born,
and birth must rise for that which dies.

What happens thus, unfailingly,
is that which must. It can't be fit
to grieve for what thus comes to pass. – 2.27

All things that have but come to be
were first unmanifest. They're only
manifested in between.

And when in course of time they pass,
they are unmanifest again.

What is there here to fuss about? – 2.28

Some make a mystery of seeing
this, some make a mystery
discussing it or hearing it;
but it can never thus be known. – 2.29

This that lives in all our bodies
cannot ever be destroyed.
It always *is*, before all time.

Therefore, there is no need to grieve:

for all those things that come to be,
that come to pass and pass away;

for anything that comes to be,
that comes to pass and passes on. – 2.30

Moreover, it's not right for you
to shrink from doing what you must,
considering your own duty here.
A warrior has no better option
than to fight as duty calls. – 2.31

When warriors are called unsought
to fight in such a war as this,
they count themselves as fortunate.
For it provides an open door
that leads towards a higher state. – 2.32

But if you don't engage in this
just war that duty asks of you,
then you turn back from your own nature:
from what's right and honourable
for you. And that will bring you ill. – 2.33

If you are killed, you will attain
to a transcendent state. Or, if
you win, you will enjoy the world.

So, Arjuna, resolve your doubts.
Stand up and face what you must fight. *– 2.37*

Hold comfort and discomfort as
the same. So also gain and loss,
defeat and victory. Be ready
thus to fight. No taint of ill
can then become attached to you. *– 2.38*

Establishment in Truth

And then (as shown below in 2.39-72), Kṛṣṇa takes Arjuna beyond his present situation on the battlefield, to describe how spiritual discipline can lead to an establishment in truth. That establishment is the true 'samādhi' or 'absorption' which Yoga aims at. It is not an altered state, which may be further altered. Instead, it is a final return to one's own, unaltered nature (svarūpa). That's what each one of us has always been. There permanence is found at last, where time and change do not apply:

This understanding has now been
explained to you, through reason and
analysis. But, Arjuna,
you also need to hear of it
as it applies in actual practice:
joining back to set one free
from bonds of action in the world. *– 2.39*

And here, no progress meets with ruin;
no reverse or loss is found.

For where such practice is well-founded,
even just a little bit
protects unfailingly against
the greatest insecurity. *– 2.40*

Here, there is just one single-minded
resolution, settling back
into the inmost ground of self.

For, those who are not resolute
get caught up in their changing minds:
which keep on branching off, in
different directions, endlessly. *– 2.41*

Some who are not inspired by truth
play games instead with talk of knowledge,
dressed in showy forms of speech.
They say there's nothing more than this. *– 2.42*

Identified as wishing minds,
they only seek some higher state
that mind conceives: producing forth
the fruits of birth and action in
a world profuse with partial acts,
possessively pursuing power. *– 2.43*

Attachment to possessive power
leads away from consciousness.

Those led away are thus deprived
of their own knowing ground. For them,
no inner resolution is
established as an understanding
joining back into itself. *– 2.44*

The knowledge that is learned from texts
shows only nature's qualities.
You need to free yourself from these:
from all opposing qualities
that may appear or disappear.

Beyond all effort seeking gain
or keeping hold of what's been gained,

you need to stand in changeless truth:
established finally in self. – *2.45*

For one who knows impartial truth,
all texts are just about as useful
as a water-tank, when there
is water flowing everywhere. – *2.46*

It is your business just to act
with full attention to your work,
to give your best to what you do.

That given, what results is never
yours. The fruits of action don't
belong to you. Obtaining them
should not become your cause to act.

Nor, giving up that cause, should you
become attached to idleness. – *2.47*

So Arjuna, stand disciplined.
Give up attachment. Be the same
in gain or loss. And carry out
all acts from there. That even
attitude, of equanimity,
is just what's meant by 'discipline'. – *2.48*

For, action moved by distant fruits
must be inferior to that
which rises up from understanding
clarified by discipline.

It is in understanding that
you need to seek your rightful home,
where you can never be disturbed.

Those who are motivated by
objectives yet to be achieved
are pitiable, Arjuna. – *2.49*

Where discipline joins back within,
to understanding; there all actions,
good and bad, are given up:
left to the world where they belong.

Thus, it is for this joining back
that you must discipline yourself.

Expressed in actions, discipline
forms capability and skill. *– 2.50*

Those who are wise have joined back in.
By letting go the fruits of action,
they attain an unaffected
state, set free from bonds of birth. *– 2.51*

When understanding goes beyond
all its deluded coverings,
then you will come to that impartial
knowledge where what has been heard
and what remains yet to be heard
can make no real difference. *– 2.52*

Your understanding is confused
by going off divergently,
in various ways you've heard about.

But when it stands absorbed within,
beneath all movement, undisturbed;

then you will find that unity
which harnesses all exercise
and focuses all discipline. *– 2.53*

Arjuna asked:

What may be said of one who is
established in true knowledge and
stands there absorbed? How does that person
speak, sit down and move about? *– 2.54*

Kṛṣṇa replied:

When all desires, going deep
into the mind, have finally
been given up, a person comes
to lasting peace and happiness:
in self alone, all by itself.

When someone gets to live there quite
spontaneously, remaining always
undisturbed, no matter what
takes place; that someone is then said
to be 'established in true knowledge'. *– 2.55*

Such a one, of steady understanding,
stays unshaken inwardly:
no longer driven by
possessive want, nor by desire,
fear and rage, through all the
miseries and joys that mind gets into.

Such a one, who stands upon
unchanging ground, is called a 'sage'. *– 2.56*

Whatever happens, good or bad,
someone whose knowledge is established
stays impartial everywhere:
quite unaffected by complacency
when things go well, or by
frustration at receiving ill. *– 2.57*

When someone draws all senses in,
back from their objects — like a tortoise
drawing back its limbs — then
knowledge is found there established, for
that someone thus returned within. *– 2.58*

When an embodied mind abstains
from objects, then for it they

disappear. But still, a taste for them
remains. For one who sees beyond
the mind, even that taste must
disappear — dissolved in its own end. *– 2.59*

The senses are by nature turbulent.
With brutal force, they hijack
mind — which rightfully belongs
to the inspired striving that
spontaneously expresses
consciousness, the inmost principle. *– 2.60*

But when all senses are controlled,
one who is disciplined may
settle back, to live at peace: absorbed
into the final truth of self.

Where knowledge is established, there
each faculty is — of its own
accord — kept perfectly controlled. *– 2.61*

From thought of objects, which is nothing
else but consciousness, attachment
to those objects is produced.

Then, with attachment comes desire,
from desire anger grows. *– 2.62*

With anger, there's confusion; with
confusion, mind's distortions bring
misunderstanding; and from that,
what one is oneself is lost. *– 2.63*

Where faculties are moved direct,
self-disciplined from truth of self,
they are not just attracted or
repelled by objects in the world.
They are thus freed from drivenness.

With faculties thus freed by inner
discipline, someone who acts
toward objectives in the world
may act from truth of self,
and there find lasting clarity. *– 2.64*

In clarity of quiet peace
all troubles and dissatisfactions
are resolved and brought to end.

For one who comes to clarity
of unaffected consciousness,
clear understanding stands directly
back, upon unshifting ground. *– 2.65*

For one who does not join back in,
truth is not rightly understood.
Someone who stays at odds within
can't rightly come to understand.

For one who does not come to truth,
there is no peace. For one thus restless,
how can there be happiness? *– 2.66*

The mind, which follows the dictates
of senses driven here and there,
is like a restless, blowing wind.

It carries off the knowledge that
it thinks it owns, just like a
blowing wind keeps carrying away
a boat that's drifting on the sea. *– 2.67*

So, Arjuna, for one whose knowledge
is established, all objective
faculties are anchored fully
back within: beneath the driven
objects that they act towards,
seen in the changing world outside. *– 2.68*

One who achieves complete control
stands wide awake in what is dark,
unconscious night — for any being
seen created in the world.

Created beings are awake
to what a sage sees as a night:
where true awareness is submerged
in dreams of blind obscurity. *– 2.69*

As waters flow into an ocean
full within, unchanging at
the depth where it stands in itself;

so also all desires flow into
the heart that comes to peace. But that
is not what's moved to seek desire. *– 2.70*

Where all desires are left behind,
the inner principle lives on
spontaneously, free from all want,
not limiting the truth of self
with petty thoughts of 'I' and 'mine'.

Thus, one attains to lasting peace. *– 2.71*

This is the state where everything
has been achieved. Where it's attained,
all foolishness is at an end.
It is the end of time itself.

By taking one's own stand in it,
all is extinguished, all complete. *– 2.72*

Part 3 — Learning and Enquiry

SOUND AND SEEING

The Sense of Sound

According to a traditional conception, we can think of the entire universe as made of sound. This conception may be introduced by going down through a series of five levels, called the 'tanmātras'.

Literally, the word 'tanmātra' means 'that-merely' or 'that-measuring'. ('Tat' means 'that', and 'mātra' means 'merely' or 'measuring'.) As 'that-merely', a tanmātra is a subtle essence, to which more obvious appearances may be reduced. As 'that-measuring', a tanmātra is a way of measuring or viewing our experience of the world. So the tanmātras are a progression of subtle essences, found through deeper ways of looking at the world.

In particular, there are five tanmātras, corresponding to the five traditional elements of 'earth', 'water', 'fire', 'air' and 'ether'. And they also correspond to the five senses: of smell, taste, sight, touch and sound.

- The first tanmātra (gandha) is that of 'earth' and 'smell'. Here, 'earth' can be interpreted as objective matter, which is divided into particular objects. Each object is a piece of matter; and together all such objects make up an external world. At this level, experience is viewed through the kind of perception that identifies a particular object, as something different from other things. That kind of perception is represented by the sense of smell, which sniffs out particular things. As for example when a dog sniffs out a trail of scent. Or when we speak of 'smelling a rat', to imply a sense of detection that zeroes in on something particular which has gone wrong.

- The second tanmātra (rasa) is that of 'water' and 'taste'. Here, 'water' can be interpreted as flowing energy. Each particular object is conceived to be a gross appearance, made of something more subtle than what previously appeared. It is not a separate piece of matter; but, instead, it is a pattern of energy currents, flowing from and into other patterns. At this level, experience is viewed through a sympathetic activation of energy in the perceiving organism. That kind of perception is represented by the sense of taste. It is clearly moved to act in sympathy with the flavours that it perceives. As it perceives an attractive or repulsive flavour, its own perceiving action is attracted or repelled accordingly.

- The third tanmātra (rūpa) is that of 'fire' and 'sight'. Here, 'fire' can be interpreted as meaningful information. Each apparent form or pattern is conceived to have a meaning, and thus to represent something that has to be interpreted. At this level, experience is viewed through the interpretation of apparent form. That kind of interpretation is represented by the sense of sight. It shows us visual shapes and forms that clearly have to be interpreted, to tell us what is thus perceived.
- The fourth tanmātra (sparśa) is that of 'air' and 'touch'. Here, 'air' can be interpreted as conditioned quality. Each representation is conceived to be made up of relative qualities, which have to be evaluated. At this level, experience is viewed through the qualitative evaluations of intuitive judgement: as represented by the sense of touch.
- The fifth tanmātra (śabda) is that of 'ether' and 'sound'. Here, 'ether' can be interpreted as pervading continuity. Each variation of quality is conceived to show a common continuity of underlying principle. At this level, changing experiences are viewed through the penetration of insight: to show an underlying continuity that they share in common. That kind of insight is represented by the sense of sound. It hears the changing sounds of words, and understands through them a continuity of meaning and consciousness that they express.

Thus, among the faculties that take perception in, the sense of sound is accorded a special place. It represents the deepest level of understanding: reflecting back from changing appearances to a changeless ground of consciousness that is expressed. From that inmost ground, the outward faculty of speech draws meaning and expresses it in sound.

Vibration and Light

In traditional learning, with its intensive use of recitation and memory, experiences of listening and speaking are central. A student learned by hearing and reciting, far more than by reading what was written down. Thus it was only natural to make a profound investigation into the microcosmic and macrocosmic experiences of sound.

In that investigation, sound is taken to be a special kind of movement, called 'vibration'. This is a repeated movement, about a central point of origin. In this kind of movement, there is a repeated cycle of disturbance: from an originating, central state of equilibrium and rest.

As our bodies speak and hear, we experience physical vibrations in our chests and throats and ears. At the lower notes of sound, the frequency is slow; and so we notice the throbbing movement of individual cycles that make up the vibration. As the pitch of sound gets higher, the frequency increases, and we are less able to notice the individual vibrations.

When the pitch is high enough, we do not notice the individual vibrations at all. There, we only notice shapes and meanings and qualities of sound, produced by vibrations whose movements are too fast for us to perceive directly. Thus we conceive of subtle vibrations — which our senses cannot see directly, but which produce perceived effects in our experience.

Like modern physics, traditional conceptions make much use of this idea of subtle vibrations, behind the forms and names and qualities that we perceive. In particular, forms are conceived to be made up from pulsating currents of vibrant energy; names are conceived to achieve their representation and meaning through a radiant resonance of sympathetic vibration; and qualities are conceived to show a vibrant swinging to and fro between opposites (like pain and pleasure, depth and height, heat and cold).

Thus, beneath apparent forms and names and qualities, more subtle vibrations are conceived. But where do they take place? At their most subtle, they take place beneath the changing surface of appearances, in the background continuity of space and time. This background continuity is called 'ākāśa' or the 'ether'.

But there is an inherent problem here. Whatever changes and movements occur, the background continuity persists beneath them. In its underlying nature, there is no change, nor any movement. To understand the changes that occur, some kind of disturbance must be conceived as added on to their unchanging background. That disturbance is its subtle vibration. From that vibration comes the entire universe of differing appearances, of changing qualities and names and forms.

In modern physics, the concept of sound is restricted to physical vibrations, in various bodies and substances that are externally perceived. But, in older traditions, this is not so. Concepts of sound and vibration are extended into mental experience: to include what we hear and perceive and think and feel within our minds. And further, there is a questioning of how these concepts extend beyond the mind as well: to a background continuity beneath all physical and mental appearances.

There, at that background continuity, it must be understood that sound is not a vibration in any object or substance which is physically or mentally conditioned. The background continuity is neither physical nor mental. It is itself beneath all changing attributes, of body or of mind. By conceiving a vibration there in it, we are adding something quite extraneous to what it is itself. It is this added on vibration that makes the continuity appear to be conditioned and changeable.

Hence the inherent paradox. The concept of vibration has been extended to the point where it is breaking down. The concept has been extended — beyond the physical and mental — to a subtle vibration that produces the world's appearances. But it produces them from a changeless background, where there is neither movement nor conditioning. So then, beneath all movement and conditioning, from where does this vibration come?

It is conceived to come from underlying consciousness — which is the essence of both light and sound. That consciousness is the essential principle of seeing and illuminating. And it is also the essential principle of hearing and speaking:

- By its very nature, of illuminating knowledge, consciousness illuminates appearances. From that illumination, all perception comes.
- By its very nature, of manifesting expression, consciousness vibrates with life. It keeps on bursting out into perceived appearance, and drawing back again. The cycle keeps repeating: projecting out and then immediately drawing in, as each appearance is perceived. From that vibration, all manifestation is expressed.

Seen in the world of appearances, illumination and vibration are actions, involving change and movement. But in consciousness itself, they are not so.

The illumination of consciousness is not a changing act, which is put on at one time and taken off at another. No action needs to be put on, for consciousness to shine. It does not shine by any changing act, but just by being what it always is. Its shining is thus changeless, and involves no movement in itself. Appearances are lit by its mere presence, as it stays unmoved within itself.

So also the vibration of consciousness. As it bursts out into appearance or draws back in, it seems to change; but the change is only in appearance. Outwardly, a change appears; but in itself, consciousness remains unmoved and unaffected, just as it always is. As differing appearances keep getting manifested forth and drawn back in, each manifests the unchanged nature of consciousness. As the cycle keeps repeating, it is just a repetition of that unchanged nature, over and over again.

To the apparent world, consciousness vibrates forth into change. But, for consciousness, that vibration is just its own nature, remaining utterly unchanged. Thus, consciousness is pure activity: the unmixed principle from which all acts arise and change is brought about. And that pure principle of all activity remains itself unmoved by change.

Shining Out

This concept, of pure illumination as the source of all activity, is expressed in the Sanskrit words 'sphoṭa' and 'sphuraṇa'. The word 'sphoṭa' conveys a sense of sudden blossoming or bursting forth: from uncreated timelessness into the created appearances of passing time. And it combines this sense of bursting creativity with a further sense of clear illumination that makes things evident. The word 'sphuraṇa' conveys both these senses; and it adds a further sense of continued repetition: so as to imply an activating vibration and an unceasing brilliance.

Here is the report of a conversation in which Ramaṇa Maharṣi describes 'sphuraṇa' as 'I'-'I': as a repetition of the true, unchanging 'I', which is pure consciousness:

> *M:* ...'I AM that I AM' sums up the whole truth.... any form or shape is the cause of trouble. Give up the notion that 'I am so and so.' Our *śāstras* [scriptures] say: *aham iti sphurati* (it shines as 'I').
>
> *D:* What is *sphuraṇa* (shining)?
>
> *M:* (*Aham, aham*) 'I'-'I' is the Self; (*Aham idam*) 'I am this' or 'I am that' is the ego. Shining is there always. The ego is transitory. When the 'I' is kept up as 'I' alone, it is the Self; when it flies at a tangent and says 'this', it is the ego.[17]

And here is the report of another conversation, in which Ramaṇa Maharṣi talks of '*Ahaṁ* sphūrti' as an 'incessant flash of I-consciousness'. 'Aham' means 'I', and 'sphūrti' is just another grammatical form of 'sphuraṇa':

> *M:* Yes, when you go deeper you lose yourself, as it were, in the abysmal depths; then the Reality which is the *Ātman* [Self] that was behind you all the while takes hold of you. It is an incessant flash of 'I-consciousness'; you can be aware of it, feel it, hear it, sense it, so to say. This is what I call '*Ahaṁ sphūrti*'.

[17] Venkataramiah 1984.

D: You said that the *Ātman* is immutable, self-effulgent, etc. But if you speak at the same time of the incessant flash of I-consciousness, of this '*Ahaṁ sphūrti*', does that not imply movement, which cannot be complete realization, in which there is no movement?

M: What do you mean by complete realization? Does it mean becoming a stone, an inert mass? The *Ahaṁ vṛtti* ['I'-acting] is different from *Ahaṁ Sphūrti*. The former is the activity of the ego, and is bound to lose itself and make way for the latter which is an eternal expression of the Self. In Vedāntic parlance this *Ahaṁ Sphūrti* is called *Vṛtti Jñāna* [the pure activity of knowledge].... *Svarūpa* [the true nature of reality] is *Jñāna* [knowledge] itself, it is Consciousness.[18]

In these conversations, Ramaṇa Maharṣi is speaking of an ultimate subjective principle, which is the essence of both knowing and doing. It is at once pure illumination and pure activity, unmixed with anything physical or mental. Each personal ego is a confused mixture of consciousness with body and mind. Beneath the confusion, the real 'I' is unmixed consciousness, the changeless source and essence of all apparent activity. All seen activities and happenings are its expressions. Accordingly, all the entire universe may be conceived as its speaking: as what it says to us.

That source is common to each one of us and to all else. It's only by returning there that our confused activities, of body and of mind, can come to knowledge and clarity. It's only there that we learn anything. Traditional conceptions of learning are thus centred upon that source, where doing and knowing come together.

In particular, that source is the meeting point of sound and light. Here is Ramaṇa Maharṣi's description:

> In the course of conversation, Maharṣi said that the subtle body is composed of light and sound and the gross body is a concrete form of the same.

---

[18] Sastri 1993.

Figure 8

	ĪŚVARA [God] UNIVERSAL	JĪVA [personality] INDIVIDUAL
gross	Universe	Body
subtle	Sound and light – *Nāda, Bindu*	Mind and *Prāṇa*
primal	*Ātmā* (Self) *Param* (transcendental)	*Ātmā* (Self) *Param* (transcendental)

The Lecturer in Physics asked if the same light and sound were cognizable by senses.

M: No. They are supersensual. It is like this:...[see figure 8, above].

They [sound and light] are ultimately the same.

The subtle body of the Creator is the mystic sound *Praṇava* [the mantra 'Om'], which is sound and light. The universe resolves into sound and light and then into transcendence — *Param.*[19]

Chanting and Enquiry

The coming together of sound and seeing is not just a matter of theory and conception. It is central to the practice of traditional learning, through the intensive use of formal recitation.

When a text is recited, the immediate practice is that of sound. The first effect is from the shape and form of sound, as pronounced by the speaker. It is like listening to music. The passing shapes of sound affect the hearing mind. They act upon the mind so as to influence attention, energy and mood. When shape of sound is used

---

[19] Venkataramiah 1984.

like this, to enable particular effects upon the hearing mind, it is described by the Sanskrit word 'mantra', which means a 'mental device'.

As shapes and sounds of words are heard, they are also understood to have a meaning, by which something more is seen. Through meaning, the hearing mind experiences a subtle and internal seeing, beneath the gross sounds that are externally heard. In that internal seeing, there is a reflection of attention back: from changing shapes at the mind's surface, to a continued understanding at the background of experience.

Thus, beneath its changing shapes and sounds, language has a second aspect: of meaningful seeing, which continues through the changes of shape and sound. This second aspect of language is described by the Sanskrit word 'vicāra' which means 'thought' and 'enquiry'.

In the practice of traditional learning, both aspects of language are highly developed:

- The *mantra* aspect is one of subtle force and power, through which the sound of words impels the hearing mind to change its state in some specific way.
- The *vicāra* aspect is one of reflective thought and enquiry, through which the meaning of words is considered and questioned.

In short, the *mantra* aspect is sheer force of sound; the *vicāra* aspect is reflective seeing.

Both these aspects are meant to be intensified by repetition. By repeated recitation, the mind is meant to focus more intently on the shape of sound, and thus to get thrown further and further towards the change of state intended by the mantra aspect. By repeated reflection, there is meant to be a progressive investigation of meaning: as the mind keeps questioning and clarifying its own assumptions, so as to go deeper and deeper into the meaning of what is said.

As the repetition continues, both aspects are meant to reinforce each other. The mantra sound induces an altered state of mind, which is meant to go together with a reflective enquiry into clearer seeing. Through continued repetition, both sound and seeing are meant to get increasingly internalized, until they reach a meeting point where the internalization is complete:

- The sound proceeds from recitation with the mouth to recitation in the mind. Then in the mind, the sound is meant to proceed from explicit forms and names of thought to tacit qualities and values of feeling — which go further and further down, into the background of experience. The eventual aim is the background itself. The intention is that there, at the background, the sound of speech dissolves into its silent essence. That is its living source. From there, expression is inspired: in a way that is completely natural and spontaneous, quite free from all the deliberated artificiality of thoughts and words.
- For seeing to be clarified, mere verbal argument must lead to genuine questioning, of prejudiced and preconceived assumptions. The eventual aim is to get beneath all prejudice and preconception: so that one comes to a pure seeing, at an inmost ground where no assumptions prejudice or preconceive what's seen.

The meeting point of sound and seeing is meant to be found there, at that inmost ground from which all sounds and seeings come.

From a narrowly 'modern' point of view, we think of learning by heart as a merely formal and unthinking memorization, which does not bother to question what has been slavishly memorized. But the same phrase, 'learning by heart', has a more basic meaning, which is essential to traditional learning. It refers to a sustained process of absorbing both the sound and meaning of a text into the depth of one's own heart, far beneath the outward forms of recitation and the deliberated interpretations of thought.

Such learning by heart is far from lazy or slavish imitation. Instead, it is a matter of making the text and what it says one's own. That requires an intensive familiarization with the text and a relentless questioning of what is said. The learning process is designed to be sustained until the text is fully familiar and its meaning is perfectly clear. In the course of time, the familiarization must be so thorough and the questioning so rigorous that what is learned goes far beneath all passing words and thoughts. The long term aim is thus an independent understanding that is spontaneously expressed in what an individual feels and thinks and does, in her or his own right.

Learning from Source

Implicit in this traditional approach is a reflection back to an inner, common source: shared by the microcosm of individual experience and the macrocosm of the external universe. A student learns by going down beneath the changing sounds of learning, to that unchanging source from where the world is understood. This is described, a little allegorically, in the *Bṛhadāraṇyaka Upaniṣad*, 4.5.8-11:

- First (in 4.5.8-10), there is a description of changing sound and how it may be understood. The understanding is achieved by holding one's mind to the instrument that plays the sound, and thus coming to the player: the inner source that is expressed.
- Second (in 4.5.11), there is a description of seeing. Here, the forms of learning, personal experience and the whole universe are described as differentiated smokes and vapours, breathed out from that one inner source which is beyond all limitation:

> The outward sounds of drumbeats can't
> be captured. But, by holding on
> to just the drum, or to the drummer,
> what get's spoken there is grasped. *– 4.5.8*
>
> The outward sounds blown from a conch
> cannot be captured and kept held.
> And yet, by holding to the conch,
> or to the one who blows the conch,
> what's spoken there is understood. *– 4.5.9*
>
> The outward sounds played from a vīṇā
> can't be captured and kept held.

And yet, by holding to the vīṇā,
or the one who plays the vīṇā,
there what's said is understood. *– 4.5.10*

As fire burns up sap-filled fuel,
smokes and vapours issue forth
in differentiated ways.

So too, breathed out of the unlimited,
which has now come to be,

is this *Ṛg-veda, Yajur-veda,*
Sāma-veda, the *Atharva-veda,*
history and myth,
the arts and sciences,
the teachings of philosophy,
verse-compositions, aphorisms,
explanations, commentaries,

sacrifices, offerings,
what's eaten, drunk,
this world, the other world,
and all created things.

They are the breaths of *that* alone. *– 4.5.11*

LEVELS OF EXPRESSION

The Science of Language

How does meaning come to be expressed in sound? This question is investigated in the traditional science of Sanskrit linguistics.

In Sanskrit, the word for grammar is 'vyākaraṇa'. It is an abstract noun from the verb 'vi-kṛ', which means to 'make different' or to 'analyse'. So 'vyākaraṇa' means 'analysis', and it refers to the same science that we study today as linguistic analysis.

But, in the traditional view, language is not just an external construction — which builds words from letters, and sentences from words. Names are not just objects representing other objects and their properties and relationships. Verbs are not just connecting names that represent the actions of various objects upon each other. Instead, language is the living experience of speaking and listening, as people act and interact and learn.

Thus, in its analysis of language, Sanskrit grammar was not confined to formulating abstract rules of linguistic construction. Through grammarians like Pāṇini, classical Sanskrit was developed into a highly formal language, with a complex set of rules that was described with the most astonishing sophistication and brevity: more so perhaps than in any other tradition of which we know. But the study of language went far beyond that, to a basic questioning of language use and meaningful experience. Thus grammar was extended, through linguistic analysis, into philosophical enquiry.

Of such linguistic philosophy, the classic example is Bhartṛhari's *Vākyapadīya*. In classical learning, it was a standard text for advanced students of grammar. As usual, we are not sure when it was composed, but we have a reliable report that it was already established in the traditional curriculum of learning by the seventh century CE. The report is from the Chinese traveller I-tsing, who visited India then.[20] He tells us that it was among the works which

[20] Coward 1976; and also Majumdar 1988.

even Buddhist students were taught, alongside their Buddhist studies, at the great monastery of Nālandā.

In the manner of a traditional treatise, Bhartṛhari begins the *Vākyapadīya* with a statement of basic principle:

> The changeless essence of the word
> is all there is. It has no start;
> nor does it stop or come to end.
>
> It manifests transformed: through aims
> and objects, as they come to be.
> From it proceeds the changing world.[21] *– 1.1*

Here, we are presented with the terms of an enquiry that the treatise intends to make. First, it is going to look for a changeless principle that underlies all our experience of language and speech. And second, it is going to interpret language in the broadest sense, to include all experience. Everything in the world, in everyone's experience, is going to be taken as an expression of the changeless principle that is being sought.

How can that principle be found? For those who share his Vedic heritage, Bhartṛhari points out that it is the source of their tradition: reflected and described in the Vedas:

> Reflecting it, the Vedic texts
> are means by which it may be found.
>
> Though it is one, it's seen approached
> in many ways; by those great seers
> from whom traditions are passed on,
> each one of them in its own way. *– 1.5*
>
> Of that same truth, all sorts of
> explanations are put forth, by monists
> and by dualists: depending

---

[21] This and ensuing translations from the *Vākyapadīya* have been freely made from Bhartṛhari 1976, with help from Iyer 1965 and Pillai 1971.

on their differing ideas,
born from their own opinions. *– 1.8*

But, in the Vedas, unmixed truth
is spoken of, as knowledge in
itself. It's there associated
with the one-word mantra 'om',
not contradicting any way
in which its truth may be explained: *– 1.9*

Subsequently, for his fellow grammarians, Bhartṛhari describes how their own discipline is a means to the same goal that the Vedas represent.

For those who are intelligent,
the foremost of the Vedic sciences
and the best discipline –
established in reality –
is the analysis of speech. *– 1.11*

It is a direct path to that
same light which is at once the
purest virtue and the final essence
of all speech. This path proceeds
by trying to achieve correct
distinctions in the forms of speech. *– 1.12*

All tying down of truths perceived,
in objects and their functioning,
consists of words expressed in speech.

But we don't clearly recognize
the truth of words, in due respect
to the analysis of speech. *– 1.13*

Linguistics is a passageway
to freedom in all disciplines.

Wherever learning is concerned
linguistics there appears: as that

investigative therapy
which may be used to clear away
the taints of speech in what is said. –1.14

All classes of the things we see
are tied back to generic names.

So too among all disciplines,
on this that analyses speech,
the others must at last depend. –1.15

Differences and Knowledge

In the above passage, to show the central position that he gives to linguistic analysis, Bhartṛhari points to an intimate connection between seeing and speaking. The way we see things depends essentially on how we name them. For example, suppose that someone looks at some tall branching shape and recognizes it as a 'tree'. That perception depends on the way that trees are named, in general. It depends on the generic name: 'tree'. As we speak, we use such general names to distinguish different kinds of things. And we carry on the differentiation by using more particular names for more particular things: as for example when we say 'this tree' or 'that tree' or 'this palm tree' or 'that oak tree'.

According to Bhartṛhari, such differentiation is a floating overlay of disturbed affectation (upaplava), seen superimposed upon the true nature of speech:

The show of seeming differences,
displayed in knowledge and in speech,
is always just an overlay
of affectation floating by.

Thus, speech is overlaid by forms
that are produced successively,
affected by successive change.

And knowledge then seems to depend
on objects that are to be known. –1.86

This stanza is explained in a Vṛtti commentary that is traditionally said to have been written by Bhartṛhari himself:

> In itself, knowledge has no differentiation, no form. All forms of things that may be known are taken on additional to it. Hence it appears with its own light reflected back, by the formation of differences. It is thus that we speak of 'five trees' or 'a herd of twenty cattle'.
>
> The self that speaks contains within itself all seeds, all potencies. It appears through a created show of different sounds — which make it manifest successively, at the times when they are shown. Through that, by taking on extraneous differences of form, the true essence of speech gets overlaid by affectation. This we know as the speaking of our minds. Partless, it is taken to be otherwise.
>
> Thus, it is said:
>
> Without an object to be known,
> pure knowledge does not enter use.
>
> Unless succession is obtained,
> speech cannot aim at anything
> for anyone to think about.

Here, two kinds of differentiation are described. On the one hand, there is a gross differentiation: of objects known externally, in an outside world of space and time. On the other hand, there is a more subtle differentiation, which requires only time. This subtle differentiation is called 'krama' or 'succession'. It is intermediate between undifferentiated knowledge and the differentiated world.

Three Levels

In Bhartṛhari's description, different appearances are superimposed on knowledge, through a succession of passing states. In each state, knowing continues, while some differentiated object appears. The differentiation is a changing appearance. In itself, knowing is unchanged. But it appears to change, through the passing affectations that express it in our minds.

The essence of that expression is indivisible. But, through our passing mental states, we mistake it to be divided. Thus, through successive states, a differentiated world appears: expressing an undivided unity that speaks through seeming differences.

To explain this conception further, Bhartṛhari distinguishes three levels of speech:

- In '*vaikharī*' or 'elaborated' speech, external sounds and symbols are articulated, as we act towards the objects of an outside world. Our experience of this world is an elaborated construction: built by relating different objects together, in space and time.
- As we act towards objects, our minds express and interpret meaning in them. In this experience of meaning, objects are related back to our knowledge of them, as our minds pass through a succession of knowing states. This mental level of language is called '*madhyamā*' or 'mediating'.
- As our minds progress through passing states, knowledge carries on beneath the change. This continuing, subjective knowledge is called '*paśyantī*' or 'seeing'. In Bhartṛhari's *Vākyapadīya,* it is a pure and unconditioned seeing, quite unmixed with any passing states or differentiated objects.

In the Vṛtti commentary on stanza 1.142, these three levels are explained:

> *Vaikharī* (the elaborated) is jointly known, in concert with other people, through its objective sound. It is the form that's heard: particular, restricted to each case. Connected, it touches upon other things, and is thus liable to interpretation. It is articulated by varied syllables, and in other ways that colour its manifestation: both in well-established modes and in degenerate formations. That is the case when it is manifested in [the sound of] a spinning axle, or in a drum, or in a flute, or in a vīṇā. It is thus that we conceive of its unmeasured variety.
>
> *Madhyamā* (the mediating) is seated backwards, within. It seems comprehended through succession, made up of mind alone. But it is followed by the subtle functioning of living

breath. As some would say, its manifest succession is only a wrapping that's put on around it, and this succession is liable to be withdrawn.

Paśyantī (seeing) is that in which succession is withdrawn. It is just being, in the absence of differentiation. Thus, it is potency: where all succession is contained, at rest. That is continual activity, found in complete absorption back within. It's that which gets obscured, itself completely pure. In it, all form is known contained, all form is utterly dissolved, no form at all appears. It comes into appearance through separated objects, through their connection together, and through their total dissolution. It's thus that we conceive of it, measureless through all variety.

Some say that in all states of speech, human development proceeds from an established distinction of right use from wrong. However, the seeing mode of paśyantī is utterly unmixed and unconfused, untouched by all corrupted use. It is beyond all usage in the world. It is approached by attaining to correctness of knowledge (jñāna), through the analysis of speech. Or through union (yoga) with the prior source of speech. So it is said in the tradition that some follow....

Again, it has been said:

> Arranged in their respective places,
> different elements of speech
> are carried, spoken, in the air.
>
> That forms *elaborated* speech.
> It's a recording, carried out
> through acts of living energy
> that functions forth from those who speak.
>
> Mind in itself is made of forms
> that follow on successively,
> replacing what has gone before.
>
> The functioning of living energy
> is thereby left behind,

as *mediating* speech goes on
with its continued functioning.

But *seeing* is that partless essence
always present, everywhere.
In it, succession is absorbed.

There's only light in its true nature,
as it is itself, within.
That is a subtle speaking where
no disappearance can be found....

It reaches its conditioned form
by mixing it, with a variety
of differing disturbances
that seem to float on it.

But that, which seems elaborated,
is pure being in itself.
It is untouched, quite unaffected
by its show of qualities.

The Essence of Speech

Above, in Bhartṛhari's *Vākyapadīya* and its Vṛtti commentary, the seeing of paśyantī is identified as the true essence of speech. But it has two aspects:

- Seen in itself, it does nothing. It is at once pure light and pure being, quite unmixed with any changing acts or differentiated show. It stands self-illuminated: shining by its own nature, not by any acts that get put onto it.
- Seen from the world of change and show, it does everything. It is the common source from which all acts and happenings arise. Everything perceived arises from its unseen potentiality.

In its first aspect, paśyantī is pure consciousness, where knowing and being are at one. In the second aspect, seen from the world, the seeing of paśyantī is what psychologists describe as the 'unconscious'. It is a hidden reservoir of 'unconscious' seeing at the underlying depth of mind.

That reservoir contains all the potentialities that get manifested in a person's experience, in the course of time. There, past experiences have been absorbed and have left behind their saṁskāras (latent tendencies), which are now bearing fruit or are maturing to bear fruit in the future.

And there, in that 'unconscious' store of mind, are the intuitive potentialities of insight — which enable us to recognize common qualities and meanings and forms in different objects. In Sanskrit, this recognition is described by the word 'ākṛti'. Literally, 'ākṛti' means 'underlying formation' or 'inner form'. In this sense, it is related to the English words 'inform' and 'information'. Like these English words, it has both objective and subjective aspects.

On the one hand, an ākṛti is something shared in common by different objects: some common principle of quality or meaning or form that is found to underlie their differences. On the other hand, precisely because an ākṛti is a common principle, its recognition is essentially intuitive. Its recognition must arise at the subjective depth of insight, beneath the differences of objective perception.

By recognizing that different objects share a common principle or ākṛti, we see that they are of the same type and so belong to the same class. In Sanskrit, the word 'jāti' is used to mean both 'type' and 'class'. For example, the jāti of a tree or a human being is the general class into which this particular tree or human being has been born. And the same word 'jāti' also describes the common type that this tree or human being shares with other members of the class.

These two words 'jāti' and 'ākṛti' are thus alternative descriptions for the same thing. They both describe a common principle that different instances are seen to share. In 'jāti', the description is approached objectively, because the word implies outward birth ('jā' means to 'be born'). In the word 'ākṛti', the description is approached subjectively, because the word implies a reflection back (ā-) from outward action (kṛti). In either case, the particular object is perceived outside, in the differentiated world. And the common principle is understood within, at the unseen depth of seeing.

According to Bhartṛhari, that subjective depth is being in itself. All things of any kind, throughout the universe, are its particulars. This is made explicit by a stanza that is quoted, as revealed authority, in the Vṛtti commentary on the *Vākyapadīya*, 1.1:

> It's that which stands, the inmost form:
> the common, universal principle
> of every different class.
>
> From it are born all kinds of
> changeable particulars: as rainy
> thunderclouds are born from air.

Levels and Ground

After Bhartṛhari, his distinction of three levels was elaborated a little, by separating the two aspects of paśyantī: on the one hand its appearance of storing latent potentialities, and on the other its true essence of self-illuminating unity. Accordingly, what Bhartṛhari had called 'paśyantī' was now divided into two levels, and the previous three levels became four.

This slightly elaborated conception, of four levels, was used in the development of traditional cosmologies, particularly in Śaivite systems of theology. There, paśyantī was the guiding insight and the creative inspiration of a divine intelligence: manifested universally in the world at large and individually in every person. A summary interpretation is shown in figure 9 (next page).

In this division, the name 'paśyantī' or 'seeing' is not now given to the final ground, but instead to a level immediately above it. Here, paśyantī is the accumulated seeing of insight, along with all the potentialities that are awakened and expressed from it. It is here that the process of learning develops our capabilities, in the course of experience. It's here that common principles are understood in different things: so that what has been learned from previous things, experienced in the past, can be applied to further things, experienced in the present and the future. It's by returning here that mis-understandings can be clarified and mistakes corrected; so that learning may progress towards better things, clearer perception and truer knowledge.

The final ground is called '*parā*' or 'beyond'. It is both knowing in itself and being in itself. There, consciousness is self-illuminating light, whose very being is to shine. That shining is its knowing and its being, illuminating everything that anyone experiences. Thus, in the end, knowing and being are found identical. Each is the same, self-shining ground that's found beneath all differences.

Figure 9

Level of expression	***Microcosm of individual experience***	***Macrocosm of the external universe***
Vaikharī (elaborated)	Personal articulation of words and symbols	Changing world of perceived objects
Madhyamā (in between)	Succession of mental states, through which symbols are formed and meanings are interpreted	Flow of happenings, through which objects take shape and convey meaning
Paśyantī (seeing)	Quiet insight and latent potentiality, continuing at the depth of mind	Unseen guidance and divine inspiration of a universal intelligence
Parā (beyond)	Ultimate identity of knowing and being	

LANGUAGE AND TRADITION

Natural Development

In the course of history, how do words form? How has language come about and grown, so as to carry meaning in the present? A very old conception of such cultural development is built into the Sanskrit language.

Literally, 'saṁskṛt' means 'well-formed' or 'fully done': from 'saṁ-' meaning 'unitedly' or 'fully', and 'kṛ' meaning to 'make' or to 'do'. Thus 'saṁskṛti' means 'culture' or 'refinement'. And the name 'Sanskrit' is given to a language that has been specially refined for the cultivation of learning and education.

By contrast, the word 'prākṛt' means 'wild' or 'raw' or 'natural'. The prefix 'pra-' means 'before' or 'prior to' or 'underlying'; so 'prākṛt' carries the sense of 'prior to doing' or 'underlying action'. Thus, 'prakṛti' means 'nature'. And the name 'prākṛt' is used to describe various ordinary languages of everyday usage, in ancient and classical India.

In short, Sanskrit was the specially developed language of classical education; and the prākṛts were untutored languages of natural, everyday use. But does it follow then that Sanskrit is a more artificial construction, inherently less natural than the untutored prākṛts? No, it does not, according to the old conceptions. That is not the way they see their own tradition.

As we are told by the classical grammarian Bhartṛhari, language and tradition are each considered at different levels. At the base, there is an inmost ground of unaffected, timeless seeing (paśyantī). At the surface, there is an elaborated construction (vaikharī) of outward words and symbols. In between (madhyamā), there is a living process that expresses knowledge outwardly, through a succession of changing states.

The history of learning is thus considered biologically. The elaborated structures of language are a living growth, which develops as an expression of continuing knowledge. On the surface, it may seem that systematic learning developed by an artificial invention — which assembles fabricated words and symbols into formal structures, like fabricated parts are assembled into an engineered machine. However, such formal structures do not express knowledge by themselves. They express it through a living history, in which they are handed on from generation to generation.

And in that living history, learning is developed by renewal. As the constructions of learning change, they are developed as renewed expressions of knowledge. Without such a renewal of living knowledge, learning is merely artificial and no longer genuine. Its constructions may be clever on the surface, but they have lost their natural grounding in the knowledge that they should express.

Thus, in the traditional view, development is not essentially a matter of construction. More fundamentally, learning is developed by a living process that keeps on reflecting back to source, from where it is continually refreshed. That source is knowledge, at its inmost ground. From there, development is naturally inspired. By reflecting back there, systems of learning can be developed to a high degree of refinement, without losing their natural grounding in an unconstructed source beneath all changes and developments.

This kind of naturally grounded refinement is conceived to be exemplified by the Sanskrit language. It was a special language of disciplined learning, cultivated alongside the prākṛts, the languages of ordinary, habitual speech. But they were compromised by the careless corruptions of everyday usage, while Sanskrit was very carefully refined by analytic systems that protected it from such corrupting compromise. This analytic refinement is described in a Tamil discourse by the late Kāñcī Śaṅkarācārya, Candraśekharendra Sarasvatī:

> Sanskrit has no syllable that is indistinct or unclear. Take the English 'word'. It has neither a distinct 'a-kāra' ['a' sound] nor 'o-kāra' ['o' sound]. There are no such words in Sanskrit. Neither is the 'r' in 'word' pronounced distinctly, nor is it silent.
>
> Sanskrit, besides, has no word that cannot be traced to its root. Whatever the word, it can be broken into its syllables to elucidate its meaning. Sanskrit is sonorous and auspicious to

> listen to. You must not be ill disposed towards such a language, taking the narrow view that it belongs to a few people.
>
> To speak Sanskrit is not to make some noises and somehow convey your message. The sounds, the phonemes in it are — as it were — purified, and the words and sentences refined by being subjected to analysis. That is why the language is called 'Sanskrit'. The purpose of Śikṣā [trained pronunciation], and in greater measure of Vyākaraṇa [grammar], is to bring about such refinement.
>
> To speak the language of Sanskrit itself means to be refined, to be cultured. As the language of the gods, it brings divine grace. The sounds of Sanskrit create beneficial vibrations of the nāḍīs [living energy currents] and strengthen the nervous system, thereby contributing to our health.[22]

This refinement, with its analytic systems, is considered as a natural growth, grounded in a living source that is its natural base. The grounding comes from those who found the tradition and develop its systems. The major founders and developers are recognized as sages, who have returned to source and thus express it naturally.

Gifted by Seers

In particular, the analytic systems of classical Sanskrit were conceived to have been developed by sages like Pāṇini, Patañjali and Bhartṛhari. And before this classical systematization, the language was founded and developed through the vision of Vedic seers, called 'mantra-draṣṭās'. In that phrase, the choice of words is telling. The word 'mantra' refers to the chanted statements of the Vedas and the Upaniṣads. And the word 'draṣṭā' means very simply a 'see-er'. So the tradition is telling us that the foundation of its spoken sounds lies in the seeing of its founding seers.

These seers have not *created* the statements that they hand down to us. Instead, the sacred texts are handed down as something that

---

[22] From Candraśekharendra Sarasvatī Svāmī 2000 — part 7, chapter 5.

the seers have *seen*, by reflecting down to an uncreated foundation. That uncreated depth of seeing is the originating source from which the tradition has been handed down. The late Kāñcī Śaṅkarācārya again provides a clear description:

> If ours is a primeval religion, the question arises as to who established it. All inquiries into this question have failed to yield an answer. Was Vyāsa, who composed the *Brahma-sūtra*, the founder of our religion? Or was it Kṛṣṇa Paramātman, who gave us the *Bhagavad-gītā*? But both Vyāsa and Kṛṣṇa state that the Vedas existed before them. If that be the case, are we to point to the ṛṣis, the seers who gave us the Vedic mantras, as the founders of our religion? But they themselves declare: 'We did not create the Vedas.' When we chant a mantra, we touch our head with our hand, mentioning the name of one seer or another. But the sages themselves say: 'It is true that the mantras became manifest to the world through us. That is why we are mentioned as the "mantra ṛṣis". But the mantras were not composed by us but revealed to us. When we sat meditating with our minds under control, the mantras were perceived by us in space. Indeed we saw them — hence the term "mantra-draṣṭās" [see-ers of the mantras]. We did not compose them.' [The seers are not 'mantra-kartās' or 'makers of the mantras'.]
>
> All sounds originate in space. From them arose creation. According to science, the cosmos was produced from the vibrations in space. By virtue of their austerities, the sages had the gift of seeing the mantras in space, the mantras that liberate men from this creation. The Vedas are apauruṣeya (not the work of any human author) and are the very breath of the Paramātman [the ultimate Self] in his form as space. The sages saw them and made a gift of them to the world.[23]

What does the Śaṅkarācārya mean when he speaks about the sages seeing vibrations in space, from which the cosmos was produced?

---

[23] From Candraśekharendra Sarasvatī Svāmī 2000 — part 2, chapter 1.

Here, the word 'space' refers to the old concept of 'ākāśa' or 'ether'. It describes a background continuity of space and time, underlying all physical and mental experience. This background continuity is both external and internal. It is shared by both the outer macrocosm of the universe and the inner macrocosm of individual experience, as the Śaṅkarācārya explains in a further discourse:

> There is a state in which the macrocosm and the microcosm are perceived as one. Great men there are who have reached such a state and are capable of transforming what is subtle in the one into what is gross in the other. I am speaking here to those who believe in such a possibility.
>
> When we look at this universe and the complex manner in which it functions, we realize that there must be a Great Wisdom that has created it and sustains it. It is from this Great Wisdom, that is the Paramātman [the ultimate Self], that all that we see are born; and it is from It that all the sounds that we hear have emanated. First came the universe of sound and then the universe that we observe. Most of the former still exists in space. All that exists in the outer universe is present in the human body also. The space that exists outside us exists also in our heart. The yogins have experience of this 'hṛdayākāśa' — this 'heart-sky' or this 'heart-space' — when they are in samādhi (absorbed in the Infinite). In this state of theirs, all differences between the outward and the inward vanish, and the two become one. The yogins can now grasp the sounds of space and bestow the same on mankind. These successions of sounds that bring benefits to the world are indeed the mantras of the Vedas.
>
> These mantras are not the creation of anyone. Though each of them is in the name of a ṛṣi or seer, in reality it is not his creation. When we say that a certain mantra has a certain sage associated with it, all that we mean is that it was he who first 'saw' it existing without a beginning in space, and revealed it to the world. The very word 'ṛṣi' means 'mantra-draṣṭā' (one who saw — discovered — the mantra), not 'mantra-kartā' (i.e.

not one who created the mantra). Our life is dependent on how our breathing functions. In the same way, the cosmos functions in accordance with the vibrations of the Vedic sounds — so the Vedic mantras are the very breath of the Supreme Being.[24]

Growth from Seed

Is the Śaṅkarācārya claiming that the Vedic texts of his religion exhaust all truth and leave no room for other texts? No, he is not, as he makes clear again:

> If the cosmos of sound (śabda-prapañca) enfolds all creation and what is beyond it, it must naturally be immensely vast. However voluminous the Vedas are, one might wonder whether it would be right to claim that they embrace all activities of the universe. 'Anantāḥ vai vedāḥ', the Vedas themselves proclaim so (the Vedas are endless). We cannot claim that all the Vedas have been revealed to the seers. Only about a thousand śākhās or recensions belonging to the four Vedas have been revealed to them.[25]

But then, given this endless multiplicity of sound and world, how can a common truth be found, in so many different things? The Śaṅkarācārya explains that this is always possible through a return to the living source from which the multiplicity has arisen, like a large tree has grown from living seed. Here is what he says:

> What we call 'this' (idam) is not without a root or a source. Indeed, there is no object called 'this' without a source. Without the seed, there is no tree. The cosmos with its mountains, oceans, with its sky and earth, with its man and beast, and so on, has its root. Anger, fear and love, the senses, power and energy have their root. Whatever we call 'this' has

---

[24] From Candraśekharendra Sarasvatī Svāmī 2000 — part 3, chapter 8.

[25] From Candraśekharendra Sarasvatī Svāmī 2000 — part 5, chapter 12.

a root. What we see, hear and smell, what we remember, what we feel to be hot or cold, what we experience — all these are covered by the term 'idam'. Intellectual powers, scientific discoveries, the discoveries yet to come — all come under 'idam' and all of them have a root cause. There is nothing called 'this' or 'idam' without a root. Everything has a root or a seed. So the cosmos also must have a root cause; so too all power, all energy, contained in it.

To realize this truth, examine a tamarind seed germinating. When you split the seed open, you will see a miniature tree in it. It has in it the potential to grow, to grow big. Such is the case with all seeds.

The mantras have 'bījākṣaras' ['seed letters' or rather 'seed syllables']. Like a big tree (potentially) present in a tiny seed, these syllables contain immeasurable power. If the bījākṣara is muttered a hundred thousand times, with your mind one-pointed, you will have its power within your grasp.

Whatever power there is in the world, whatever intellectual brilliance, whatever skills and talents, all must be present in God in a rudimentary form. The Vedas proclaim, as if with the beat of drums: 'All this has not sprung without a root cause. The power that is in the root or seed is the same as the power that pervades the entire universe.' Where is that seed or root? The Self that keeps seeing all from within, [that Self which sees] what we call 'idam', [that Self] is the root.

When you stand before a mirror, you see your image in it. If you keep four mirrors in a row, you will see a thousand images of yourself. There is one source (or root cause) for all these images. The one who sees these one thousand images is the same as the one who is their source. The one who is within the millions of creatures and sees all 'this' is Īśvara [the Lord]. That which sees is the root of all that is seen. That root is knowledge and it is the source of all the cosmos. Where do you find this knowledge? It is in you. The infinite, transcendent knowledge is present partly in you — the whole is present in you as part.

Here is a small bulb. There you have a bigger bulb. That light is blue, this is green. There are lamps of many sizes and shapes. But their power is the same — electricity, electricity which is everywhere. It keeps the fan whirling, keeps the lamps burning. The power is the same and it is infinite. When it passes through a wire, it becomes finite. When lightning strikes in flashes, when water cascades, the power is manifested. In the same way, you must try to make the supreme truth within you manifest itself in a flash. All Vedic rites, all worship, all works, meditation of the mahāvākyas, Vedānta — the purpose of all these is to make the truth unfold itself to you — in you — in a flash.

Even the family and social life that are dealt with in the Vedas, the royal duties mentioned in them, or poetry, therapeutics or geology or any other śāstra are steps leading towards the realization of the Self. At first the union of 'Tat' and 'tvam' ('That' and 'you') would be experienced for a few moments like a flash of lightning. The *Kena Upaniṣad* (4.4) refers to the state of knowing the Brahman experientially as a flash of lightning happening in the twinkling of an eye. But with repeated practice, with intense concentration, you will be able to immerse yourself in such experience. It is like the electricity produced when a stream remains cascading. This is mokṣa, liberation, when you are yet in this world, when you are still in possession of your body. And, when you give up the body, you will become the eternal Truth yourself. This is called 'videhamukti' (literally bodiless liberation). The difference between jīvanmukti [liberation while living in the body] and videhamukti [liberation on departing from the body] is only with reference to an outside observer. For the jñānin [liberated sage], the two are identical.[26]

In this conception, the knowledge that tradition shows is truth itself.

---

[26] From Candraśekharendra Sarasvatī Svāmī 2000 — part 5, chapter 34.

It is a true knowing that is at once the source and ground of all experience. All things that we experience are its expressions. They all arise from it and stand on it. To realize it, one has only to return to it and stand established there, in one's own experience.

That is what the tradition tells us, through the sayings of sages who have returned to an establishment in this same truth that underlies our own experience now. This present truth is the ancient knowledge that the tradition has always expressed and teaches us today.

What's here described as 'knowledge' is completely timeless and individual. It is not a built-up knowledge: cultivated in our social institutions of technology and science, or of art and organized religion. Instead, it is an underlying knowledge that remains the same, as it is differently expressed in changing cultural and intellectual structures. As cultural descriptions change, this underlying knowledge stays unchanged. It is quite unaffected by all changing circumstances and all passing times in which it gets expressed. For it is always true, quite plainly and unconditionally true, at the centre of each individual's experience.

For example, in modern physics, we can say that Einstein knew more than Newton. Or we can say that discoveries in chemistry have brought modern chemists more knowledge of their subject than was known before. Or that some growth or decline of artistic techniques and imagery has brought artists to a greater or lesser knowledge of their art. Or that some change of doctrine or faith has affected the theological or devotional knowledge of a religious community.

But, in a tradition like Hinduism, where knowledge is considered changeless, it would be meaningless to say that a twentieth century sage like Ramaṇa Maharṣi knew more than Śrī Śaṅkara did many centuries before, or that Śrī Śaṅkara knew more than the sages of the Upaniṣads, or that the sages of the Upaniṣads knew more than tribal sages before the development of civilization.

Elaboration over Time

The knowledge of all sages is conceived to be the same. Each of them knows the same truth. The only difference between them is the way in which they express their common knowledge. In earlier times, the expression tends to be more condensed and implicit: like a germinating seed. As time progresses, the expression may grow to become more explicitly articulate, with a fuller explanation of its reasoning: just as a growing plant may show a developing elaboration of manifested potency that was previously latent within a germinating seed.

For example, consider the mantra 'om'. It is one of those 'bījākṣaras' or 'seed syllables' that are conceived to have been seen by ancient sages, in the background continuity of space and time. Falling deeply back into the depth of individual experience, some sage perceived this sound 'om' and passed it on to the tradition: as a sacred mantra of prime significance.

This significance is not just an artificial convention. It is latent naturally, in the sound itself. The very shape of sound is such that when it is recited, it directs the listening mind towards a progressive activation of its significance. Through the science of Śikṣā or 'phonetics', this naturally inherent significance is explained by analysing the syllable 'om' into three component letters: 'a', 'u' and 'm'. Through philosophical enquiry, the three letters are interpreted as states of waking, dream and sleep. And the states are interpreted as analysing the nature of experience and reality.

In the tradition of texts, these explanations are progressively elaborated. Traditional scholars tell us that the Vedas often make an implicit reference to the syllable 'om', in many passages where the word 'akṣara' is used. ('Akṣara' means 'changeless' in general; and it is often used to mean a 'changeless syllable' in particular — with 'om' being the prime unchanging syllable, representing all expression and experience.) In some of the earlier Upaniṣads (particularly the *Chāndogya*), 'om' is explicitly described as a beginning and ending syllable of Vedic chanting: a syllable associated with threefold knowledge and thus signifying everything. In the *Praśna Upaniṣad* (5.1-7), it is described as a symbol with three elements for meditation: in which one element leads to greatness in the changing world of human beings; two elements together lead to expansion in an intermediate world associated with the mind; and all three elements together lead to an ultimate principle of light itself, represented by the sun.

In the *Māṇḍūkya Upaniṣad,* the entire text of twelve stanzas is devoted to a concise, but analytic discussion of the mantra 'om': how it represents three states of experience and an unvoiced reality that underlies them all. Subsequently, Gauḍapāda composed a *kārikā*: of which one chapter comments on the verses of the *Māṇḍūkya Upaniṣad,* and the remaining three chapters extend the analysis to a systematic exposition of non-dual philosophy. After that, Śrī Śaṅkara composed a *bhāṣya* commentary, further explaining both the *Māṇḍūkya* verses and Gauḍapāda's *kārikā* on them.

And to this day, the syllable 'om', the *Māṇḍūkya Upaniṣad* and its various commentaries continue to be further discussed and explained. All this growth of reasoning and explanation is manifested forth from the implicit potency contained within the sound 'om'; just as a many-branching tree, with all its leaves and blossoms, is manifested from the living essence of a seed.

This is how the tradition grows and develops, according to its own conception. A living source of timeless knowledge is expressed in germinating seeds of culture, which grow into our built-up structures of religion and art, technology and science. It is in this sense that traditional scholars sometimes say that the Vedas inherently contain all cultural and scientific developments. They are then thinking of the Vedas (including those lost or undiscovered) as comprising all the seeds that sages may discover, by going back into the depth of their experience.

Interpreted too crudely, this kind of thinking can of course become mind-boggling and absurd; but in its essence it is simple and does not conflict with any genuine development. The essence is a timeless ground to which each individual may return, in her own or his own experience. Conceiving that unchanging ground as knowledge in itself, all cultural and scientific developments are then conceived as its changing expressions.

Over the course of many generations, the expressions are built up: in religious, artistic, technological and scientific institutions. But this development depends upon the ever-present ground of living experience, from where the forms of knowledge are renewed and come alive. All genuine developments are inspired from that living ground; and so they are best carried out by sages who have come to oneness with that ground and stand established there.

In its own view, the whole tradition rises from the realization of its guiding sages. Their knowledge, in the end, is individual, though utterly impersonal as well. It's taught from one individual to another, as a return to common ground: beyond all personality, beneath all social and cultural institutions.

Interpretation and Retelling

Freedoms of Choice

As learning is continually renewed from generation to generation, by different people and in changing circumstances, old texts are liable to be interpreted in different ways. This changing use of texts is described in Bhartṛhari's *Vākyapadīya*:

All arguments and inference
depend upon intelligence.
They're nothing but the power of words.

Where formal logic blindly follows
words expressed in outward speech,
it's just a verbal mimicking
that ties no concrete meaning down.
It cannot record anything.
Such logic is not found in texts
of genuine authority. *– 1.137*

As shapes and forms and colours seen
and other sights have, each of them,
their special capabilities;
so also words are each perceived
to have their own particular
effects, like the elimination
of contaminating waste. *– 1.138*

Just as these words accord with virtue
so they also lead to it.

They are the words of honest people,
to be spoken by good people
aiming to improve their state. *– 1.139*

It's commonly acknowledged that
unseen effects may be achieved
by chanting from the sacred texts.

But it is always possible
to say conflicting things about
what's in the texts and what they mean. *– 1.140*

... Therefore, some sacred text is made authentic, and a settled standpoint is established. There, whatever reason finds fit and proper, confirmation is attained. [From Vṛtti commentary on 1.140]

Linguistics is a discipline
whose aim is knowledge, clarified
from errors of mistaken use.

It is recorded through an
uncut continuity, of learning
that is called to mind by those
who've learned it well and hand it down. *– 1.141*

... From generation to generation, the intent remembered is reconstituted, over and over again, through an unbroken succession. In an established tradition of common practice that has not been recorded in words, it's only the unbroken practice of successful learning that gets remembered. [From Vṛtti commentary on 1.141]

In this passage, Bhartṛhari is describing the interpretation of texts that are regarded as authoritative. The word he uses for such a text is 'āgama'. It is derived from the root 'gam', meaning to 'go' or to 'move'. To this root is added the prefix 'ā-', meaning 'near' or 'back'. So 'āgama' implies a coming back, near to a source of origin. In fact, the word 'āgama' is often used to mean a 'source'. And when a text is treated as a source of traditional authority, it may be called an 'āgama'. It is thus considered near to an ultimate origin, of which it is a close representation. In listening to the text, and following its meaning, one is meant to experience a coming back, towards the final source that is expressed.

In the above passage, Bhartṛhari points out that reasoning is an essentially practical capability, depending on intelligence and carried by the power of words. So abstract rules, derived from the mere form of words, can never be enough to understand the meaning of a text (1.137). The meaning inherently includes 'unseen effects' that make it possible to interpret the texts in different and conflicting ways (1.140).

Thus, Bhartṛhari points to an essential freedom of interpretation, which is inherent in the use of authoritative texts. Moreover, in the Vṛtti commentary (on 1.140), a further freedom is described: of choosing a text that is 'made authentic', as 'a settled standpoint is established'.

These two freedoms, of selection and interpretation, are essential to the actual practice of a living tradition. For, in practice, such a tradition is 'a continuity of learning, called to mind by those who know it well and hand it down' (1.141). This calling to mind is inherently selective; as, 'from generation to generation, the intent remembered is reconstituted, over and over again', so that 'only the unbroken practice of successful learning is remembered' (Vṛtti commentary on 1.141).

Intensive Use

Since an authoritative text is considered close to final source, its statements are taken to be rich in meaning, with a condensed significance that may unfold itself through many different aspects. Such a condensed statement is liable to an intensity of use, through a sustained repetition and reflection in which the same text may be rather differently interpreted on differing occasions. From this intensive usage come the two inherent freedoms:

- on the one hand, to select particular statements and passages upon which attention is intensively focused;
- and on the other hand, to make particular interpretations that may differ widely, in accordance with their changing contexts and situations.

Over many thousands of years, the Sanskrit language has been specially cultivated and refined, for this intensive usage of recited texts — with its implicit freedom of selection and interpretation.

Here, Sanskrit is rather different from ordinary spoken languages, and from most modern scientific and technical languages that have been developing since the introduction of printing and subsequent media of communication.

For, Sanskrit is especially inclined towards the *intensive* statement of inner ideals and principles, abstracted metaphorically and analytically from the outward world of varying particulars. By contrast, ordinary spoken languages are inclined towards everyday descriptions of particular circumstances. And modern scientific or technical languages are inclined towards *extensive* description of the diverse information that modern media have now made so much more widely available.

Thus, in the modern world, we tend to have become somewhat unfamiliar with the kind of intensive statement that is found in Sanskrit and other such ancient languages of education. In particular, we often fail to take proper account of the flexible interpretation that is implied.

For example, the codes of conduct in the Dharma-śāstras are often considered on the model of modern jurisprudence, as though the Dharma-śāstras were the printed legislation that some modern state applies through standardized bureaucratic procedures in its administrative offices, its law courts and its police. In fact, of course, the Dharma-śāstras were no such thing. They were not at all a politically enacted legislation, meant to be applied through the official administration and law-enforcement of some political government in overall control. Instead, they were statements of social and cultural ideals: designed to make allowance for community and personal differences that are conceived to overlie a common principle of 'humanness' (puruṣa) where true equality is ultimately found.

In practice, these social and cultural ideals were not applied in any one way that was officially standardized, across the very different times and places in which they came to be used. Instead, they were applied through an essential flexibility of interpretation, to a great variety of very different communities, in widely varying localities and circumstances.

Poetic Ambiguity

In allowing for such flexibility, the Sanskrit language has developed an extraordinary capacity for difference of interpretation. Here is an example, in a story told by the late Kāñcī Śaṅkarācārya, Candraśekharendra Sarasvatī:

> There is no tonal variation in poetry as there is in Vedic mantras. The unaccented poetic stanza corresponding to the accented Vedic mantra owes its origin to Vālmīki, but its discovery was not the result of any conscious effort on his part.
>
> One day Vālmīki happened to see a pair of krauñca birds sporting perched on the branch of a tree. Soon one of the birds fell to the arrow of a hunter. The sage felt pity and compassion, but these soon gave way to anger. He cursed the hunter, the words coming from him spontaneously: 'O hunter, you have killed a krauñca bird sporting happily with its mate. May you not have everlasting happiness.'
>
> mā niṣāda pratiṣṭhāṁ tvam
> agamaḥ śāśvatīḥ samāḥ
> yat krauñca-mithunād ekam
> avadhīḥ kāma-mohitam
>
> Unpremeditatedly, out of his compassion for the birds, Vālmīki cursed the hunter. But, at once, he regretted it. 'Why did I curse the hunter so?' When he was brooding thus, a remarkable truth dawned on him. Was he not a sage with divine vision? He realized that the very words of his curse had the garb of a poetic stanza in the Anuṣṭubh metre. That the words had come from his lips, without his being aware of them for himself (in the same way as he had, without his knowing, felt compassion and anger in succession), caused him amazement.
>
> It occurred to him that the stanza he had unconsciously composed had another meaning. The words aimed at the hunter were also words addressed to Mahāviṣṇu. How? 'O consort of Lakṣmī, you will win eternal fame by having slain one of a couple who was deluded by desire.' Rāvaṇa and his

> wife Maṇḍodarī are the couple referred to here, and Rāvaṇa was deluded by his evil desire for Sītā. Śrī Rāma won everlasting fame by slaying him. Without his being aware of it, the words came to Vālmīki as poetry. Realizing it all to be the will of Īśvara [God], the sage composed the *Rāmāyaṇa* in the same metre.
>
> The 'śloka' (without the Vedic tonal variation) was born in this manner.[27]

This story describes how epic poetry was born in Sanskrit, from the intense inner experience of a sage. And this intensity is shown to produce a stanza with two very different meanings. Significantly, the ambiguity is not shown to rise from any objective calculation in the composer's mind. Instead, it arises spontaneously from a subjective intensity that gives the stanza a special richness of meaning. The richness unfolds in two interpretations that seem to conflict objectively, though each is valid in its own way and has its own contribution to make.

Objective Analysis

From an objective point of view, ambiguities of meaning show a failure of linguistic precision. If a statement has conflicting interpretations; then, objectively, its meaning is thus imprecise. This is as true in Sanskrit as in any other language. There is no lack of respect for formal and objective precision in traditional Sanskrit. In fact, traditional Sanskrit linguists and analysts have taken great pains in developing the language to an extraordinary degree of formal and objective precision: as for example in Pāṇini's rules for generating grammatical forms, or in the Mīmāṁsā and Nyāya analyses of textual exegesis and logical argumentation.

However, along with these objective analyses, there is a recognition that they each define a limited and partial point of view. And this partiality gives rise to many different views, thus leaving us

---

[27] From Candraśekharendra Sarasvatī Svāmī 2000 — part 8, chapter 4.

with a problem of conflicting appearances that have somehow to be reconciled. In the end, the reconciliation has to be subjective. It is achieved by standing back from the differentiation of objective perceptions, into a deeper subjectivity that underlies the differences.

Thus, beyond its formal and objective precision, the Sanskrit language also developed a deeper precision that is essentially informal and subjective. That deeper precision is expressed in ambiguities of meaning which are inspired directly from an intensity of inner experience, beneath all outward determination of diverging names and forms. Such inwardly inspired ambiguities are then precisely used: to show us different aspects of a common reality that cannot be determined by outward descriptions, but must be realized reflectively within.

This use of ambiguity is relatively obvious in the imaginative symbols and metaphors of art and poetry, ritual and myth, religious worship and belief. But, through analytical discussion, particular traditions try to develop more abstract concepts that apply more universally and are thus less ambiguous in their meaning. It may then appear that there is no proper place for ambiguity of meaning, in a discussion that is analytic.

Again, this is only a partial and somewhat misleading appearance, in some objective view that has been restricted by basing it upon a constructed foundation of limiting concepts and assumptions. In effect, this conceptual foundation forms a logical but limiting framework, within which analytical discussion serves to work out the details that build up an objective picture. When such a foundation is being used to build upon, then of course there is no proper room for ambiguity of meaning in the discussion that derives the details and builds up the picture.

Reflective Questioning

Beyond this building of objective pictures, there is a further and more fundamental use of analytic discussion. That further use is skeptical and reflective. It investigates the foundations of our built-up pictures, by using words and concepts in a reflective way that throws their meaning into question. Here, ambiguity of meaning can be properly and positively used, as different meanings are investigated on the way to underlying truth.

Such use of ambiguity is illustrated in a story from the *Chāndogya Upaniṣad*. The story starts with the words of Prajāpati, the father of all created things:

> That which is self dispels all ill:
> untouched by age, decay and death
> and grief. It does not hunger, does
> not thirst. It's that for which all thought
> and all desire is only truth.
>
> It's that which is to be sought out,
> just that which we must seek to know.
> Whoever finds and knows that self
> attains all worlds and all desires. *– 8.7.1*

These words are heard by the gods and the demons, who then say among themselves:

> Well let us seek that self:
> that self which seeking one attains
> all worlds and all desires. *– from 8.7.2*

Accordingly, Indra travels from the gods and Virocana from the demons, into the presence of Prajāpati. For thirty two years they live with him, observing the chaste and humble life of student discipline. Finally, Prajāpati asks them why they have come. They repeat the words that they have heard he said, and then they ask to know the self he speaks about. He replies:

> This principle of humanness
> that's seen in seeing is the self.
> It does not die. Nor has it fear.
> It is complete reality. *– from 8.7.4*

Indra and Virocana are puzzled by these words, and so they ask:

> Then, Sir, what is it that's perceived
> in water, or in a mirror here? *– from 8.7.4*

Prajāpati replies:

> Within all these, just this
> itself is seen perceived. *–from 8.7.4*

He makes them look at their reflections in a pan of water, and asks them what they see. They say:

> We both of us, Sir, see it all:
> the self that is reflected here,
> down to the hairs and fingernails. *–from 8.8.1*

Next, Prajāpati tells them to dress in all their finery, as chieftains of the gods and demons. Again, he makes them look at their reflections in a pan of water and asks them what they see. They reply:

> Just as we are, Sir, well-adorned,
> well-dressed, well-groomed; so also these
> are well-adorned, well-dressed, well-groomed. *–from 8.8.3*

Prajāpati points out that what they see is only self:

> It is this self
> that does not die.
> Nor has it fear.
> It is complete reality. *–from 8.8.3*

At this reply, Indra and Virocana now feel a sense of satisfaction. So they take their leave and go away, thinking that they have understood. But Prajāpati looks sadly after them, saying to himself:

> They go away, not having realized
> or understood the self.
> Whoever takes to such a doctrine,
> whether they be gods or demons,
> shall in time be overcome. *–from 8.8.4*

Virocana goes back to the demons and proclaims his doctrine to them:

Here, self alone is to be magnified,
and self alone is to be served.
Here magnifying self alone
and serving self, one thus obtains
both worlds: this world and that beyond. *–from 8.8.4*

The Upaniṣad comments then (in 8.8.5) that this is the doctrine which we call 'demonic'. It is a doctrine of personal selfishness: held by one who is ungiving and faithless, quite unprepared to make any personal sacrifice. It amounts to dressing a lifeless body with clothes and ornaments that have been begged from somewhere else, in the vain hope that this extraneous dressing up will somehow win some further state of life.

Indra takes a different course. On the way back home to his fellow gods, he is troubled and dissatisfied:

Just as this self gets to be
well-adorned here in a body that
is well-adorned, or gets to be
well dressed and groomed here in a body
that's well-dressed and is well-groomed;

so also it gets to be blind
here in a body that is blind.
And in a lame or crippled body,
it gets crippled or gets lamed.
So too, it even gets destroyed,
here when the body is destroyed.

I see no satisfaction here. *–from 8.9.1*

Thus Indra turns around and goes back to Prajāpati, to live there as a humble student for another thirty two years. Then Prajāpati tells him:

This which journeys free in dream
enabling mind to magnify,

> this is the self.
> It does not die.
> Nor has it fear.
> It is complete reality. *–from 8.10.1*

Again, Indra feels satisfied by what he hears and goes away. But again, on his way back home, he is troubled by doubt:

> It's true that even if this body
> here gets to be blind, the dreaming
> self may not thereby be blind.
> So too, if body here is lame,
> the dream self is not thereby lame.
>
> Indeed, it doesn't suffer from
> this body's ills. Nor by this body's
> death does it get killed. Nor by
> the body's lameness is it lame.
>
> And yet, in dream, it is as if
> they kill the self found there; as if
> they strip it bare; as if it comes
> to know dislike and suffering;
> as if it weeps and grieves as well.
>
> I see no satisfaction here. *–from 8.10.1-2*

Thus, Indra comes back again to Prajāpati, to live as a student for a third period of thirty two years. Then Prajāpati tells him:

> That is just this, where one who sleeps
> perceives no dream, but is withdrawn
> back into unity and peace.
>
> This is the self.
> It does not die.
> Nor has it fear.
> It is complete reality. *–from 8.11.1*

For a third time, Indra feels satisfied, starts out for home and on the way is troubled by dissatisfying doubt:

> This deep sleep self, such as it is,
> it does not rightly know itself
> as 'I am this'; nor does it know
> these things created in the world.
>
> It thus becomes a something gone
> to where all things have been destroyed.
>
> I see no satisfaction here. *–from 8.11.1*

Thus, yet again, Indra comes back to Prajāpati and tells his doubt. Once more, Prajāpati says that he will explain further. But this time he adds that 'there is really nothing else, other than this'; and he asks Indra to live there only five years more (8.11.3). When the five years are over, he finally enlightens Indra, by distinguishing a deathless self that lives within our dying personalities:

> This body is just mortal, Indra.
> It is always held by death.
> And yet it is a dwelling place
> of bodiless, undying self.
>
> Whatever is found mixed with body
> is inevitably held
> by pleasure and unpleasantness.
>
> Thus, for existence mixed with body,
> there's no true deliverance
> from pleasure and unpleasantness.
>
> But pain and pleasure cannot touch
> existence that is bodiless. *– 8.12.1*
>
> As a draught animal is harnessed
> to a cart, so too this life
> is harnessed to the body that
> is added onto us by birth. *–from 8.12.3*

Where sight is settled down as this
that underlies pervading space –
continuing through everything –
that is the principle which sees.

The faculty of sight is just
an instrument that's used to see.

What knows 'I smell this' is the self.
The faculty of smell is just
an instrument that's used to smell.

What knows 'I say this' is the self.
The faculty of speech is just
an instrument that's used to speak.

What knows 'I hear this' is the self.
The faculty of hearing is
an instrument that's used to hear. *– 8.12.4*

What knows 'I think this' is the self.
Mind is its shining sight within.

That self in truth is this that sees,
through shining sight of inner mind,
all these desires here. It is
itself at peace and happiness. *– 8.12.5*

That is in truth this self, to which
the gods pay heed, here in this state
beyond all petty narrowness.
Because of that, all states and worlds
and all desires are held by them.

Whoever finds and knows that self
attains all worlds and all desires. *– from 8.12.6*

This story tells us about a sustained reflection into the meaning of 'ātman' or 'self'. At the start, there is an intriguing text, which promises 'all worlds and all desires' to one who comes to knowledge of the self. To find this knowledge, Indra and Virocana come to live as humble students in the presence of Prajāpati, the father of creation.

Virocana does not persist beyond his first interpretation that the self is a physical body in an outside world. So he returns to a demonic arrogance that self is to be magnified by seeking bodily dominion in this world and that beyond.

Indra's first interpretation is similar, but he keeps questioning persistently beyond it. Thus he is led through a series of different interpretations to an ultimate realization of impersonal self, beyond all physical and mental faculties. Similar descriptions of a deathless and fearless and complete self are repeated over and over again (in 8.7.1, 8.7.4, 8.8.3, 8.10.1, 8.11.1, 8.12.6). Quite often, the exact same words are repeated from before, but in a different context that changes the interpretation; until the meaning is finally refined into a realization of unconditioned truth, beyond all the conditioned descriptions that lead towards it.

This story illustrates how differences and changes of interpretation are considered an inherent part of investigation into truth. That applies no less to an analytically reasoned approach than to a poetic or metaphorical one. And it affects both individual enquiry and the collective development of culture and tradition. Accordingly, to understand the Hindu tradition, it helps to distinguish two kinds of precision that have been specially developed in the Sanskrit language, to an extraordinary degree:

- First, an objective precision that enables highly formalized discussions, intended to narrow down particular meanings in their particular contexts.
- Second, a subjective precision that inspires the unfolding of a rich variety of meanings in different and changing contexts.

Because of its intensive oral character, the Sanskrit language is able to combine these two kinds of precision in a way that has become quite unfamiliar to us today, in our modern languages that have developed a much more extensive expression of information suited to the use of printing and other modern media.

Changing Times

From this unfamiliar combination of objective and subjective precision, there results a characteristic problem of translation:

- On the one hand, literal translations tend to become extremely awkward and technical and difficult to understand, as they attempt to reproduce the objective precision. Moreover, each time a word is literally translated, a particular interpretation is chosen and meaning is thus narrowed down. So literal translation cannot reproduce the original richness of meaning; and it is forced to restrict itself to some particular interpretation that it has narrowed upon. This can be very misleading, if it is somehow thought that being literal means being fully faithful to the original.
- On the other hand, free translations may be more graceful and more clearly understood; but they depend more directly on the judgement of a translator, to be faithful to the spirit of the original. Here, the approach is subjective rather than objective. The translator reflects from the original to an understanding found expressed in it, and the translation is composed as a new expression of that understanding. This is not just an objective translation word by word, but more essentially a subjective retelling by reflection back to underlying meaning. And here also, as the retelling takes place, choices of meaning are made; so that some richness of meaning is lost from the original.

In either case, no matter how literal or free a translation may be, the loss of richness must be clearly understood. And where a special richness of meaning is compressed into a relatively few words, as in ancient and classical languages like Sanskrit, we need especially to understand how far each translation gives only one of many possible interpretations that show different aspects of the original.

Today, our main access to ancient and traditional texts is through translations made available by modern media. But in traditional times, before the use of printing, it was not so. In the Hindu tradition, before the nineteenth century, relatively little use was made of translation from Sanskrit.

For most traditional Hindus, Sanskrit was their common language of classical education. For those who were classically educated, their standard training of intellect was attained through learning the rigorous and complex formalities of the Sanskrit language. So, for those who were prepared to train their intellects, there was no need for any translated texts.

If a Sanskrit text was found difficult to understand, it was not accessed by reading a translation; but instead by a further examination of the original, through textual commentaries and explanations and elaboration, under the guidance of a living teacher. Over the generations, various different schools of thought were developed through such commentary and elaboration of the ancient texts.

As Sanskrit learning developed and continued through classical and medieval times, it played a major role in the development of more ordinarily spoken languages, or 'vernaculars' as they have come to be called. But this widespread and popular influence of Sanskrit learning did not take place through scholarly and institutional translations into the vernacular. Not nearly to the same extent that Greek and Roman classics and the Jewish and Christian Bibles were translated into European vernaculars by scholars and academics associated with church and university institutions.

Instead, in the Hindu tradition, the popularization of Sanskrit learning was brought about through vernacular retellings by inspired individuals: who did not speak so much from scholarship or institutional authority as from a renewed return to the same underlying source that had inspired the older Sanskrit texts. Following the tradition of Sanskrit epics and Purāṇas, the new vernacular retellings freely modified the old stories and ideas, to suit the changing and differing circumstances of changing times and differing communities.

These new retellings gave rise to vernacular literatures with classics of their own, in an overall process of vernacular popularization whose records go back a millennium and a half (to the early devotional literature of Tamil in the south). In the process, there has been a progressive broadening of the tradition: from a somewhat elite emphasis on intellectual education in classical Sanskrit, towards a more popular and emotional spirit of religious worship and spiritual devotion, expressed in the vernacular languages that ordinary people speak. And it is from there that the Hindu tradition is being modernized today, in the everyday lives of those who now inherit it.

SCHOOLS OF THOUGHT

Śāsana — Traditional Instruction

In Sanskrit, the instruction given from teacher to student is called 'śāsana'. This word comes from the root 'śās', meaning to 'chastise', 'correct', 'rule', and hence to 'instruct' or 'teach'. There is an etymological connection here with the English words 'chastise' and 'chaste'.

As this etymology shows, the traditional instruction called 'śāsana' was authoritarian and disciplinarian in its approach. The teacher was meant to exercise a position of authority, to discipline the students under his care. A traditional teacher may thus be called a 'śāstrī', which means a 'chastiser', a 'ruler', and hence a 'master' who is in command of both his students and his subject.

But, more essentially, a teacher is called a 'guru', which literally means 'heavy' and is related to the English word 'gravity'. The word 'guru' is thus used for a family elder who is not to be taken lightly, but approached instead with a devoted reverence. When a teacher is called a 'guru', it implies that the teacher is a kind of spiritual parent, to the students who have been entrusted to his care.

Hence the ancient ideal that teaching should take place in a 'guru-kula', which means literally a 'teacher-family'. According to this ideal, as students were being educated, they were supposed to live in a profoundly intimate family relationship with the teacher, from whom they would learn by living example and watchful care, as children learn in a loving relationship with a much respected and beloved parent.

The teacher thus exemplified the discipline and knowledge of tradition, which was handed down through a delicately personal and deeply respectful relationship between teacher and student. The basis of discipline here is not a tyrannical fear that destroys a student's sense of independence, by imposing instruction from outside. Instead, as the word '*in*struct' implies, traditional discipline was essentially meant to inspire trust and to awaken knowledge from within, through a careful nurturing that would progressively strengthen a student's ability to think and question and learn independently. It was thus that a student was meant to come eventually to knowledge, for himself or herself.

In early classical texts like the Upaniṣads, the *Rāmāyaṇa* and the *Mahābhārata,* we are told of small guru-kulas or schools that consisted of a single teacher, with the students living at the teacher's home or otherwise in close proximity nearby. Further, there are indications of larger centres of learning, like the city of Takṣaśilā, where a number of small family-centred schools were located near each other.

From the chronicles of Chinese Buddhists who travelled to India, we have accounts of large, centrally administered institutions of learning: in particular the Buddhist monastery of Nālandā, which functioned from the fifth to twelfth centuries CE. In its heyday, it had several thousand students, with a centrally organized administration and academic curriculum, as in a modern university. Along with specifically Buddhist studies, a general Sanskrit learning was taught, including the four Vedas and other brahmanical subjects.

There are some indications that such large institutions were also organized for brahmins and other Hindus. For example, the seventh century traveller I-tsing mentions that Nālandā's fame was rivalled by a centre of learning at the town of Valabhī in Kāṭhiavār, and there is a reference in the *Kathāsarit-sāgara* (xxxii, 42-43) confirming that brahmins went there for advanced studies.[28] And further, through textual references and historical inscriptions, the late Kāñcī Śaṅkarācārya Candraśekharendra Sarasvatī has shown evidence for large Vedic teaching institutions called 'ghaṭikāsthānas'.[29]

But, as the Śaṅkarācārya points out, even in such large institutions, the teaching was centred upon the guru-kula ideal of teacher and pupils living together as an intimate spiritual family in which learning is passed on. For even in the large institutions, individual

---

[28] See Majumdar 1988.

[29] See Candraśekharendra Sarasvatī Svāmī 1991, part 5.

students would be subject to a closely parental kind of supervision and guidance from individual teachers, who taught them and lived with them and were responsible for their practical and intellectual and moral welfare.

Thus, whether in small single-teacher schools or in larger institutions, traditional learning was centred upon the individual teacher: as a spiritual parent who passed on knowledge directly and individually, through a direct, living relationship with individual students. In this sense, traditional learning was primarily individual, rather than institutional. It was primarily focused on the inner education of the individual student, rather than the outward construction of institutional systems and technologies.

There were of course traditional institutions which grew progressively in size, enabling the organization of larger systems and more elaborate technologies. But all systems and technologies were considered as only the outward trappings of knowledge. In themselves, they are not knowledge itself. They can, however, be used to train a student's capabilities and intellect and character, and to clarify judgement and understanding. It is in this way, primarily, that systems of ideas and technologies were used in traditional learning.

In Sanskrit, an intellectual system or a science is called a 'śāstra'. The same word 'śāstra' is used today for modern science as well. But where modern sciences are taught primarily through organized schools, universities and institutes, a traditional śāstra was taught primarily by 'śāstrīs' who were individual teachers. And where modern learning and sciences depend broadly upon extensive amounts of information that various institutions collect and organize and distribute with the aid of mechanized media, traditional learning and its śāstras depended far more intensively upon a relatively few texts that could be passed on from teacher to student.

To suit their intensive usage, the basic texts of a śāstra are highly condensed. Typically, a traditional śāstra is based upon a founding text that is made up of extremely concise aphorisms, called 'sūtras'. The sūtras are conceived as a product of intense thought by someone of profound insight, who thus distils a substantial body of experience into its bare essentials. From this distillation of experience, a sūtra text lays out the essential principles of a subject, through a restricted number of terse and bare statements that are designed to be recited and remembered, for further consideration and reflection.

Such a founding text is both short and comprehensive. It covers an entire subject, and it does so shortly and systematically, through a judicious and highly economical use of a few compressed statements. But there is of course a price to be paid, for such extreme economy of statement. There is no room in the text to explain what its bare statements mean, and how they are to be applied.

A founding text was therefore explained through textual commentaries, and further levels of explanation were provided by commentaries upon commentaries, in a consequent tradition of texts. In the living tradition, the texts were continually explained and interpreted anew, through teaching and discussion, to meet the needs of the present time and occasion. It was thus that the texts came to life, in the actual practice of living education.

According to the conventions of traditional Hindu learning, the old texts were taken to be authoritative, more than any organized institutions. For a traditional student, the teacher stood personally, as a living individual, for the knowledge that was taught. And for both teachers and students, the texts stood more impersonally, as collective representations, for the traditions of learning that were handed down through them. So much so that the same word 'śāstra' is used both for the traditional intellectual systems and for the texts through which they were transmitted. An intellectual system is called a 'śāstra', and so also a basic text that transmits it.

By thus according authority to old, established texts, it was collectively assumed by teachers and students that these texts had something true to say, if correctly interpreted and understood. So the aim of traditional teaching was to bring out that truth in the texts, through a carefully reasoned appeal to the common experience of speaker and listener. For the śāstras or intellectual systems in particular, the reasoning was highly analytic and systematic. A student of the śāstras was meant to learn how to reason clearly and vigorously, so as to interpret the texts for himself or herself, upon a firm basis of common experience that was shared with others.

Thus, while starting from its conventions of didactic and textual authority, traditional instruction and learning were aimed at reasoning and knowing things independently. The aim was to go beyond all merely formal and external authority; by falling back upon an inner basis of experience, which different people somehow share. But then, what kind of knowledge can be learned like this?

Clearly, in this kind of learning, there is a tendency towards reflective reasoning, by which an inner component of knowledge gets emphasized. That inner emphasis is shown by the Sanskrit word 'śās', meaning to 'correct'. The traditional śāstras are not primarily aimed at outward construction; but more towards inner correction, through the use of reason to cultivate and clarify our inner faculties of mind and understanding. Such a correction is achieved by reflecting down from our built-up pictures, towards an inner ground of knowing that has been mistaken and misunderstood, beneath the outward picturing that has been built on it.

Because of their systematic reasoning, the traditional śāstras may rightly be called 'sciences'; but they are not the same kind of science as modern physics. In particular, they are not meant to be tested and applied so much through external instruments and machines, in the way that modern physics has now come to be. In the older sciences, knowledge is applied more closely through the inner education of our living faculties. The application is thus less dependent on external calculations. It works more directly through the trained and educated capabilities of living individuals.

In the long history of traditional civilization in India, sophisticated external technologies were most certainly developed and organized. Despite the lack of historical chronicling, it is clear that this was a rich and vigorous civilization, both inwardly and outwardly. The inner education of the śāstras has contributed richly and vigorously to practical life and organized technology in the outside world. But in the tradition's own view, it is the inner education that has always been central. It is thus regarded as the proper source of all outward development.

In the living tradition that we inherit today, through all the destructions of India's medieval period, a great many of the external technologies are gone. But a substantial core of the śāstras still remains, very definitely centred upon the inner education of those who study them genuinely, for the knowledge that they have to teach.

Vidyās — Branches of Learning

As the śāstras built their intellectual systems, they formulated different branches of learning, through which they developed various capabilities. These branches of learning are called 'vidyās' (from the root 'vid' — to 'know').

How are the branches classified? One way of classifying them is orthodox, based on the Vedic texts:

- Each of the four Vedas is considered as a vidyā in itself: including its Saṁhitā collection of mantras, its Brahmaṇa accounts of ritual performance, its Āraṇyaka interpretation of ritual symbols and its Upaniṣad questioning towards plain truth.
- To the four Vedas are added six 'aṅgas' or limbs. The first Vedāṅga is 'Śikṣā' or 'phonetics', meant to enable a correct pronunciation and hearing of the Vedic chants. The second Vedāṅga is 'Vyākaraṇa' or 'grammar', meant to enable the right forms and relationship of words. The third Vedāṅga is 'Chandas' or 'poetic metre', meant to enable a required flow of rhythmic sound. The fourth Vedāṅga is 'Nirukta' or 'etymology', meant to enable a discernment of word meanings. The fifth Vedāṅga is 'Jyotiṣa' or 'astrology', meant to decide the appropriate time for performing various rituals and actions that have been prescribed. And the sixth Vedāṅga is 'Kalpa' or 'duty', meant to define good works and right practices that should be carried out, in the course of our living journeys through the world.
- To the Vedas and Vedāṅgas, there is a further addition of Mīmāṁsā (which interprets Vedic injunctions), Nyāya (which formulates rules for logical argument), the Purāṇas (myths and legends), and Dharma-śāstra (ethics and morality). So far, this

amounts to fourteen branches of learning, which are called the 'caturdaśa-vidyās'.

- Another four branches are sometimes added as auxiliary sciences: Āyurveda (medicine), Artha-śāstra (economics and politics), Dhanur-veda (military science), and Gandharva-veda (music). The total then becomes eighteen.[30]

But, for a modern reader, this list of eighteen vidyās must seem rather strange and very incomplete, as an accounting of the various disciplines that may be used to educate our knowledge of the world. It seems to allow no proper place for modern disciplines: like physics and mathematics, biology, linguistics and culture studies, psychology and philosophy. How then can we relate the old vidyās to our modern education? Where did the old learning allow for what we study in our modern disciplines? A broad analysis has already been suggested in the third column of figure 7 (on page 112).

Let us first consider ***mathematics and physics***. Mathematics was called 'gaṇita' or 'calculation', and it may be included in the Vedāṅga of Jyotiṣa or astrology. This Vedāṅga may also be taken to include the modern physical science that we now call 'astronomy'. In fact, the disciplines of mathematics and physics were most definitely investigated and practised in ancient times. Our records show that Pythagoras's theorem was known and used in ancient Egypt, in ancient Iraq and in ancient India. The use of this theorem is clearly described in the Sanskrit *Śulba-śāstras,* many centuries before its formulation by Euclid in classical Greece. (See footnote 10, page 41.)

What's new in Euclid is not the measured and calculating use of mathematical deductions. That had been developing from long before. Euclid's contribution was instead a new way of formulating mathematics, in a manner that is suited to transmitting it through written documents. This way of formulation is to state explicit

---

30 As described in Candraśekharendra Sarasvatī Svāmī 2000 — part 5, chapter 3.

hypotheses, and to show how mathematical results are derived from them. Through this explicit formulation, of hypotheses and deductions, we make calculating models of structures in the world. And we use these models to predict some particular results in the phenomena that nature shows us.

In the last few centuries, since Galileo and Newton, this mathematical modelling has greatly developed the kind of sciences that we now call 'physical'. The modelling works mechanically, through the use of printing and other media that have increasingly mechanized our recording and processing and transmission of information. But the mechanization has a restricting effect. Its calculating method is restricted to an external world of structured space. This is the world to which we apply our physical sciences. And we think of these sciences as 'modern', in the sense that they have been greatly developed in recent times.

So, when we speak of 'modern physics', it can be useful to remember two things:

- First, as we use the word 'modern' here, it does not quite mean 'new'. Modern physics is in fact an old science — whose roots go a long way back, into an ancient past. This science is 'modern' only in the sense that it has received a special emphasis in recent times, so that a large part of it has been developed recently.
- And second, as we use the word 'physics' now, it has a meaning that has been restricted recently. In older times, before Newton and Galileo, the words 'physics' and 'physical' were used in a far broader way than they are today. In their older usage, these words referred to all of nature, which the Greeks called 'phusis'. That nature includes activities of mind, which are today excluded from the external world of modern physics.[31]

---

[31] To show this recent restriction of meaning, here is a quotation from *The Oxford English Dictionary*, Oxford University Press, England, 1933 (from the entry 'Physics'):

footnote continued on next page ...

Next, after mathematics and physics, let us consider the discipline of ***biology***. It is concerned with bodies that we take to be alive. So, in the sciences of life, there are two aspects of concern. On the one hand, there is the living body — with its structures, its mechanisms and its chemistry. On the other hand, there is an organic functioning, whereby consciousness becomes expressed, in the physical activities of living bodies in the world.

Of these two aspects, the first involves a judicious use of modern physics. And the second requires a rather different approach, through a subjective reflection back into the consciousness that's somehow found to be expressed. This combination of two aspects can be clearly seen in the sciences of bodily medicine.

In modern Western medicine, the bodily aspect has been greatly emphasized, through the use of modern physical technology and through recent advances in anatomy and bio-chemistry and molecular biology. This emphasis has of course been very useful, in its own way, as it has applied some advances of modern physics to our descriptions and our treatment of living bodies and their behaviour in the world.

... footnote continued from previous page

Physics...

1. Natural science in general; in the older writers *esp.* the Aristotelian system of natural science; hence natural philosophy in the wider sense.... The application of the term has tended continually to be narrowed. It originally (from Arist.) included the study of the whole of nature (organic and inorganic); Locke even included spirits (God, angels, etc.) among its objects. In the course of the 18th cent., it became limited to inorganic nature, and then, by excluding chemistry, it acquired its present meaning...

2. In current usage, restricted to The science, or group of sciences, treating of the properties of matter and energy, or of the action of the different forms of energy on matter in general (excluding Chemistry, which deals specifically with the different forms of matter, and Biology, which deals with vital energy).

But there is also a sense in which biology cannot be treated merely as a branch of modern physics. No mere branch of modern physics can address the living aspect of organic functioning. As things stand at present, when we speak of 'physical biology' or 'bio-physics' or 'bio-chemistry' or 'molecular biology', these disciplines are no more than special branches of modern physics. They have no way of conceiving life in its essential sense, as expressing a subjective consciousness in the bodies and the happenings that nature manifests to us.

So, while some branches of physics can work in a helpful partnership with medicine and with other sciences of life, no branch of physics can itself be a life science. When a doctor treats a patient, for the purpose of some living therapy, there is always something more involved than mere physics and mechanical technology. There is an organic functioning that has to be treated quite differently — through living faculties that work subjectively, by arising from within.

In India, that organic functioning is investigated in the medical discipline of Āyurveda, in various ritual disciplines that are exemplified in the Vedas, and in other disciplines like astrology and alchemy. These sciences are essentially biological.

It may seem strange to think of ritual and astrology and alchemy in this way, as biological sciences, but there is a good reason for it. These sciences are founded on a correspondence that they essentially conceive between the macrocosm of the world at large and the microcosm of each person's experience. The entire world is here conceived as a living macrocosm, with a generic life and mind. It thus inherently expresses a subjective consciousness, through all its ordered functioning, its intelligible meanings and its valued qualities.

Third, after biology, we may consider ***linguistics and the study of culture***. In the Veda-based list of disciplines, linguistics is prominently represented by the first four Vedāṅgas: Śikṣā or phonetics, Vyākaraṇa or grammar, Chandas or poetic metre, and Nirukta or etymology. This prominence accords with a central role which linguistics has played in classical systems of education; not just in India, but also in China, in the Middle-east and in the West.

In such classical systems, a student's education was centred upon the systematic study of a classical language — like Sanskrit or Hebrew or ancient Greek or Latin or Mandarin Chinese. Such a classical language was taught through its corresponding linguistic science, including its formal analysis of phonetics, grammar and semantics. This linguistic analysis was the initiating centre of a classical student's training of mind. Just as, today, a modern student starts out with a basic training that is centred upon mathematics and physical science and the use of computers and machines.

Accordingly, as we think of scientific disciplines today, we tend to model them on the calculating approach of modern physics. But classical sciences have long been modelled somewhat differently, upon the educating use of reason in linguistic analysis.

In modern physics, a reflection into mind is excluded from the application of ideas. The theories of modern physics must be applied through the calculation of external results, which are observed and implemented through external instruments and machines, in an objective world that does not include reflection back through mind into a subjective consciousness. This restriction is essential to the standardization of knowledge in modern physics. It is standardized externally, by specifying outward instruments and machines that are observed and used through our external bodies.

In classical linguistics, ideas and theories are more broadly applied. Their application includes both objective calculation and subjective reflection. On the one hand, objective rules are formulated, for the calculation of word forms and use. And on the other hand, a reasoning analysis is used reflectively, for an investigation that turns back into mind, in search of clearer meaning. The application of linguistics thus includes a subjective aspect, which educates our living faculties of expression and understanding. The application works through those living faculties, as they keep learning from the process of experience in our minds.

The older sciences are thus more broadly modelled than modern physics. They take a broader view of science, which has long been exemplified by classical linguistics. That broader view allows for a consideration of arts and humanities as scientific disciplines. But it also opens up a problem of cultural relativity. Each language, each art and each human discipline is culture specific. Each depends on artificial forms and conventions that differ from one culture to another. How then can any language or art or discipline attain to the impartiality of science? Through any of the languages or arts or disciplines we cultivate, how can we ever describe or investigate impartial principles, which are shared in common by our differing cultures?

One way of answering this question is to recognize that our descriptions are always cultural constructions, made up from culture-specific symbols and conventions. This makes our descriptions partial and variable, as expressions of knowledge. From this partiality and difference, our sciences must turn their investigation back, reflectively, towards impartial and common principles that are thus found expressed. It's only such impartial principles that can provide the common standards which our sciences require.

Fourth, after linguistics and the humanities, we can ask about the science of ***psychology***. In modern systems of education, psychology has come to be treated as a separate science, because of the exclusion of mind from modern physics. In older systems, before the mind was thus excluded, it was treated as a natural component of consideration, in a variety of different disciplines — including medicine, ritual, astrology, alchemy, linguistics, creative arts and the humanities. In classical Sanskrit learning for example, we do not find much mention of a separate 'mano-śāstra' or 'science of the mind'.

However, there is one ancient discipline that is specifically aimed at the capabilities of mind. This is the discipline of meditative practice. In Sanskrit, this discipline is called 'yoga' or 'harnessing'. It seeks to expand intuition and to purify character, by repeated exercises of withdrawal from the restless turning at the narrow focus of attention. Withdrawing back into the depth of mind, a meditator seeks to develop penetrating judgements and subtle intuitions that transcend the usual limitations of the mind in space and time.

Such meditative practice is the basis of traditional psychology. In this sense, we may speak of 'Yoga-śāstra' as a major science of the mind. Its immediate concern is with the control of 'citta-vṛtti' or the 'turning of mind'. In Sanskrit, each passing state of mind is called a 'vṛtti' or a 'turning'. This term 'vṛtti' is thus used to describe our mental states as cyclic transformations, each of which arises through an outward turning from a common background that stays present in them all.

It's through this outward turning that the mind experiences what happens in the world. As anything that happens is perceived and taken in, it leaves behind a conditioned tendency. In Sanskrit, such tendencies are called 'saṁskāras'. They are assimilated at the underlying background, where they continue quietly, like dormant seeds of unmanifested potency. From that background, they influence the turning of the mind, from one state of experience to another.

That background is the depth of mind. It's there that knowing carries on. From there, each state of mind must rise. Back there, each passing state is taken in and gets absorbed. It's only by returning there that changing mind can be arrested and controlled.

Fifth, after psychology and meditation, we may go on to the questioning discipline of ***philosophy***. This discipline is purely educational. It is not meant to calculate results, in our physical and mental pictures of the world. It's only meant to clarify what's true, by questioning all pictures we assume in our physical and mental calculations. In Sanskrit, philosophy is commonly called 'tattva-śāstra', which simply means the 'science of truth'. ('Tattva' means 'that-ness', and hence 'reality' or 'truth'.)

In the Veda-based list of eighteen disciplines, neither Yoga nor tattva-śāstra are explicitly mentioned. Instead, they are included implicitly, as undisclosed parts of the listed disciplines. In particular, they get to be described in the Upaniṣad portion of the four Vedas, and in various commentaries and treatises that followed later on.

As philosophy and Yoga were thus more explicitly described, there came to be a further list, of six 'darśanas' or 'seeings'. Each

Darśana is a school of philosophy, with its own way of looking at the world.

Darśanas — World Views

The six Darśanas are Vaiśeṣika, Nyāya, Sāṅkhya, Yoga, Mīmāṁsā and Vedānta. As summarized in figure 10, they can be grouped in

Figure 10

Vaiśeṣika-Nyāya	Assumes an *external world* of differentiated objects.	Analyses the *structure* of descriptions and arguments.	Body
Sāṅkhya-Yoga	Assumes a manifesting *nature* that produces appearances before the light of *consciousness*.	Explains how nature manifests appearances of world, through an evolving *process* that expresses consciousness.	Mind
Mīmāṁsā-Vedānta	Examines differentiated actions and appearances, in search of underlying *potencies* and *principles*.	Mīmāṁsā is concerned with the achievement of desired results, through the *causal potency* of prescribed actions. Vedānta asks for an impartial truth that is independent of all change and difference. The questioning reflects *beneath all causality* of action and result.	Consciousness*

**Note*: Mīmāṁsā is concerned with the causal aspect of consciousness, whereby nature is motivated to produce particular manifestations in the world.

Vedānta is concerned with a reflective investigation towards the inmost being of consciousness, which shines by its own light. There, consciousness is known in identity, by merely being what it is. By that very being, consciousness illuminates itself. Its knowing light is the source from which all appearances get lit.

three pairs, corresponding to a three-fold division of body, mind and consciousness.

'***Vaiśeṣika***' means 'differentiation' or 'particularity'. In the Vaiśeṣika system, a differentiated world is described — a world that extends through a variety of differences and changes, in outward space and time. The differentiation starts with five padārthas or categories. They are: dravya or substance, guṇa or quality, karma or action, sāmānya or association, viśeṣa or difference, and samavāya or inherence.

The differentiation continues further, within the basic categories. Thus, substance is differentiated into nine substances: earth, water, fire, air, ether, time, space, self and mind. Of these nine substances, the first seven are made up of aṇus or fine particles. No particle can be perceived in isolation, by itself, for it has no extension in the structured space of world. It's only by association that these particles form structures that extend in space and can be thus observed.

Each self or ātman is a special substance that is all-pervading, unbounded and unlimited by space or time. That pervasion is inherent in the self's capacity to know of different things, in different parts of space and time. But in this knowing of differences, a mediation is implied, in between the knowing self and the world of differences.

The mind is thus conceived as a mediating substance, enabling self to know the world. Like the self, each mind continues on through time. But, unlike the self, each mind is affected by a changing particularity. Impelled by activating self, the mind associates with particular sense organs, at particular moments in time. Through this association, the mind is found to function towards particular objects, which then affect the mind with their changing particulars.

'***Nyāya***' implies a return to authentic standards of correct procedure. The Nyāya system develops a description of the world which is similar to Vaiśeṣika. As in Vaiśeṣika, knowing is described as an action that proceeds from self, through mind and body, towards objects in the world. This act of knowing is cultivated and refined through formal logic, which organizes bodily perceptions and meaningful descriptions into formally ordered structures.

In Sanskrit learning, Nyāya is primarily used for Tarka-śāstra or rhetoric, the science of meaningfully ordered exposition through logical argument. Four means of knowledge are distinguished: pratyakṣa or perception, anumāna or inference, upamāna or analogy, and śabda or testimony. Inference is further analysed as of three kinds: from cause to effect, from effect to cause, and from particular perception to abstract principle.

As can be seen from the third kind of inference, Nyāya logic is not merely a formal deduction that could be carried out mechanically, on a computer. A living induction is essentially involved, with a reflection back into the depth of mind, from differing perceptions at the surface of attention to underlying principles that are found shared in common.[32]

'***Sāṇkhya***' means 'making known' or 'reckoning'. In the Sāṅkhya system, our experience is accounted through a distinction of two principles: puruṣa and prakṛti. Puruṣa is consciousness, the knowing subject in each personality. Prakṛti is nature, including all activities of body, sense and mind.

In this conception, nature is self-manifesting. It shows itself to each one of us, as it produces all the perceptions, thoughts and feelings that appear and disappear, in our observing and conceiving minds. Accordingly, for each of us, nature is the objective or known part of experience, containing all activities that change. And consciousness is the subjective or knowing part, which witnesses the actions and their change. That witnessing is not a changing act, but an actionless illumination that continues through the change.

Here, knowing is conceived quite differently from Nyāya and Vaiśeṣika. It's not a knowing that goes out, through action, towards objects in the world. Instead, it is a witnessing that stays unmixed

---

[32] The foregoing description of Vaiśeṣika and Nyāya has been aided by Heinrich Zimmer 1953.

and unaffected in the mind. What then is the effect of that witnessing? How is it relevant to nature's actions in the world?

This question is answered by the phrase 'puruṣārtha'. As nature's acts produce their show of changing appearances, these acts are described as 'puruṣārtha'. They are done 'for the sake of consciousness', the witnessing principle for whom the show takes place. All nature's show is animated by an inner inspiration which arises from pure consciousness within. This inspiration is the living energy called 'prāṇa'. As it arises, it inherently expresses its illuminating principle of consciousness, from where and for whose sake it is inspired.

Thus consciousness becomes quite naturally expressed, in all of nature's functioning. It is expressed in all the ordered structures, all the meaningful significance and all the valued qualities that nature manifests. Wherever any order is recognized, or any meaning is interpreted, or any value is judged in nature's phenomena, the recognition or interpretation or the judgement requires an implicit reflection back into a knowing principle of consciousness, found in each living individual and in nature as a whole.

Implicitly, whenever we make any sense of nature, we reflect back into consciousness, in the microcosms of our individual experience. By understanding nature thus, through a reflection back within, we are treating nature as we would a living being with whom we share an underlying kinship of common, inner life. Implicitly, but often without properly acknowledging it, we thus keep treating nature as alive.

In the Sāṅkhya conception, the acknowledgement is made explicit. The world as a whole is described as a living macrocosm, with a generic life and mind. A correspondence is conceived between the universal macrocosm and each individual microcosm. All our perception and interpretation of the world is thus described as taking place through an organic correspondence that connects our microcosmic faculties with the macrocosmic functioning of living nature in the universe outside.

The Sāṅkhya use of reason is to analyse the basic constituents and elements of nature's functioning, in world and personality. In particular, it's thus that the three guṇas and the five elements are analysed. In making this kind of analysis, Sāṅkhya provides a theoretical basis for many traditional sciences, in their descriptions of the world and their cultivation of living faculties through which those descriptions are applied. For example, the sciences of Āyurveda and astrology make use of some Sāṅkhya ideas.

'***Yoga***' means 'union' or 'harnessing'. As a school of philosophy, the Yoga system uses the Sāṅkhya analysis to develop Yoga-śāstra as a systematic science of meditative practice — meant to control and purify the mind by withdrawing it back from its changing states into its underlying depth, where it becomes absorbed into unmixed consciousness. (A brief summary of this Yoga system may be found on pages 212-13, and a longer account in the chapter on *Yogic Discipline*, pages 116-32.)

Thus, Yoga can be seen as a practical application of Sāṅkhya theory. So much so that the terms 'sāṅkhya' and 'yoga' can sometimes be used in the sense of 'theory' and 'practice' (as most famously in the *Bhagavad-gītā*).

'***Mīmāṁsā***' means 'examination'. The Mīmāṁsā system is meant to examine and interpret the Vedic texts. In particular, it is meant to interpret Vedic instructions, about the performance of required actions and duties. In this system, the Vedic gods are not approached as supernatural persons, to be worshipped with faith and devotion. Instead, they are invoked as natural powers, which get directed by the Vedic chants and rituals, for the achievement of required results.

Mīmāṁsā is thus concerned with the practical effectiveness and power of authentic speech. Here, words and acts are conceived to manifest an inner potential, inherent in their proper speaking and enactment. Each word and act is taken to include its inner potency, from where it gets its meaning and effect.

In this consideration, meaning and usage are not mere conventions, added on by artifice to outward sounds and forms. Beneath the varying conventions of cultural artifice, the meaning of a word arises more deeply, from the inner nature of its sound. That inner nature is the basis of word meaning and use. It is a depth of meaning that remains unchanged, beneath its changing expressions in our different cultures.

The methods of Mīmāṁsā were applied beyond the Vedas, to various kinds of cultural and social and political regulation. They have thus played a major part in the organization of traditional Hindu society.

'***Vedānta***' implies a culmination of knowledge (from 'veda' meaning 'knowledge' and 'anta' meaning 'end'). The name Vedānta is thus applied to some schools of philosophy that seek an ultimate knowing of impartial truth, beyond all partiality of seeing and conceiving through our senses and our minds. Historically, these schools were formed by interpretation and commentary upon the Upaniṣads (which are the ending portion of the Vedic texts). Thus known by the name Vedānta, there are three main schools.

The earliest is '*Advaita*' or 'non-dualism'. Its approach is plainly philosophical. It questions all assumed beliefs, in search of truer knowing. The questions are turned back reflectively and skeptically, upon all personal and cultural beliefs that have been assumed by the questioner. The aim is to investigate a depth of true knowing that is utterly impartial, beneath all personal and cultural assumptions that give rise to our partial pictures of a differentiated world.

It's only in these pictures that we see or hear or smell or taste or touch various objects that are different from ourselves. It's only in these pictures that we think of different objects, by which we may feel attracted or repelled. It's only in this picturing that we experience different things and make assumptions about them.

Beneath our partial pictures, no difference can be known. In particular, no object can be known as different from the self that knows it. That self can only be known in identity, as identical with its own being. There, knowing and being must be the same. There can be no duality between what knows and what is known. Accordingly, in the Advaita Vedānta system, truth is sought as a pure self that is completely 'non-dual', beneath all seeming duality of knowing subject and known object.

However, from the standpoint of religious worship, a certain conflict may be found with advaita or non-dual questioning. In the act of worship, there is implied an essential duality. God is ultimately worthy, while the worshipper is not. So long as the worship is in progress, the worshipper must feel inadequate. And God must be regarded as a greater and superior being, to whom all wishes need to be surrendered.

In order to allow for the duality of worship, an organic synthesis was made, in the second major school of Vedānta. This school is called '*Viśiṣṭādvaita*' or 'qualified non-dualism'. It conceives of God as an all-comprehending unity, including each self and each object in the world. All individual selves and objects thus participate in that one unity, which they each manifest and which supports them all. Here, knowing is a recognition of God's living unity, as it seems differently expressed in individual selves and objects.

Because all individuals depend upon that unity, none of them can have a separate existence. In this sense, they are not different from it. But here, the non-difference must be qualified. No individual self or object can be more than a component part of the entire unity. No one or more of them can thus amount to it. In that sense, it is different from them all.

In the third main school of Vedānta, the qualified non-difference is given up. In its place, an unqualified differentiation is made, between each knowing subject and the objects that are known. This third school is called '*Dvaita Vedānta*' or 'dualistic Vedānta'. Here, God is described as the creator, the ruler and the destroyer of the world. The objects of the world are taken to be real: as perceived and conceived through our bodies and our minds, by physically and mentally differentiated selves.

In this six-fold division of Darśanas or schools of philosophy, it is recognized that each has its uses, when properly applied from its own point of view. Each works in its own way towards a common goal of mokṣa or freedom. They all work towards the liberation of a changeless self called 'ātman', which is wrongly identified as a changing person in the world. Each such person suffers from ignorance, which binds our personalities to partiality and loss. The Darśanas all work towards freedom from this ignorance and suffering.

Vaiśeṣika works by carefully discerning different categories of the world that gets known, including the true nature of the selves that know it. Nyāya elaborates the differentiation, so as to analyse how reasoned argument can help to know things better.

Sāṅkhya works by distinguishing the subjective illumination of consciousness from the objective manifestation of nature's mental and physical activities. Yoga develops a practical discipline that empowers the mind to withdraw from its changing manifestations, towards a liberating absorption in unchanging consciousness.

Mīmāṁsā works by examining authentic sayings and instructions, so as to regulate required actions towards effective results. Vedānta reflects towards an ultimate principle of truth and value, which is implied by all correctness of right knowing and all motivation of effective action.

Each of these six Darśanas develops its own ways of explaining the phenomena of world. They thus develop differing world views, which both contradict and complement each other. It is then only natural that the word 'darśana' or 'seeing' has come to be used more generally; not just for these six Darśanas, but for world views in general, as developed in a variety of cultures and religions.

Accordingly, various Jain, Buddhist, Christian and Islamic schools of thought have been treated as Darśanas, along with many Hindu schools (both philosophical and theological) which have come about in the long course of Indian history. Included also is an ancient school of materialism, attributed to a sage called 'Cārvāka', who refused to accept the spiritual beliefs of traditional religious faith.

Most Hindu schools describe their goal as 'mokṣa' or 'freedom': whereby an inmost self is liberated from a degraded ego that must suffer from its bondage to outward objects in the world. The Jain schools describe their goal as 'kaivalya' or 'aloneness': in which a living being is completely purified from all degrading attachment to non-living things. And Buddhist schools describe their goal as 'nirvāṇa' or 'extinction': in which there is a cessation of all false individuality that brings about defilement and suffering, through its mistaken grasping at impermanence.

These goals are rather differently described, from the differing perspectives of their various schools. But, beneath the differences, there has been quite enough in common for some vigorous debates, in which each school has learned from the others and has contributed in return.

Approaching Truth

In the Hindu tradition, three aspects are distinguished for approaching truth. These aspects are called 'sat' or 'existence', 'cit' or 'consciousness', and 'ānanda' or 'happiness'. From these aspects, there arise three 'mārgas' or 'ways of approach'.

The existence aspect gives rise to the '*yoga mārga*' or the 'way of union'. The consciousness aspect gives rise to the '*jñāna mārga*' or the 'way of knowledge'. And the happiness aspect gives rise to the '*bhakti mārga*' or the 'way of devotion'.

Sat — Existence

> It's that which can't be seen or grasped,
> which has no family, no class,
> no eyes or ears, no hands or feet.
> It is just that which carries on,
> extending subtly everywhere,
> beyond the finest subtlety.
> It is that being which remains,
> found always changeless at the source
> of all becoming in the world.
> That's what the wise and steadfast see.
>
> – *Muṇḍaka Upaniṣad 1.1.6*

By 'sat' is meant a reality that's shown in common, by differing appearances.

Accordingly, sat may be described as '*tattva*' or 'that-ness'. It is a changeless that-ness which transcends all these changing appearances that show it to us, through these bodies and these senses and these minds. For short, it is sometimes called just 'that', as opposed to the 'this' of its manifold appearances. Since that reality is changeless, it is found to be the same in each individual, and throughout the entire universe.

Approached individually, the reality is called '*svarūpa*' or 'true nature'. A 'rūpa' is a form, appearing through some act of perception. The prefix 'sva-' means 'own'. So 'sva-rūpa' means 'one's own form'. It is the inmost form that is revealed by looking at an individual from her or his or its own point of view, without any intervention from outside.

When an individual is perceived from outside, the perception is then indirect. A perceiving mind or body intervenes, between the perceiver and the individual perceived. This intervention creates a mental or physical appearance — which is then liable to change, from changing points of view.

But when an individual is seen fully from within, there is no intervening distance between the point from which one looks and some other point to which the looking is directed. There is, accordingly, no difference between what sees and what is seen. What's seen is then no outward appearance — thus seen to differ and to change, from various outside points of view. What's seen instead is the true nature of the individual, there found exactly as it is, in a direct realization of itself.

That true nature may be sought as one's own self. Or as the self in anyone, at the centre of each living personality. Or that same nature may be sought as the reality of any object in itself, in its own individuality. And that same nature called 'svarūpa' may be sought universally: as the complete reality of the entire universe, including every object and each personality. The universe is then treated as an individual whole.

In every case, the reality called 'sat' is what stays the same, throughout the changing life of each person or each object or the universe. As life proceeds through a variety of different happenings, we see in them an ordered functioning, which somehow expresses purposes and meanings and values that we find intelligible. It's only thus that we can understand what happens, as we reflect from change and difference to a sense of purpose and meaning and value that we find shared in common with what we see.

Sat is accordingly a shared reality, which is expressed in common by all nature's life, both in our personalities and in their containing world. This gives rise to the yoga mārga or the way of union. Here, truth is approached by a progressive harnessing of personality. All faculties of body, sense and mind are harnessed back into their underlying source of life, from which they have arisen.

As the harnessing progresses, the personality becomes more integrated and its capabilities expand, beyond their usual limitations. The final aim is a complete integration, by absorption back into the underlying source, where all limitations and all differences are found dissolved.

This way of yoga is comprehensively described in Patañjali's *Yoga-sūtras*, and in the *Bhagavad-gītā*. (See the chapters on *Yogic Discipline*, pages 116-32 and *Detachment from Personality*, pages 133-48.)

Cit — Consciousness

> In *that*, the sun does not shine,
> nor do the moon and stars,
> nor these flashes of lightning.
> How, then, this fire here?
> *That* shines itself.
> Everything shines after it.
> All of this world reflects its light.
>
> *– Kaṭha Upaniṣad 5.15*

Cit is the knowing light of consciousness, found in each person's mind.

In everyone's experience, it is a subjective knowing that illuminates whatever may appear or disappear. As time proceeds in any mind, perceptions, thoughts and feelings come and go. But consciousness continues as their knowing principle. It stays present always, illuminating all appearances and disappearances. It is a common principle of knowing, found always present in all states of experience, beneath their changes and their differences.

Found as a knowing principle, consciousness is called 'prajñāna'. It's that which is prior (pra-) to all different instances of knowledge (jñāna). Where different things are told apart, we speak of a discerning knowledge called 'vijñāna', with the prefix 'vi-' implying differentiation. Where different things are put together, we speak of an associating knowledge called 'saṁjñāna', with the prefix 'sam-' implying mixture or inclusion.

But consciousness itself is neither differentiating nor associating. Its knowing is no action that tells things apart or puts them together. Its knowing is no act that it starts doing at some point of time or stops doing later on. Instead, its knowing is just what it is. Its very being is to know, to shine with knowing light. That light shines by itself, by its mere presence in all changing states that show a differentiated world.

All differences appear through changing acts of perception, thought and feeling in our bodies and minds. It is these changing acts that produce the different things we perceive or think or feel. And it is again these changing acts that put things together, in our constructed pictures and stories that describe a differentiated world. All telling things apart and putting them together are thus personal acts, which are performed by our minds and our bodies in the world.

How then can we come to a true knowledge of reality, which is shown in common by our differing descriptions of it? How can we interpret our constructed pictures and stories, so that we may know more clearly and more truly what they show? This investigation is pursued in the jñāna mārga or the way of knowledge. Here, truth is approached by questioning belief. Our descriptions are examined to uncover the assumptions that we make in them, so as to remove confusions and mistakes of unquestioned belief.

In the tradition of Hindu texts, the jñāna mārga first shows up in some philosophical chants from the Vedic Saṁhitās (see the chapter on *Creation in the Vedas*, pages 53-63). It is further shown in various passages from the Upaniṣads, which raise basic questions about the Vedic world view. But in the Upaniṣads, the questions are raised through some rather condensed and cryptic statements, without much explanation or systematic treatment of the questioning.

The systematic treatment is put forward in the Darśanas or schools of philosophy, which have developed a variety of differing world views (see the section on *Darśanas — World Views*, pages 214-22). The differences have naturally given rise to philosophical debates, through which the various schools have developed their theoretical systems, in relation to each other.

However, such debates are institutional and theoretical. Debate is what pandits or scholars do, as they construct and establish the competing views of their various different schools. This is a theoretical activity, in which each school sets out its own system of thought, in competition with other schools.

This construction of world views is not the actual practice of philosophy. It cannot be more than a theoretical preliminary, which serves to prepare a student for reflective questioning. The actual practice of philosophy does not begin till reason is reflected back from built-up ideas, so as to question the very basis of assumptions upon which the ideas have been built.

So long as reason is applied to question someone else's beliefs, then that is just a theoretical debate, which is used largely to prevent the questioner's beliefs from being opened up to question. But when the questioning turns round reflectively, upon one's own assumptions, then one's own understanding is at stake. And if such a questioning is genuine, it then amounts to an investigating experiment, in which one looks to see what clearer understanding it may lead towards.

The results of such a questioning are then inherently practical, for the new understanding gets inherently expressed in further feelings, thoughts, perceptions and actions that arise from it. It's through such questioning that we get educated, as we learn in practice from the process of experience.

The actual practice of philosophy is just that turned-back questioning. It takes place within all schools: as each student learns received ideas and gets to question what they mean, for herself or himself.

Debate and enquiry have thus two different functions. Debate is used institutionally, to set out a systematic view of world that represents a school of thought to those who see it from outside. Enquiry serves individually, for each student of a school to learn its ideas and to investigate their meaning from within. An inner education is here sought through an individual questioning, under the guidance of a living teacher. That inward and individual emphasis lies at the heart of the jñāna mārga.

Ānanda — Happiness

It is just this essential savour
that is quite spontaneous and natural.
It's only when one reaches this true savour
that one comes to happiness.
For what could be alive at all,
what could move with energy,
if there were not this happiness –
here at the background
of all space and time,
pervading the entire world?

– Taittirīya Upaniṣad 2.7

Ānanda is happiness, the happiness that's sought in all feelings and desires.

That happiness is not a passing state of mind. It is not a 'happy' state of satisfied desire, alternating with 'unhappy' states where desires fail to be achieved. When we speak of 'happiness', the suffix '-ness' implies a common principle. That principle is common to both happy and unhappy states. Happiness is just that principle of value which both happy and unhappy feelings show.

When someone feels happy, this feeling is positive. It feels at one with 'hap', with what has *hap*pened to take place. By contrast, when someone feels unhappy, this feeling is negative. It feels itself at odds with 'hap', with what is seen to have *hap*pened here. In either case, a common principle of happiness is shown.

In feelings that are happy, the principle of happiness is positively shown, by a positive acceptance of one-ness with what happens. In feelings that are unhappy, exactly the same principle is negatively shown, by a negative avoidance of disruptive differences between what feels and what is felt to happen.

That principle of happiness is not just personal. It is not merely 'nanda', the personal enjoyment that so differs from person to person, as we pursue our many different objects of desire. It's more specifically described as '*ā*nanda', with the prefix 'ā-' implying a return back to an underlying depth. By ānanda is meant an experience of enjoyment that is shared in common, beneath all differences of personality and world.

In coming back to that depth of enjoyment, all personal pleasures must be left behind, in search of a truer happiness. All desire for partial objects must be given up to a truer love, for something that is more complete. All falsely independent ego must be surrendered, in devotion to a self that is truly free. This approach is called the 'bhakti mārga' or the 'way of devotion'.

One use of the bhakti mārga is concerned with religious worship. Here, truth is approached through devotion to a worshipped God, whose form is conceived by telling stories and performing rituals. A form of God is thus imagined and worshipped, through stories and rituals that appeal to the liking and desires of a personal worshipper. Such an appealing form of God is called an 'iṣṭa-mūrti', which means an 'embodiment of liking and desire'.

In this kind of worship, God is approached through personal desire, although the final aim is to surrender all desires to an ultimate value that is represented by God's form. Through personal attentions of worship, a devotee's love is meant to grow towards a final fulfilment, in which everything is seen as an expression of the ultimate. In that fulfilment, no matter what is done, nor where attention is directed, the devotee sees always the pervading goodness and truth that has been shown by the worshipped form.

In the Hindu tradition, there is a great variety of different religious sects. They each have their stories and rituals, their beliefs and practices, their written and chanted texts, their world views and schools of thought, their institutions and their teachers. Through this variety of sects, the tradition has kept growing, in the course of its long history. That's how it has come down to us, in both classic and vernacular languages.

But, underneath the sectarian variety, there is a further use of devotion that is shared in common. This use is individual. It occurs in the relationship of teacher and disciple. For a disciple, the teacher stands for truth that has been taught. So love for truth gets naturally expressed in a spiritual devotion towards the teacher. But this is a very delicate matter of sensibility, where an impersonal truth is seen expressed in the person of a teacher.

Such a devotion must arise unforced and unpretended, of its own accord. It must be felt from an impersonal depth of being, from far beneath all words and thoughts and all their spoken or conceived intentions. All teaching works by leading back to that unspoken depth, through clearer knowing and uncompromised devotion.

An Afterword — For a Globalizing World

TRADITION AND THE LIVING INDIVIDUAL

Individual Centering

When we speak of India and the West, in a globalizing world, there is at stake an issue of how knowledge is learned and handed down. As learning gets passed on, there is an interplay between two different aspects.

On the one hand, knowledge passes down in a living tradition of direct contact, from person to person. Here, a living teacher guides each student individually, through an education that trains qualitative skills and clarifies discerning faculties within the living individual.

But on the other hand, as learning is transmitted from generation to generation, individuals use ideas, techniques and instruments that get organized in cultural and social institutions. Thus knowledge comes to be represented outwardly — by theoretical and technical systems that get to compete politically, for institutional predominance.

In India, there has long been a tendency to emphasize the inner aspect of knowledge, and thus to centre learning upon the individual. The tendency has been to see a subjective and individual learning as primary and central, with objective and institutional approaches treated as auxiliary and peripheral. This individual centering is shown in a common understanding of spiritual and religious practice, shared alike by Hindu, Jain and Buddhist traditions.

Each of these three traditions shares a basic aim that is centred upon the individual, in an essential sense. The aim is one of freedom or enlightenment. And it is meant to be achieved in practice, by individuals who seek beyond the limitations and the ignorance in which they feel caught. In Sanskrit, the individual seeker is called a 'sādhaka', which literally means an 'achiever' or an 'attainer'. And the work of seeking is called 'sādhana', which means 'achievement' or 'attainment'. In this essential sense, individual achievement takes a central place in the actual practice of spiritual enquiry. The central aim is not the establishment and organization of religious institutions. Instead, it is an ultimate enlightenment that is sought by individuals.

Moreover, to attain enlightenment, it is stressed that outward forms must lead within, to something deeper that they show. What institutions do is to collect and pass on outward forms — of texts, ideas and practices. These forms take meaning through their use by living individuals. However much the texts, ideas and practices are valued and held sacred by tradition, it is through an individual teacher that they are interpreted and brought to life. Such a teacher represents, in person, a living knowledge that is learned through outwardly transmitted forms. The relationship of teacher and disciple is intensely individual, at the living centre of traditional instruction and transmission.

The forms that are transmitted have come down, through a line of teachers and disciples, from an original founder who established the tradition. In Sanskrit, such a founder of tradition is called an 'ācārya'. The name implies a founding of customs and conventions on which the tradition is based. An ācārya formulates essential principles and initiates transmitting institutions on which a tradition is subsequently based. The ācārya is very much an individual, giving rise to a particular tradition, which is called a 'sampradāya'. From such individual ācāryas different traditions form and grow — each with its own systems of ideas and practices, organized in its own institutions.

In short, there are three ways in which Indian spiritual traditions are centred upon the individual. They centre on the individual seeker or 'sādhaka', upon the individual teacher or 'guru' and upon the individual founder or 'ācārya'.

All of these three are greatly emphasized in Hinduism, where it is generally accepted that new ācāryas can found new traditions or sampradāyas in the present. In Jainism and Buddhism, the individual seeker and the living teacher are emphasized in a way that is similar to Hinduism, but there is rather less emphasis upon living individuals as founders of tradition. For Jains do not consider any current teachers on a par with Mahāvīra, and Buddhists similarly do not think of any current teachers on a par with the Buddha Gautama.

Reconciling Different Views

Where knowledge centres on the individual, there is of course a problem that different individuals see things from different points of view. The relativity of different views must somehow be acknowledged and reconciled.

In *Jainism,* our experience of the world is acknowledged as 'anekānta', which means 'not alone' or 'non-exclusive'. Things in the world are seen in various ways that seem to contradict each other. But, in fact, there is no finally exclusive view that rules the others out and stands quite on its own. As things work out in practice, our different views are non-exclusive. They come to compromise and work together, each contributing its relative and partial descriptions. This partiality is classically epitomized in the story of several blind men, who come upon an elephant. As they grab hold of trunk and legs and tail and other different parts, they describe the animal quite differently. Such is our experience of the world.

In contrast to our relative experiences, the knowledge of enlightenment is described as 'kevala', meaning 'on its own' or 'absolute'. Through purifying practices that lead to enlightenment, there is a crossing over, from worldly experiences to 'kevala-jñāna' or 'absolute knowledge'. That knowledge is impartial and complete, because it is completely on its own, uncompromised by any mixture or confusion with other things. Accordingly, Jains speak of enlightenment as 'kaivalya', meaning by that a complete 'aloneness' or final 'absolution'.[33]

In *Buddhism,* the world's experiences are spoken of as 'anitya' or 'impermanent'. Here, there are no lasting things; but only changing occurrences, in a causal chain called 'pratītya-samutpādana' or 'dependently conditioned arising'. In this world of dependent

[33] For this Jain conception, see Upadhye 1975.

change, no independent absolutes arise. Wherever such absolutes are intellectually described, the description is no more than a changing and relative view, which does not in itself address the actual problem.

The actual problem is 'duḥkha' or 'suffering', caused by the inevitable frustrations of desire for impermanent and changing things. So long as desire keeps on grasping at impermanence, the problem must remain. The only way out is to bring this futile grasping of desire to an end, through practical accomplishment.

That accomplishment is carried out through physical and mental practices — which are meant to bring about a clear understanding of the world's impermanence, and hence to extinguish finally the ongoing chain of causation that perpetuates each person's entanglement with suffering. Accordingly, Buddhists speak of enlightenment as 'nirvāṇa', meaning by that a complete 'extinction' or 'cessation' of entanglement in change and limitation.[34]

In *Hinduism*, there is a marked duality in the way that descriptions are used. On the one hand, there are descriptions of a relative and changing world. On the other hand, there are descriptions of a changeless and absolute reality, expressed in the relative appearances of world. In either case, the descriptions themselves are relative and changing, for they are made in the apparent world. But where they describe a changeless absolute, they point beyond all change and relativity, to something quite beyond themselves. These descriptions are conditioned and thus compromised by their circumstances in the world. But even so, they are meant for a questioning beyond, towards an uncompromised reality that is completely free of all conditioning and circumstance.

Accordingly, Hindus speak of enlightenment as 'mokṣa' or 'freedom'. In particular, it is the freedom of uncompromised reality, whose relative appearances are seen in the conditioned world. The world is then spoken of as 'bandhana' or 'bondage'. Where we are

---

[34] For this Buddhist conception, see Gethin 1998, pages 60-79 and 140-47.

taken to be persons in this world, all our lives and all our views are bound by the conditioning of circumstance.

Such a conditioning must bring in relativity, with all its conflicting interests and partial views. The conflicts and the partialities can only be resolved by returning back, from relative and compromised appearances, to an uncompromised and impartial reality that they all show in common.

To search for that reality, each sādhaka or seeker must go deeper into her or his own view of it. This requires an intense commitment to a particular approach that is specifically suited to the seeker — who seeks from a particular situation of place, time and personal inclination. But, in committing thus to a particular approach, it gets taken to be central, by its followers. Their commitment inherently requires that they put it at the centre of their concern. For them, while they follow it with full intent, through to its final end, it must be the best way of looking. Its view must then be better than all other views.

In the Hindu tradition, there is a marked emphasis upon this intense commitment, of each approach to its own view. Many different approaches are acknowledged, but one thing is characteristic of the tradition as a whole. Each differing approach describes itself as the centre, for its followers. For them, its view is the best of all, with all other views peripheral to it.

In this way, the tradition as a whole has many centres, inherently. The many centres are inherent in the individual nature of teaching and learning. Each teacher is a living centre of tradition, for each student or disciple who is taught. Each teaching puts forward a particular view — called a 'darśana' — in which a student needs to be intently centred, at the time of learning from it.

Such darśanas, or views, are many and varied. They are associated with different sampradāyas or sectarian traditions, which have been established by their respective ācāryas, or founding teachers. Each sampradāya has its own social and cultural institutions, its own temples and maṭhas, with its own teaching lineages that are traced back to their founding ācāryas. It's through these many different sampradāyas that Hinduism has been organized, as a living tradition that continues very much alive into the present.

But then, how do the different sampradāyas relate to each other, so as to form the tradition as a whole? It is a well-known characteristic of Hinduism that its different sects are not formally organized together, under any overarching institution whose authority is accepted in common. And correspondingly, sectarian differences of view are not formally reconciled, in any single system of consistent doctrine.

Instead, the differences are reconciled upon a basis that is essentially informal. The basis is an understanding that each different view expresses a reality which is described in common. No matter how much any view may focus on its own particular descriptions, with their particularities of name and form and quality, these are only means to a reality that is beyond them. Each approach is thus a focusing of some particular means, towards a common reality that's found beneath the differences. It's only there that differences are truly reconciled.

This understanding is sometimes made explicit; and sometimes it is left tacit, as confusing differences are brought into the open, to be discussed and clarified. In either case, whether left tacit or made explicit, this understanding of a common reality enables a many-centred organization of the Hindu tradition. The tradition as a whole has many centres of support, like the many trunks of an old banyan tree. The trunks aren't held together by some formally constructed organization, but just by the sustaining ground from which they grow. From that ground, they grow and branch into a rich profusion of bewildering variety.

The same profusion is also described as a 'functioning anarchy'. The traditions of Hinduism are 'anarchic' in the sense that they are not governed from above, under the overall command of a supervising organization. But they each function with a natural life that relates them from within, as they express a living kinship that is rooted in their common ground.

Personal and Individual

In all three traditions, Hindu, Jain and Buddhist, knowledge is investigated through an inherent correspondence between the universal and the individual — between the outer macrocosm of the universe at large and the inner microcosm of an individual's experience. But this raises a rather delicate question, of how an 'individual' may be conceived. In a person's mind and body, who or what is it that finds experience of the world to be inadequate? And who or what thus travels through experiences of world and personality, in search of enlightenment?

In *Jainism*, an individual is conceived as a transmigrating soul, called a 'jīva' or a 'living being'. Each soul is inherently sentient or knowing. That's what is meant by calling it 'living'. But the world has also an objective or known component — which is made up from matter, movement, rest, space and time. This objective component is 'ajīva' or 'not living', and it is thus inherently insentient or unknowing.

Through 'karma' or 'action' in the world, the living soul is associated with non-living things, in what is called a 'kārmaṇa-śarīra' or a 'kārmic body'. The body is both gross and subtle, as physical and mental actions bring an influx of attachments to the non-living and the unknowing. The attachments limit and degrade the soul's experience, and they make its knowledge partial.

But, through special actions that reduce and destroy the attachments, the soul's experience can be purified, until it reaches a final stage of 'kevala-jñāna', where knowledge is entirely impartial and unmixed.[35]

In *Buddhism*, an individual is conceived as a changing complex of physical and mental personality. Through bodily senses — of sight, sound, smell, taste and touch — a changing variety of physical form (called rūpa) is experienced in the world outside. And in the mind

---

[35] For this Jain conception also, see Upadhye 1975.

are experienced mental activities of feeling (vedanā), recognition (saṁjñā), inclination (saṁskāra) and awareness (vijñāna).

Our personal experience is thus described pragmatically, as an inherently complex process of transforming activity. The process necessarily involves a complex interdependence of different particulars, which require skilful management towards a transformation that is sought. Ultimately, the transformation sought is a positive perfection of experience, which is finally uncompromised by any trace of suffering or dissatisfaction.

To attain that perfection, Buddhists advocate a dispassionate examination of experience, through a 'middle way' that skilfully negotiates between two opposing alternatives. Detachment is here cultivated on the one hand from passing change, and on the other hand from a causal continuity of complex interdependence between varying particulars. Thus progressing to detachment, from changing and dependent things, it is realized that no independent and unchanging self can be constituted anywhere, in any of the changing complexities that we experience through our bodies and our minds. Nothing physically or mentally experienced can rightly be described as a single individual, uncomplicated and uncompromised by difference and change.

No such individual, calling itself 'I', could then rightly be perceived by body or conceived by mind. This view is described by a teaching that Buddhists call 'anātmā' or 'not self'. The Buddha is reported to have described it thus:

> Therefore, monks, all body ... feeling ... recognition ... volition ... conscious awareness whatsoever, whether past, present or future, whether gross or subtle, inferior or refined, far or near, should be seen by means of clear understanding as it really is, as 'this is not mine, I am not this, this is not my self'.[36]

---

[36] From Gethin 1998, page 137, quoting the *Majjhima Nikāya* (i.138-39,232-33).

According to this teaching, experience is defiled by a personally grasping attachment of 'mine'-ness, which produces a false sense of self and individuality. Accordingly, a path to perfection is prescribed, through practices that progressively eliminate the grasping and thus lead to an eventual clearing of the falsity.[37]

In *Hinduism*, there is again a marked duality in the way that descriptions are used. On the one hand, there are descriptions of a changing personality, whose body, senses and mind keep being changed by their own physical and mental activities. On the other hand, there are descriptions of an essentially unchanging self, which is meant to be distinguished from all changing body, sense and mind.

Each person is described as a 'vyakti' or a 'manifestation', which appears through 'ahaṅkāra' or 'ego'. Literally, 'ahaṅkāra' means 'I-acting' — from 'aham', which means 'I', and '-kāra', which means 'acting'. Accordingly, this ego is an acting 'I'. It is a changing act that manifests the 'I', in partial activities of body, sense and mind.

The self within is called 'ātman'. Its inner nature is described as 'avyakta' or 'unmanifest'. It is pure spirit or pure subject, quite unmixed with the changing objects and activities that manifest it. So it stays unaffected and unchanged, through all its changing manifestations, which keep on expressing it in the apparent world.

Here, the dual use of description must be clearly understood. On the one hand, the manifested world is described constructively, by putting different things together. In this world, manifested individuals are described, as persons made of many parts and playing various different roles. These manifested persons are called 'vyaktis'. But none of them is truly individual. Each one is a dependent complex of changeable components, driven by conditioning from circumstance outside. This kind of description is inherently pragmatic. It serves mainly to discuss a variety of

---

[37] For this Buddhist conception, see chapter 6, especially pages 135-39, in Gethin 1998.

practical activities — intended to achieve results, in manifested personalities transacting with a manifested world.

But on the other hand, words can also work in quite a different way, to search for what is '*a*vyakta' or '*un*manifest'. The description is then inherently reflective. Instead of building its construction up, it searches down, into its own foundation. The search turns back upon itself, to look for its own basis of support. In particular, the concept of ātman is thus used reflectively. It's meant to question our habitual sense of personal ego, in search of an underlying self that stands completely on its own, unsupported from elsewhere. Where ego's seeming individuality is compromised by divisions from within and by influences from outside, the word 'ātman' asks for a true individuality that is completely indivisible and independent.

Such an individuality is *not* a theoretical assumption prescribed for belief in some person's mind. Instead, it is essentially beyond all prescriptions and beliefs, in any mind. And it implies a search of such intensity that mind and partiality are utterly dissolved.

In different schools and sects of Hinduism, that search and its results are differently described. But the question of a final individuality is central to the tradition as a whole.

Ancient and Medieval Institutions

In India's history, such differing descriptions and approaches have been carried down through different institutions, acting both in hostile competition and in mutual contribution towards each other.

Our earliest living records are the Vedic texts, which have a powerfully oral character, handed down directly from person to person, through a very careful training in their mantra chanting. Through this directly personal transmission, they have survived the passing of many institutions and material records, over an extraordinary length of time. In fact, because their survival has been so long and so independent of material documentation, we are unsure about their early history.

In particular, we are unsure about the relationship between the Vedas and the Indus civilization. Current research is greatly changing our picture of this relationship; but, where the history of knowledge is concerned, it would perhaps be fair to say that two things are becoming clearer:

- First, in both the Vedas and the Indus civilization, we see an inner emphasis on the unwritten and unpublished aspect of knowledge, in a way that is characteristic of Indian history as a whole. The Indus sites show a development of science and technology that is quite comparable to contemporary developments in Egypt and Iraq. But, in the Indus region, there is far less by way of public monuments and written documents, to publish and record historical achievements in material form. Similarly, the Vedic texts show a great cultivation of technical and spiritual learning, but in a way that is not meant for writing or publication in material documents and monuments. There is, accordingly, a common emphasis on living knowledge that is independent of its material expressions in the course of public history.
- However, from this very independence of living knowledge, there arises a second consideration — that the Vedic tradition would not need to have any simple and confining relationship with the Indus or any other civilization. The Vedas show a tradition that extends far back in time, before the development of settled agriculture and the growth of cities. Since that tradition was independent of settled farms and townships, it would not need to be confined or even centred within the geographic limits of any civilization. Instead, its living practice could well have flourished also in tribal or nomadic areas, thus bridging out into relationships with other cultures and traditions found elsewhere. Moreover the Vedic tradition could well carry on in time, beyond the collapse of city-centred civilization.

In the case of the Indus civilization, our current evidence suggests that it declined and collapsed in a period of centuries soon after 2000 BCE. But many of its techniques and ideas continued, in regional cultures that carried on its developments of skill and learning. The development of Vedic learning could thus well have continued flourishing, through the decline of Indus cities, into a decentralized medieval period of rather more than a thousand years. And from there, the same Vedic tradition could well have gone on, into its more evident role in the subsequent phase of Indo-Gangetic civilization, which started taking shape in the centuries before 500 BCE.

Around this date of 500 BCE, our written records start to give a clearer picture of Indian history. One reason is that we start getting Jain and Buddhist records, telling us about the lives and times of Mahāvīra and the Buddha. These Jain and Buddhist records are more clearly historical than those in the Vedic and Hindu tradition.

For the Hindu tradition has long had a special limitation, in its recording of public history. In this tradition, from the Vedas onwards, the transmission of learning has been specially centred upon individual teaching lineages, often passed down in particular communities and families. Stories and teachings from the past have thus been handed down in a rather idiosyncratic way, embellished with an intimate mixture of myth and ritual that is idiosyncratic to their transmitting lineages.

With the growth of Jainism and Buddhism, there was a shift of emphasis — towards a more universal organization of learning in monastic institutions. In such a universal organization, people come together, from different communities with different myths and rituals. Some idiosyncrasies of mythical embellishment get thereby ironed out and left behind, in a process of coming to some institutional consensus, upon plainer and more public records of historic teachings and events.

In the Jain and Buddhist traditions, such instituted processes took place in the centuries that followed Mahāvīra and the Buddha, in the latter part of the first millennium BCE. From this formative period of classical Indian civilization, these two traditions have accordingly produced institutional accounts that tell us their own history. In particular, the accounts show us Mahāvīra and the Buddha as historic persons with historic teachings — rather more so than the ṛṣis and the sages of the Vedas and the Upaniṣads, or than the incarnations and the teachers in Hindu epics and Purāṇas.

In the Hindu tradition, some similar processes of instituted organization did take place, partly in response to inroads from Jain and Buddhist competition. But an emphasis on teaching lineages continued alongside temple and monastic institutions; society continued to be differentiated into hereditary communities called 'jātis'; and history continued mixed with idiosyncratic myths.

A prime example of this is the life of Śrī Śaṅkara, who established the classic system of Advaita Vedānta philosophy. Much emphasis is placed upon the teaching lineage from which he came; and he went on to found five prominent monastic institutions called 'maṭhas', with a number of monastic orders that carried on his tradition through different lineages. He accepted the ritualistic varṇa ranking of different jāti communities; but in his biography there is also a famous incident that shows up the limitations of such social differentiation, when he accepts a polluting untouchable as a fellow teacher from whom he has something to learn (see pages 25-27).

There is however, a problem with Śrī Śaṅkara's biography. Our earliest records of it are medieval texts, which were composed long afterward and which don't tell us when he lived. In the stories of his life, there are no incidents that connect him definitely with any datable kingdoms or kings or historic persons. In the maṭhas that he founded, there are records of teaching lineages that go back to him; but calculations back through these give us conflicting dates which have not been reconciled and which modern academics tend to dismiss as much too early.

Currently, modern academics tend to place Śrī Śaṅkara somewhere near the end of India's classic period, around the eighth or ninth centuries CE. But these datings are largely conjectural, arguing that Śrī Śaṅkara must be later than various doctrines which he is conjectured to be confirming or refuting. As things stand at present, we do not rightly know whether Śrī Śaṅkara lived at the end of India's classic period, as modern academics estimate, or whether he lived rather earlier, as the traditional records suggest.

Śrī Śaṅkara's main work was in the development of classical philosophy. But, in the classic period, another stream of development was also taking place, more broadly in society. This was the growth of bhakti or religious devotion, which made an emotional appeal not just to those who were educated in Sanskrit but also to more ordinary people in their common speech. This bhakti movement was conveyed through the purāṇic literature in Sanskrit and through songs and stories in the many different vernaculars of local speech. Corresponding to the different gods who could be worshipped, different sects arose, with sectarian organizations that were centred upon temple institutions.

Around the end of the first millennium CE, a series of invasions began, from Islamic countries north-west of India. The invasions damaged many classic institutions, and brought in a medieval period. Buddhist monasteries were destroyed, and Buddhism disappeared from the mainland of India. Many Jain and Hindu temples were destroyed, but Jainism and Hinduism survived, through difficult political and social conditions.

In a way, the Hindu tradition was even enriched by its medieval difficulties. It fell back upon its proliferating diversity, as it went on developing its devotional traditions, in their differentiated sects and in their different regions and vernaculars. Thus, regional languages and literatures developed, incorporating classic learning for wider classes of people. New Hindu sects continued to be formed, to meet new needs in changing times. And accommodation was made with Islamic communities, by considering that their religion also seeks a common truth which is beyond sectarian differences. As Islamic domination collapsed and gave way to colonial British rule, a similar accommodation was made with Christianity.

Free-Thinking Individualism

But British rule brought a new stimulus, with a profound impact on India's medieval traditions. These traditions were medieval in the sense that their learning was oriented backward, to a remembered past that was idealized in classic texts. By the latter part of the eighteenth century, when British rule began, Islamic, Jain and Hindu traditions were all caught up in a backward-looking stage of resignation to decline and decay.

To that medieval stage of Indian society, colonial rule brought in a forceful stimulus of new learning from the West. The stimulus is twofold. On the one hand, it has had a *Westernizing* aspect, which brings Western forms of learning and their new sciences into an obvious competition with older forms and sciences inherited through India's medieval traditions. On the other hand, the same stimulus has a *modernizing* aspect, which is further reaching and more positive towards the older learning.

As Western learning now impacts on older traditions, it comes down through a process of modernization that started more than five centuries ago, with the introduction of printing in fifteenth century Europe. Thus, Western learning is the product of a modernization that arose from a medieval stage of its own. In that medieval stage, Western learning was scholastic and authoritarian. It looked back, through scholastic doctrines, to the Christian bible and to some classic texts from ancient Greece and Rome. Its doctrines were dependent on authority, sanctioned by a universal Catholic church that was centrally administered from the supreme position of the pope in Rome.

But, following the introduction of printing, a change of emphasis has come about: from scholastic doctrine to independent questioning, from instituted authority to self-reliant individualism. The change is one of attitude, but it gets expressed in a modernizing process of great cultural and social upheaval, as old ideas and beliefs come into question.

In Europe, this modernizing process can be seen extending over many centuries: through the humanism of the renaissance; through protestant movements of church reform; through the scientific and industrial revolutions; through the growth of nation states; through colonial exploration and expansion all over the world; through enlightenment ideas of reasoned progress; through socialist and democratic reforms of politics and government; and through a globalization of trade, commerce, science and education, as links with other parts of the world are improved by better transport and new media of communication.

In India, a corresponding modernization is in process, but the process is more recent. It was only in the nineteenth century that Indian classic and vernacular traditions began to change their orientation — from faithfully reciting texts transmitted by respected elders, to asking questions for oneself about the flood of information that has come to be available through printing and subsequent media.

This change is illustrated by the relationship between Śrī Rāmakṛṣṇa and Svāmī Vivekānanda, in late nineteenth century Bengal. Śrī Rāmakṛṣṇa's education was very much traditional and oral. In many ways, he was a culmination of the rich devotional traditions in medieval Indian bhakti. His personal approach was very much inclined towards devotional surrender, through an abiding faith in old forms received from past tradition. And yet, he handed that tradition on to his chief disciple Svāmī Vivekānanda, in whom he encouraged a rather different approach of independent questioning.

In fact, through Indian history, there has always been an essential co-operation between these two approaches — of personal surrender through devoted faith and independent reasoning through skeptical enquiry. In medieval Indian society, declined conditions brought an overwhelming emphasis upon religious faith and surrender, so that self-reliant independence was somewhat confined to sannyāsīs or other such renouncers who had given up their social ties. From an early age, Svāmī Vivekānanda was much attracted to sannyāsīs and their independent ways. And further, his sense of independence was reinforced by a school and college education in English and Western learning. Under Śrī Rāmakṛṣṇa's instruction, Vivekānanda became a sannyāsī, along with some fellow disciples. After their teacher's passing, they went on to organize the Rāmakṛṣṇa Mission, with an independent-minded way of using new media to record and organize the old traditions, in modern times.

Svāmī Vivekānanda is specially remembered by many modern Indians, because he was so effective in reconciling a dynamic tension between two streams of liberating influence, which continue very much into the present. One stream is the liberating effect of English and Western education, going back to Rāmmohan Roy and the Hindu College in early nineteenth century Bengal.[38] The other stream

---

[38] See Majumdar 1981.

goes deeper back, into the living traditions that India has inherited from ancient times. These traditions are fundamentally concerned with the liberation of each individual, through a discerning search for dispassionate knowledge and impartial truth. So there is a basic agreement here, with modern individualism and its independent questioning.

Academic Institutes and Living Knowledge

Why then the apparent conflict that still keeps on erupting, between new institutes of learning and India's old traditions? To get a balanced view, it might help to recognize that there are problems on both sides.

On the Indian side, the main problems are those of transition, from a recently medieval past where painful force of overwhelming circumstance had brought about an attitude of backward-looking resignation. From there, the transition now is towards a more self-reliant individualism, making use of present opportunities that come from new advances in modern science and education. As this transition takes place, India is today a rather conflicted and confusing mixture of the modern and the medieval.

An enormous legacy of living tradition has come down through a medieval past; but it has come so richly and so recently that there has not been time to interpret it in modern terms. In particular, it still tends to be expressed in a cryptic and authoritarian way that conflicts with the openness and independent questioning of modern education. Such an authoritarian manner makes the old learning look like mere belief, accepted superstitiously or dogmatically upon blind faith, without a proper testing by experience.

For a modern student or a modern reader, the old ways of teaching and expression are off-putting and confusing. Because their statements were condensed, for oral transmission, they could not spell out detailed information and open explanations, in ways that are now commonplace through printing and electronic media. So the old statements were intended for a far more intensive use than modern readers can easily appreciate. That use was initiated by a formal learning, in which old texts were faithfully recited and repeated and thus memorized. But the understanding and the testing were essentially informal. They came later on, through subsequent experience — as the old statements were repeatedly remembered, with a deepening reflection on their meaning, in the course of an individual's life.

Thus, beneath the authoritarian manner of old learning, a profound investigation was implied, through a persistent testing of sustained experience. The testing is more individual than institutional. It is unlike the testing of modern academic sciences and their industrial technologies, whose standards are maintained by national and global institutions. And here, there is a major problem on the part of new academic institutions, which modern Indians have enthusiastically adopted from the West. These institutions have inherited a bias that has been deeply ingrained by their development, through some two thousand years of European history, starting with the Roman empire and the Christian church.

From Christ's early teaching that 'the kingdom of God is within you', the Catholic church grew into an organized religion that came to call itself the 'Holy Roman Empire'. As the name suggests, this was a centrally administered establishment, with a tendency to propagate and to enforce its doctrines through external means that were decidedly material and political. It's from this church establishment that modern universities and schools have developed in the history of the West.

Moreover, as Western science grew and became more prominent in universities and schools, it reinforced the same external tendency that they had inherited from their church origins. Though Western science shifted emphasis from authoritarian doctrine to empirical investigation, it has maintained and reinforced a longer-standing Western bias, towards the institutional aspect of learning. In particular, as modern sciences have developed in the West, they are inherently dependent on a growing documentation of printed and electronic information, which has to be maintained and organized by a corresponding growth of institutional administration. And as these highly documented sciences are tested and applied, they are similarly dependent on a growing technology of material instruments and machines, which must again be institutionally organized.

In short, through the Western development of modern schools and universities, they have come to be ingrained with a long-standing bias that favours the written word and the organized academy. That favour is achieved at the expense of living traditions, which have come down through individual teaching from one person to another, going back to ancient times. In modern Europe and America, such traditions have been much impoverished and driven underground, by the prevailing bias of Western church religion and academic science.

But in India, and in other such civilizations, the situation is quite different. For here, a rich legacy of old tradition is still very much alive. As it is taught by living teachers, it centres on an inner knowing, whose experience is essentially direct and immediate, beneath its expressions in external media and institutions. Our living legacy of old tradition is thus spiritual. Its teaching centres closely on an inmost source of unmediated spirit, from where all knowledge of the world is mediated to arise.

To those who take such spiritual traditions seriously, institutes of learning are a 'necessary evil'. They are described explicitly as such by the late Śrī Candraśekharendra Sarasvatī, a very traditional and much respected ācārya of the Śaṅkara lineage at Kāñcīpuram, in the twentieth century. In speaking of the institutions founded by Śrī Śaṅkara, he tells us that they are 'Śaṅkara's work for a necessary evil'. And he says that though he is the head of such an institution, he must speak out in favour of the individual teacher. In particular, he says:

> It is when a guru is on his own as an individual, without the backing of an institution, that he has greater reason to remain pure of heart and mind.[39]

---

[39] From Candraśekharendra Sarasvatī Svāmī 1991.

The quotation illustrates a basic distinction that is made in the Indian tradition, between two kinds of learning. One kind is indirect, built up from mediating forms and organized in institutes. The other kind investigates beyond the indirectness, in search of an immediate truth that is quite free of all impurities.

The first kind of learning is *objective and institutional.* Its indirectness compromises it with a degree of partiality and wrong. But, as the late Kāñcī ācārya said, it is needed to spread education through society and to maintain standards in a conflicted world.[40] There is no major disagreement here, between the old traditions and new universities or schools.

The second kind of learning can't be tested or applied by institutions. Its goal of truth is sought beyond all instituted forms and standards. So, as the Nāsadīya sūkta says, the search has always been pursued by 'inspired individuals, searching in their hearts with keen intelligence'.[41] The search is thus profoundly *subjective and individual.* It's meant to question back so far that it throws radically into question just what's meant by these two words: 'subjective' and 'individual'.

In old traditions that are still alive, particularly in India, the second kind of learning is considered as essential. For it is taken to access an inner truth that is outwardly expressed in the objective structures of instituted learning. All instituted learning is thus taken to derive its value and its meaning from a truth of living spirit that is inwardly accessed. That spiritual approach is essentially subjective, as indicated clearly by the Sanskrit word 'ātmīya'. And yet, despite its subjectivity, it is given precedence, over all objective learning that is institutionally tested and applied.

It is here that there remains a problem, in the way that Indian traditions are portrayed by modern schools and universities, both in India and the West. The problem is that these schools and universi-

---

[40] From Candraśekharendra Sarasvatī Svāmī 1991.

[41] 'hṛdi pratīṣyā kavayo manīṣā', *Ṛg-veda* 10.129.4.

ties are still very strongly biased, in favour of an objective learning that falls within their institutional domain. And they suffer from a corresponding prejudice, against the spiritual and subjective learning that is given precedence in old traditions.

That subjective learning works by cultivating the faculties and clarifying the perspectives of those living individuals who make use of it. So it is tested and applied in the living practice of those individuals, as they go about their business and their lives. The tests and the applications of such learning must of course extend beyond all institutional jurisdictions; but that can hardly make it incompatible with a truly modern education, nor reduce its value as an essential means to knowledge.

And yet, modern academics carry on with an ingrained reluctance to admit the validity of a subjective approach to knowledge. It is still taken for granted that the word 'subjective' means 'personal', ignoring the fundamental question of an impersonal subjectivity in spiritual traditions. Exactness of knowledge still tends to be equated with physical sciences that are mechanically computed and applied, through an industrial technology of material instruments and machines. Biological sciences are treated as an extension of calculating physics, without yet seriously considering traditional investigations of a living energy that expresses underlying consciousness. Old sciences, like Āyurveda and astrology, are discounted by looking at their testing and their application in a narrowly mechanical way — which does not take into account their living use, through the faculties they harness and develop in their skilled practitioners.

This narrowly objective bias shows up crucially in current academic attitudes towards religion and philosophy. Religion is identified with ritual practices and systems of belief, thus distancing it from impartial knowledge. Philosophy is identified with intellectual analysis and system-building, thus restricting it to an academic exercise. In either case, there is a telling failure to admit the validity of living knowledge whose actual teaching and investigation are not rightly academic.

In the case of religion, its knowledge is denied validity by portraying it as a ritualized construction of emotional beliefs, left unexamined and untested by more careful and more rigorous investigation. This portrayal is a distant and a superficial one, which does not fit with closer views from the inside. When a religion is more deeply seen, as experienced by its genuine practitioners, it most certainly implies a search of progressively increasing care and rigour, to the point where all partiality must be surrendered to an ultimately valued truth. Thus, it turns out that devotional religion does indeed approach a finally impartial knowledge, through extremes of emotional surrender that are decidedly not academic.

In the case of philosophy, its living knowledge cannot rightly be confined to intellectual reasoning, which states assumptions and deduces theories describing structured objects in the world. Such intellectual reasoning produces dead constructions, which only come to life by asking what they mean. The living knowledge of philosophy is sought by reflective questioning — which turns back in to question all assumption of ideas and beliefs, in search of a less partial ground from where their partialities are known.

The questioning is rigorously reasoned, but increasingly subjective. As deeper questions rise, each is turned back upon its own assumptions; so as to keep enquiring into an underlying depth of mind, beneath all thoughts and feelings of intellect and intuition. So long as any thought or felt assumptions may remain, there can be no end to the enquiry. Its inward-turning logic makes it utterly relentless, pursuing its exacting reason far beyond all academic reach, as it investigates an inmost knowing where no partiality remains.

In India's long history, such an inmost knowing has been broadly acknowledged as the common source and goal of many different traditions. It's taken as their living source, from where their differing ideas and practices arise. And as their final goal, where ideas and practices come back to the living knowledge they express. Where such knowledge is concerned, only its outward forms can be recorded by institutions and described by scholars. Its actual teaching is the work of sages who have realized it for themselves. They are the ongoing founders of tradition, who alone can rightly teach its living knowledge.

Here, modern academics are presented with a delicate and challenging dilemma. On the one hand, they are told of a knowledge that they cannot rightly teach or even investigate, in their academic context. But on the other hand, they have somehow to be fair and accurate, as they describe traditions where that knowledge is alive. In order to be accurate, they must of course maintain a sharply critical examination of their own academic statements and theories. But to be fair, their descriptions must be open and receptive, to a living knowledge where their academic criticism does not rightly apply. That calls of course for a discerning judgement, in order to decide how far the criticism should extend and where it's better to be open or receptive.

Bibliographic References

Aurobindo, Shri: *The Secret of the Veda,* Sri Aurobindo Ashram, Pondicherry, India, 1999.

Bhartṛhari, *Vākyapadīyam* (text and commentaries in Sanskrit), 2nd edn., Sampurnanand Sanskrit Vishvavidyalaya, Varanasi, 1976.

Candraśekharendra Sarasvatī Svāmī: *The Guru Tradition,* at start of part 4, Bharatiya Vidya Bhavan, Mumbai, 1991.

________: *Hindu Dharma – The Universal Way of Life,* English translation of author's Tamil discourses, Bharatiya Vidya Bhavan, Mumbai, 2000.

Coward, Harold G.: *Bhartṛhari,* start of chapter 2, Twayne Publishers, Boston, 1976.

Einstein, Albert: *Mein Weltbild,* Amsterdam, Querido Verlag, 1934. Quoted from *Ideas and opinions by Albert Einstein* (New translations and revisions by Sonja Bargmann), Rupa and Co., New Delhi, 1989.

Elst, Koenraad: *Update on the Aryan Invasion Debate* (chapter 2, 'Astronomic data and the Aryan question'), New Delhi, Aditya Prakashan, 1992. <http://www.bharatvani.org/books/ait/>

Frawley, David: *Gods, Sages and Kings,* Motilal Banarsidass, Delhi, 1993.

Gethin, Rupert: *The Foundations of Buddhism,* Oxford University Press, Oxford, 1998.

Iyer, K. A. Subramania: *The Vākyapadīya of Bhartṛhari with the vṛtti, Chapter I English Translation,* Deccan College, Pune, India, 1965.

Kak, Subhash: *The Astronomical Code of the Rigveda,* Aditya Prakashan, New Delhi, 1994.

Klostermaier, Klaus: 'Questioning the Aryan invasion theory and revising ancient Indian history', *The Journal of Indian Council of Philosophical Research,* special issue 'Chronology and Indian

Philosophy', pp. 63-78, New Delhi, June 2001; alternatively published in *ISKCON Communications Journal* – Vol. 6, no. 1, June 1998. <http://www.iskcon.com/icj/6_1/6_1klostermaier.html>

Majumdar, R.C., Ed.: *The History and Culture of the Indian People, Vol. 10, British Paramountcy and Indian Renaissance*, Part II, chapters I-III, Bharatiya Vidya Bhavan, Mumbai, 1981.

________: *The History and Culture of the Indian People, Vol. 3, The Classical Age*, chapter 21, section 4, Bharatiya Vidya Bhavan, Mumbai, 1988.

Pillai, K. Raghavan: *The Vākyapadīya, Critical Text of Cantos I and II (with English Translation, Summary of Ideas and Notes)*, Motital Banarsidass, Delhi, 1971.

Ratnagar, Shereen: 'Revisionist at work', *Frontline* magazine, India, 9 February 1996.

________: *The End of the Great Harappan Tradition*, Manohar, New Delhi, 2000.

Sastri, Kapali: *Sat-darshana Bhashya and Talks with Maharshi*, page xxi, Sri Ramanashramam, Tiruvannamalai, Tamil Nadu, 1993.

Seidenberg, A.: 'The Origin of Mathematics', *Archive for History of Exact Sciences*, Vol. 19, No.4, pp. 301-42, 1978.

________: 'The Geometry of the Vedic Rituals', *Agni: The Vedic Ritual of the Fire Altar*, pp. 95-126, Vol. II, edited by Frits Staal, Berkeley, Asian Humanities Press, 1983.

Upadhye, A.N.: 'Jainism', in A.L. Basham, Ed., *A Cultural History of India*, chapter IX, pp. 103-5, Oxford University Press, Delhi, 1975.

Venkataramiah, M.S.: *Talks with Sri Ramana Maharshi*, Sri Ramanashramam, Tiruvannamalai, Tamil Nadu, 1984.

Zimmer, Heinrich: *Philosophies of India*, Appendix A, Bollingen Foundation, New York, 1953.

Index

General Index

Index of Quoted Passages